W9-BRW-366

The Short Story & You

The Short Story & You

An Introduction to Understanding and Appreciation

John S. Simmons/Malcolm E. Stern

National Textbook Company
a division of *NTC Publishing Group* • Lincolnwood, Illinois USA

The authors and publishers are indebted to John B. Karls, curriculum specialist, English Language Arts, department of elementary and secondary education, Milwaukee Public Schools, for his contribution in the development of the text.

1995 Printing

Copyright © 1987 by National Textbook Company,
a division of NTC Publishing Group,
4255 West Touhy Avenue,
Lincolnwood (Chicago), Illinois 60646-1975 U.S.A.
All rights reserved. No part of this book may
be reproduced, stored in a retrieval system, or
transmitted in any form or by any means, electronic,
mechanical, photocopying, recording or otherwise,
without the prior permission of NTC Publishing Group.
Manufactured in the United States of America.
Library of Congress Catalog Number: 86-62047

4 5 6 7 8 9 0 BC 9 8 7 6 5

Contents

Short Stories and You

The focus of this book is twofold—short stories and you. Through reading and enjoying these stories, you are encouraged to grow in your understanding of yourself and your world. For as long as there have been people, there have been stories about people. From our earliest beginnings, human beings have been curious about each other and have satisfied that curiosity with myths, legends, adventure tales, fantasy—stories. People respond to stories that have a special enduring quality—a sparkle of life, a bit of truth, a glimpse of ourselves.

All stories trace their origin to an oral tradition. For centuries, people shared accounts of their cultures through storytelling. They entertained each other with tales of great battles, of the exploits of noble ancestors and, through their stories, they kept alive their heritage. When people began to write stories, a variety of forms appeared. The form of the stories was unimportant to most audiences. The main purpose was entertainment, yet the stories also satisfied a human need to know more about human behavior.

By the nineteenth century, the loose, episodic tales of early times were replaced with a more artistic form—the short story. It is a relatively recent literary form and one that can truly be called American. The American short story as we know it was shaped by many pens, including those of Nathaniel Hawthorne, O. Henry, Jack London. Among them, the primary creator of the new genre was Edgar Allan Poe.

Poe felt that the short story should be written to stand alone and that it need not be related to a previous or subsequent episodes. He said that a story should be of such length that it could be read at one "sitting". . . a real "short" story. Poe felt that the story should have a definite internal unity; it should create a single effect and every part should reinforce that effect. For Poe, the single effect was usually terror. "The Fall of the House of Usher" offers an opportunity for you to see how well Poe put his theory into practice.

In our contemporary world, the short story has grown in popularity and surpassed many other forms of expression in terms of literary appeal. Because of its handy length, a short story can be read in a relatively brief span of time. But there is a more important feature that accounts for its popularity. It contains an intensity that draws the reader onward from the beginning of the conflict to the climax and then to the resolution. As we identify with the human situation of a particular story, we are compelled to satisfy our curiosity about how the story will end.

If reading stories were an end in itself, there might be little reason for us to read many of them. But there is more to the short story than the narration of a plot. The overall idea of a short story makes an impression on us, calling to mind similar struggles and situations when we have had to make choices. Like Sucker, we have had our feelings hurt; like Ollie in "Happy Birthday," we have all been disappointed. By experiencing these emotions through the actions of fictional characters, we can re-examine these unavoidable situations. We feel a kind of safety in our separation from the conflict and are able to draw more detached, unemotional conclusions about the best way to respond to everyday conflicts.

The five Parts of this book contain stories chosen just for you—stories of a variety of characters, such as a bridegroom of the Old West, a Yukon trailblazer, a teenage grocery clerk, a young black scholar, a German war orphan. As you read, consider the persons who took the time to compose each work and the reasons they thought a small glimpse of a make-believe world might be worth the effort. Is there something about a character's decision that is designed to make you consider your own choices? Is there a message in the way the characters learn from their failures? Is there a way you can relate to their situations by putting yourself in their shoes—just for the moment?

If you can, let go of your hold on the real world and immerse yourself in fiction. Examine the motivations of the characters. Ask yourself why they choose a particular path, even when the way leads to pain or disillusionment. Speak aloud their words. Empathize with the people you read about for the short duration of the story. Then examine the questions that accompany each selection. As you refresh your memory of the facts, delve deeper into the purpose of the story, the reason for the conclusion.

When you finish each Part, consider its theme—facing conflict, adjusting to life, encountering the unexpected, confronting prejudice, getting along. How does each story express a unique thought, yet contribute to your understanding of the unifying idea? Is it possible for so many points of view to exist? Is any one answer correct? Why don't we all think alike?

If you find yourself wondering whether there are answers to these questions, you will have arrived at an important point in your personal growth. Truly, there have always been quandaries that have left people with no conclusion. At times, the questions themselves have inspired more questions, such as why is there violence, why must we suffer pain, and why do we cause suffering to others. The existence of these questions in the human spirit is the reason for our desire to know more. As long as there are people, there will be questions. As long as there are questions, there will be stories.

PART ONE

Facing Conflict

The theme of conflict is a good place to start because it is truly universal. Rich and poor, young and old, famous and little-known, all people face conflicts. We must each decide how important a conflict is and how to deal with it. Conflicts can involve personal welfare, reputation, beliefs, wealth, family. Some decisions are arrived at very quickly; others require time to consider choices. In the final analysis, each of us must deal with conflicts in our own experience to ease burdens, uncomfortable situations and personal struggles.

Literature reflects the whole range of human experience through four basic kinds of conflicts—people against people, people against nature, people against fate, and people against themselves. It is important to sort out which conflicts are operating in each literary selection as well as in life situations because the nature of the struggle determines how we choose to combat it. In reading short stories, you can observe up close how people similar to you face conflicts and decide a course of action.

Please note that in some stories there are several kinds of conflict. In "The Bride Comes to Yellow Sky," for example, Jack, the main character, faces three conflicts: the possibility of a fight with Scratchy Wilson, his old enemy; the problem of introducing his wife to her new home; and his own feelings. Often it is the person's concern with thoughts and emotions that demands the closest attention from the reader.

Keep in mind the inner workings of each character as you read the stories and answer the questions that follow. As you formulate your responses, review the types of conflicts in each story so that you can derive the greatest understanding of each struggle.

William Carlos Williams (1883–1963)

In addition to earning a medical degree from the University of Pennsylvania and maintaining a successful pediatrics practice in his hometown of Rutherford, New Jersey, William Carlos Williams pursued a parallel career in writing. He earned fame for startlingly realistic images in *Poems* (1909), *Sour Grapes* (1921), *Spring and All* (1922), and a Pulitzer Prize for poetry in *Pictures From Brueghel and Other Poems* (1963). His most famous poems, such as "The Red Wheelbarrow," are fresh, direct impressions of the sensuous world.

Three of his novels—*White Mule* (1937), *In the Money* (1940), and *The Build-up* (1952)—form a trilogy about a single family. His short stories, which probe the strange facets of human behavior, appear in a collection, *The Farmers' Daughters* (1961). In addition, he published an autobiography, a book of essays, and notable letters. His realistic descriptions of commonplace situations, such as the one in "The Use of Force," reflect long hours spent in observing his patients, diagnosing their ailments, and healing their ills.

The Use of Force
William Carlos Williams

They were new patients to me, all I had was the name, Olson. Please come down as soon as you can, my daughter is very sick.

When I arrived I was met by the mother, a big startled-looking woman, very clean and apologetic who merely said, Is this the doctor? and let me in. In the back, she added. You must excuse us, doctor, we have her in the kitchen where it is warm. It is very damp here sometimes.

The child was fully dressed and sitting on her father's lap near the kitchen table. He tried to get up, but I motioned for him not to bother, took off my overcoat and started to look things over. I could see that they were all very nervous, eyeing me up and down distrustfully. As often, in such cases, they weren't telling me more than they had to, it was up to me to tell them; that's why they were spending three dollars on me.

The child was fairly eating me up with her cold, steady eyes, and no expression to her face whatever. She did not move and seemed, inwardly, quiet; an unusually attractive little thing, and as strong as a heifer in appearance. But her face was flushed, she was breathing rapidly, and I realized that she had a high fever. She had magnificent blonde hair, in profusion. One of those picture children often reproduced in advertising leaflets and the photogravure sections of the Sunday papers.

She's had a fever for three days, began the father and we don't know what it comes from. My wife has given her things, you know, like people do, but it don't do no good. And there's been a lot of sickness around. So we tho't you'd better look her over and tell us what is the matter.

As doctors often do I took a trial shot at it as a point of departure. Has she had a sore throat?

Both parents answered me together, No . . . No, she says her throat don't hurt her.

Does your throat hurt you? added the mother to the child. But the little girl's expression didn't change nor did she move her eyes from my face.

Have you looked?

I tried to, said the mother, but I couldn't see.

As it happens we had been having a number of cases of diphtheria in the school to which this child went during that month and we were all, quite apparently, thinking of that, though no one had as yet spoken of the thing.

Well, I said, suppose we take a look at the throat first. I smiled in my best professional manner and asking for the child's first name I said, come on, Mathilda, open your mouth and let's take a look at your throat.

Nothing doing.

Aw, come on, I coaxed, just open your mouth wide and let me take a look. Look, I said opening both hands wide, I haven't anything in my hands. Just open up and let me see.

Such a nice man, put in the mother. Look how kind he is to you. Come on, do what he tells you to. He won't hurt you.

At that I ground my teeth in disgust. If only they wouldn't use the word "hurt" I might be able to get somewhere. But I did not allow myself to be hurried or disturbed but speaking quietly and slowly I approached the child again.

As I moved my chair a little nearer suddenly with one cat-like movement both her hands clawed instinctively for my eyes and she almost reached them too. In fact she knocked my glasses off and they fell, though unbroken, several feet away from me on the kitchen floor. Both the mother and father almost turned themselves inside out in embarrassment and apology. You bad girl, said the mother, taking her and shaking her by one arm Look what you've done. The nice man . . .

For heaven's sake, I broke in. Don't call me a nice man to her. I'm here to look at her throat on the chance that she might have diphtheria and possibly die of it. But that's nothing to her. Look here, I said to the child, we're going to look at your throat You're old enough to understand what I'm saying. Will you open it now by yourself or shall we have to open it for you?

Not a move. Even her expression hadn't changed. Her breaths however were coming faster and faster. Then the battle began. I had to do it. I had to have a throat culture for her own protection. But first I told the parents that it was entirely up to them. I explained the danger but said that I would not insist on a throat examination so long as they would take the responsibility.

If you don't do what the doctor says you'll have to go to the hospital, the mother admonished her severely.

Oh yeah? I had to smile to myself. After all, I had already fallen in love with the savage brat, the parents were contemptible to me. In the ensuing struggle they grew more and more abject, crushed, exhausted while she surely rose to magnificent heights of insane fury of effort bred of her terror of me.

The father tried his best, and he was a big man but the fact that she was his daughter, his shame at her behavior and his dread of hurting her made him release her just at the critical times when I had almost achieved success, till I wanted to kill him. But his dread also that she might have diphtheria made him tell me to go on, go on though he himself was almost fainting, while the mother moved back and forth behind us raising and lowering her hands in an agony of apprehension.

Put her in front of you on your lap, I ordered, and hold both her wrists.

But as soon as he did the child let out a scream. Don't, you're hurting me. Let go of my hands. Let them go I tell you. Then she shrieked terrifyingly, hysterically. Stop it! Stop it! You're killing me!

Do you think she can stand it, doctor! said the mother.

You get out, said the husband to his wife. Do you want her to die of diphtheria?

Come on now, hold her, I said.

Then I grasped the child's head with my left hand and tried to get the wooden tongue depressor between her teeth. She fought, with clenched teeth, desperately! But now I also had grown furious—at a child. I tried to hold myself down but I couldn't. I know how to expose a throat for inspection. And I did my best. When finally I got the wooden spatula behind the last teeth and just the point of it into the mouth cavity, she opened up for an instant but before I could see anything she came down again and gripping the wooden blade between her molars she reduced it to splinters before I could get it out again.

Aren't you ashamed, the mother yelled at her. Aren't you ashamed to act like that in front of the doctor?

Get me a smooth-handled spoon of some sort, I told the mother. We're going through with this. The child's mouth was already bleeding. Her tongue was cut and she was screaming in wild hysterical shrieks. Perhaps I should have desisted and come back in an hour or more. No doubt it would have been better. But I have seen at least two children lying dead in bed of neglect in such cases, and feeling that I must get a diagnosis now or never I went at it again. But the worst of it was that I too had got beyond reason. I could have torn the child apart in my own fury and enjoyed it. It was a pleasure to attack her. My face was burning with it.

The damned little brat must be protected against her own idiocy, one says to one's self at such times. Others must be protected against her. It is a social necessity. And all these things are true. But a blind fury, a feeling of adult shame, bred of a longing for muscular release are the operatives. One goes on to the end.

In a final unreasoning assault I overpowered the child's neck and jaws. I forced the heavy silver spoon back of her teeth and down her throat till she gagged. And there it was—both tonsils covered with membrane. She had fought valiantly to keep me from knowing her secret. She had been hiding that sore throat for three days at least and lying to her parents in order to escape just such an outcome as this.

Now truly she was furious. She had been on the defensive before but now she attacked. Tried to get off her father's lap and fly at me while tears of defeat blinded her eyes.

Check Your Reading

1. What details does the doctor notice when he enters the Olson's kitchen?

2. How does Mathilda manage to thwart the doctor's attempts to examine her throat?

3. What methods of persuasion does the doctor use?

4. How do the parents hinder the doctor's progress?

5. What secret is Mathilda hiding from her parents and the doctor?

Further Exploration

1. What might have happened if the doctor had examined Mathilda without the presence of her parents?

2. Imagine that you are the doctor. What methods would you try if you were examining Mathilda? Are there ways to remove fear from terrified patients?

3. Is a doctor's "use of force" ever justified? Describe a situation in which a professional person might resort to force.

4. How would Mathilda describe this same episode? Would Mrs. Olson share Mathilda's point of view if she were the narrator?

5. Why is Mathilda crying "tears of defeat" at the end of the story? How might Mathilda see the doctor's diagnosis as a victory?

Stephen Crane (1871–1900)

Following the example of his parents and two brothers, all of whom wrote for a living, Crane left school for a few semesters at Lafayette College and Syracuse University to pursue a career in freelance reporting in New York City for the *Herald* and the *Tribune*. Close contact with the saloons and slums of his beat resulted in a masterly command of naturalistic detail, a type of writing he made famous in his first novel, *Maggie: A Girl of the Streets* (1893), and also in his classic novel of youth and war, *The Red Badge of Courage* (1895). As a result of his achievement he was hired to cover war news during the Cuban Revolution, the Greco–Turkish War, and the Spanish–American War.

In addition to novels, Crane produced verse and a collection of Civil War stories, *The Little Regiment* (1896). His best known work, "The Open Boat," resulted from a 50-hour struggle with the sea in a small dinghy after his ship was sunk near Cuba. Suffering the effects of his ordeal and of tuberculosis, Crane went to England and published two collections of stories—*The Open Boat* (1898) and *The Monster* (1899). He sought a cure for his ill health in Germany but died at the age of twenty-nine.

The Bride Comes to Yellow Sky

Stephen Crane

I

The great Pullman was whirling onward with such dignity of motion that a glance from the window seemed simply to prove that the plains of Texas were pouring eastward. Vast flats of green grass, dull-hued spaces of mesquite and cactus, little groups of frame houses, woods of light and tender trees, all were sweeping into the east, sweeping over the horizon, a precipice.

A newly married pair had boarded this coach at San Antonio. The man's face was reddened from many days in the wind and sun, and a direct result of his new black clothes was that his brick-colored hands were constantly performing in a most conscious fashion. From time to time he looked down respectfully at his attire. He sat with a hand on each knee, like a man waiting in a barber's shop. The glances he devoted to other passengers were furtive and shy.

The bride was not pretty, nor was she very young. She wore a dress of blue cashmere, with small reservations of velvet here and there, and with steel buttons abounding. She continually twisted her head to regard her puff sleeves, very stiff, straight, and high. They embarrassed her. It was quite apparent that she had cooked, and that she expected to cook, dutifully. The blushes caused by the careless scrutiny of some passengers as she had entered the car were strange to see upon this plain, underclass countenance, which was drawn in placid, almost emotionless lines.

They were evidently very happy. "Ever been in a parlor car before?" he asked, smiling with delight.

"No," she answered, "I never was. It's fine, ain't it?"

"Great! And then after a while we'll go forward to the diner, and get a big lay-out. Finest meal in the world. Charge a dollar."

"Oh, do they?" cried the bride. "Charge a dollar? Why, that's too much—for us—ain't it, Jack?"

"Not this trip, anyhow," he answered bravely. "We're going to go the whole thing."

Later he explained to her about the trains. "You see, it's a thousand miles from one end of Texas to the other; and this train runs right across it, and never stops but four times." He had the pride of an owner. He pointed out to her the dazzling fittings of the coach; and in truth her eyes opened wider as she contemplated the sea-green figured velvet, the shining brass, silver, and glass, the wood that gleamed as darkly brilliant as the surface of a pool of oil. At one end a bronze figure sturdily held a support for a separated chamber, and at convenient places on the ceiling were frescos in olive and silver.

To the minds of the pair, their surroundings reflected the glory of their marriage that morning in San Antonio; this was the environment of their new estate; and the man's face in particular beamed with an elation that made him appear ridiculous to the Negro porter. This individual at times surveyed them from afar with an amused and superior grin. On other occasions he bullied them with skill in ways that did not make it exactly plain to them that they were being bullied. He subtly used all the manners of the most unconquerable kind of snobbery. He oppressed them; but of this oppression they had small knowledge, and they speedily forgot that infrequently a number of travelers covered them with stares of derisive enjoyment. Historically there was supposed to be something infinitely humorous in their situation.

"We are due in Yellow Sky at 3:42," he said, looking tenderly into her eyes.

"Oh, are we?" she said, as if she had not been aware of it. To evince surprise at her husband's statement was part of her wifely amiability. She took from a pocket a little silver watch; and as she held it before her, and stared at it with a frown of attention, the new husband's face shone.

"I bought it in San Anton' from a friend of mine," he told her gleefully.

"It's seventeen minutes past twelve," she said, looking up at him with a kind of shy and clumsy coquetry. A passenger, noting this play, grew excessively sardonic, and winked at himself in one of the numerous mirrors.

At last they went to the dining car. Two rows of Negro waiters, in glowing white suits, surveyed their entrance with the interest, and also the equanimity, of men who had been forewarned. The pair fell to the lot of a waiter who happened to feel pleasure in steering them through their meal. He viewed them with the manner of a fatherly pilot, his countenance radiant with benevolence. The patronage, entwined with the ordinary deference, was not plain to them. And yet, as they returned to their coach, they showed in their faces a sense of escape.

To the left, miles down a long purple slope, was a little ribbon of mist where moved the keening Rio Grande. The train was approaching it at an angle, and the apex was Yellow Sky. Presently it was apparent that, as the distance from Yellow Sky grew shorter, the husband became commensurately restless. His brick-red hands were more insistent in their prominence. Occasionally he was even rather absent-minded and faraway when the bride leaned forward and addressed him.

As a matter of truth, Jack Potter was beginning to find the shadow of a deed weigh upon him like a leaden slab. He, the town marshal of Yellow Sky, a man known, liked, and feared in his corner, a prominent person, had gone to San Antonio to meet a girl he believed he loved, and there, after the usual prayers, had actually induced her to marry him, without consulting Yellow Sky for any part of the transaction. He was now bringing his bride before an innocent and unsuspecting community.

Of course people in Yellow Sky married as it pleased them, in accordance with a general custom; but such was Potter's thought of his duty to his friends, or of their idea of his duty, or of an unspoken form which does not control men in these matters, that he felt he was heinous. He had committed an extraordinary crime. Face to face with this girl in San Antonio, and spurred by his sharp impulse, he had gone headlong over all the social hedges. At San Antonio he was like a man hidden in the dark. A knife to sever any friendly duty, any form, was easy to his hand in that remote city. But the hour of Yellow Sky—the hour of daylight—was approaching.

He knew full well that his marriage was an important thing to his town. It could only be exceeded by the burning of the new hotel. His friends could not forgive him. Frequently he had reflected on the advisability of telling them by telegraph, but a new cowardice had been upon him. He feared to do it. And now the train was hurrying him toward a scene of amazement, glee, and reproach. He glanced out of the window at the line of haze swinging slowly in toward the train.

Yellow Sky had a kind of brass band, which played painfully, to the delight of the populace. He laughed without heart as he thought of it.

If the citizens could dream of his prospective arrival with his bride, they would parade the band at the station and escort them, amid cheers and laughing congratulations, to his adobe home.

He resolved that he would use all the devices of speed and plains-craft in making the journey from the station to his house. Once within that safe citadel, he could issue some sort of vocal bulletin, and then not go among the citizens until they had time to wear off a little of their enthusiasm.

The bride looked anxiously at him. "What's worrying you, Jack?"

He laughed again. "I'm not worrying, girl; I'm only thinking of Yellow Sky."

She flushed in comprehension.

A sense of mutual guilt invaded their minds and developed a finer tenderness. They looked at each other with eyes softly aglow. But Potter often laughed the same nervous laugh; the flush upon the bride's face seemed quite permanent.

The traitor to the feelings of Yellow Sky narrowly watched the speeding landscape. "We're nearly there," he said.

Presently the porter came and announced the proximity of Potter's home. He held a brush in his hand, and, with all his airy superiority gone, he brushed Potter's new clothes as the latter slowly turned this way and that way. Potter fumbled out a coin and gave it to the porter, as he had seen others do. It was a heavy and muscle-bound business, as that of a man shoeing his first horse.

The porter took their bag, and as the train began to slow they moved forward to the hooded platform of the car. Presently the two engines and their long string of coaches rushed into the station of Yellow Sky.

"They have to take water here," said Potter, from a constricted throat and in mournful cadence, as one announcing death. Before the train stopped, his eye had swept the length of the platform, and he was glad and astonished to see there was none upon it but the station agent, who, with a slightly hurried and anxious air, was walking toward the water tanks. When the train had halted, the porter alighted first, and placed in position a little temporary step.

"Come on, girl," said Potter, hoarsely. As he helped her down they each laughed on a false note. He took the bag from the Negro, and bade his wife cling to his arm. As they slunk rapidly away, his hangdog glance perceived that they were unloading the two trunks, and also that the station agent, far ahead near the baggage car, had turned and was running toward him, making gestures. He laughed, and groaned as he laughed, when he noted the first effect of his marital bliss upon Yellow Sky. He gripped his wife's arm firmly to his side, and they fled. Behind them the porter stood, chuckling fatuously.

II

The California express on the Southern Railway was due at Yellow Sky in twenty-one minutes. There were six men at the bar of the Weary Gentleman saloon. One was a drummer who talked a great deal and rapidly; three were Texans who did not care to talk at that time; and two were Mexican sheepherders, who did not talk as a general practice in the Weary Gentleman saloon. The barkeeper's dog lay on the boardwalk that crossed in front of the door. His head was on his paws, and he glanced drowsily here and there with the constant vigilance of a dog that is kicked on occasion. Across the sandy street were some vivid green grass-plots, so wonderful in appearance, amid the sands that burned near them in a blazing sun, that they caused a doubt in the mind. They exactly resembled the grass mats used to represent lawns on the stage. At the cooler end of the railway station, a man without a coat sat in a tilted chair and smoked his pipe. The fresh-cut bank of the Rio Grande circled near the town, and there could be seen beyond it a great plum-colored plain of mesquite.

Save for the busy drummer and his companions in the saloon, Yellow Sky was dozing. The newcomer leaned gracefully upon the bar, and recited many tales with the confidence of a bard who has come upon a new field.

"—and at the moment that the old man fell downstairs with the bureau in his arms, the old woman was coming up with two scuttles of coal, and of course—"

The drummer's tale was interrupted by a young man who suddenly appeared in the open door. He cried: "Scratchy Wilson's drunk and has turned loose with both hands." The two Mexicans at once set down their glasses and faded out of the rear entrance of the saloon.

The drummer, innocent and jocular, answered: "All right, old man. S'pose he has? Come in and have a drink, anyhow."

But the information had made such an obvious cleft in every skull in the room that the drummer was obliged to see its importance. All had become instantly solemn. "Say," said he, mystified, "what is this?" His three companions made the introductory gesture of eloquent speech; but the young man at the door forestalled them.

"It means, my friend," he answered, as he came into the saloon, "that for the next two hours this town won't be a health resort."

The barkeeper went to the door, and locked and barred it; reaching out of the window, he pulled in heavy wooden shutters, and barred them. Immediately a solemn, chapel-like gloom was upon the place. The drummer was looking from one to another.

"But say," he cried, "what is this, anyhow? You don't mean there is going to be a gun fight?"

"Don't know whether there'll be a fight or not," answered one man, grimly, "but there'll be some shootin'—some good shootin'."

The young man who had warned them waved his hand. "Oh, there'll be a fight fast enough, if any one wants it. Anybody can get a fight out there in the street. There's a fight just waiting."

The drummer seemed to be swayed between the interest of a foreigner and a perception of personal danger.

"What did you say his name was?" he asked.

"Scratchy Wilson," they answered in chorus.

"And will he kill anybody? What are you going to do? Does this happen often? Does he rampage around like this once a week or so? Can he break in that door?"

"No, he can't break down that door," replied the barkeeper. "He's tried it three times. But when he comes you'd better lay down on the floor, stranger. He's dead sure to shoot at it, and a bullet may come through."

Thereafter the drummer kept a strict eye upon the door. The time had not yet been called for him to hug the floor, but, as a minor precaution, he sidled near to the wall. "Will he kill anybody?" he said again.

The men laughed low and scornfully at the question.

"He's out to shoot, and he's out for trouble. Don't see any good in experimentin' with him."

"But what do you do in a case like this? What do you do?"

A man responded: "Why, he and Jack Potter—"

"But," in chorus the other men interrupted, "Jack Potter's in San Anton'."

"Well, who is he? What's he got to do with it?"

"Oh, he's the town marshal. He goes out and fights Scratchy when he gets on one of these tears."

"Wow!" said the drummer, mopping his brow. "Nice job he's got."

The voices had toned away to mere whisperings. The drummer wished to ask further questions, which were born of an increasing anxiety and bewilderment; but when he attemped them, the men merely looked at him in irritation and motioned him to remain silent. A tense waiting hush was upon them. In the deep shadows of the room their eyes shone as they listened for sounds from the street. One man made three gestures at the barkeeper; and the latter, moving like a ghost, handed him a glass and a bottle. The man poured a full glass of whisky, and set down the bottle noiselessly. He gulped the whisky in a swallow, and turned again toward the door in immovable silence. The drummer saw that the barkeeper, without a sound, had taken a Winchester from beneath the bar. Later he saw this individual beckoning to him, so he tip-toed across the room.

"You better come with me back of the bar."

"No, thanks," said the drummer, perspiring; "I'd rather be where I can make a break for the back door."

Whereupon the man of bottles made a kindly but peremptory gesture. The drummer obeyed it, and, finding himself seated on a box with his head below the level of the bar, balm was laid upon his soul at a sight of various zinc and copper fittings that bore a resemblance to armor plate. The barkeeper took a seat comfortably upon an adjacent box.

"You see," he whispered, "this here Scratchy Wilson is a wonder with a gun—a perfect wonder; and when he goes on the war-trail, we hunt our holes—naturally. He's about the last one of the old gang that used to hang out along the river here. He's a terror when he's drunk. When he's sober he's all right—kind of simple—wouldn't hurt a fly—nicest fellow in town. But when he's drunk—whoo!"

There were periods of stillness. "I wish Jack Potter was back from San Anton'," said the barkeeper. "He shot Wilson up once—in the leg—and he would sail in and pull out the kinks in this thing."

Presently they heard from a distance the sound of a shot, followed by three wild yowls. It instantly removed a bond from the men in the darkened saloon. There was a shuffling of feet. They looked at each other. "Here he comes," they said.

III

A man in a maroon-colored flannel shirt, which had been purchased for purposes of decoration, and made principally by some Jewish women on the East Side of New York, rounded a corner and walked into the middle of the main street of Yellow Sky. In either hand the man held a long, heavy blue-black revolver. Often he yelled, and these cries rang through a semblance of a deserted village, shrilly flying over the roofs in a volume that seemed to have no relation to the ordinary vocal strength of a man. It was as if the surrounding stillness formed the arch of a tomb over him. These cries of ferocious challenge rang against walls of silence. And his boots had red tops with gilded imprints, of the kind beloved in winter by little sledding boys on the hillsides of New England.

The man's face flamed in a rage begot of whisky. His eyes, rolling, and yet keen for ambush, hunted the still doorways and windows. He walked with the creeping movement of the midnight cat. As it occurred to him, he roared menacing information. The long revolvers in his hands were as easy as straws; they were moved with an electric swiftness. The little fingers of each hand played sometimes in a musician's way. Plain from the low collar of the shirt, the cords of his neck straightened and sank, straightened and sank, as passion moved him. The only sounds were his terrible invitations. The calm adobes preserved their demeanor at the passing of this small thing in the middle of the street.

There was no offer of fight—no offer of fight. The man called to the sky. There were no attractions. He bellowed and fumed and swayed his revolvers here and everywhere.

The dog of the barkeeper of the Weary Gentleman saloon had not appreciated the advance of events. He yet lay dozing in front of his master's door. At sight of the dog, the man paused and raised his revolver humorously. At sight of the man, the dog sprang up and walked diagonally away, with a sullen head, and growling. The man yelled, and the dog broke into a gallop. As it was about to enter an alley, there was a loud noise, a whistling, and something spat the ground directly before it. The dog screamed, and, wheeling in terror, galloped headlong in a new direction. Again there was a noise, a whistling, and sand was kicked viciously before it. Fear-stricken, the dog turned and flurried like an animal in a pen. The man stood laughing, his weapons at his hips.

Ultimately the man was attracted by the closed door of the Weary Gentleman saloon. He went to it and, hammering with a revolver, demanded drink.

The door remaining imperturbable, he picked a bit of paper from the walk, and nailed it to the framework with a knife. He then turned his back contemptuously upon this popular resort and, walking to the opposite side of the street and spinning there on his heel quickly and lithely, fired at the bit of paper. He missed it by a half-inch. He swore at himself, and went away. Later he comfortably fusilladed the windows of his most intimate friend. The man was playing with this town; it was a toy for him.

But still there was no offer of fight. The name of Jack Potter, his ancient antagonist, entered his mind, and he concluded that it would

be a glad thing if he should go to Potter's house, and by bombardment
induce him to come out and fight. He moved in the direction of his
desire, chanting Apache scalp-music.

When he arrived at it, Potter's house presented the same still front
as had the other adobes. Taking up a strategic position, the man howled
a challenge. But this house regarded him as might a great stone god.
It gave no sign. After a decent wait, the man howled further challenges,
mingling with them wonderful epithets.

Presently there came the spectacle of a man churning himself into
deepest rage over the immobility of a house. He fumed at it as the winter
wind attacks a prairie cabin in the North. To the distance there should
have gone the sound of a tumult like the fighting of two hundred Mexicans.
As necessity bade him, he paused for breath or to reload his revolvers.

IV

Potter and his bride walked sheepishly and with speed. Sometimes
they laughed together shamefacedly and low.

"Next corner, dear," he said finally.

They put forth the efforts of a pair walking bowed against a strong
wind. Potter was about to raise a finger to point the first appearance of
the new home when, as they circled the corner, they came face to face
with a man in a maroon-colored shirt, who was feverishly pushing
cartridges into a large revolver. Upon the instant the man dropped his
revolver to the ground and, like lightning, whipped another from its
holster. The second weapon was aimed at the bridegroom's chest.

There was a silence. Potter's mouth seemed to be merely a grave for
his tongue. He exhibited an instinct to at once loosen his arm from
the woman's grip, and he dropped the bag to the sand. As for the bride,
her face had gone as yellow as old cloth. She was a slave to hideous
rites, gazing at the apparitional snake.

The two men faced each other at a distance of three paces. He of
the revolver smiled with a new and quiet ferocity.

"Tried to sneak up on me," he said. "Tried to sneak up on me!" His
eyes grew more baleful. As Potter made a slight movement, the man
thrust his revolver venomously forward, "No, don't you do it, Jack
Potter. Don't you move a finger toward a gun just yet. Don't you move
an eyelash. The time has come for me to settle with you, and I'm goin'
to do it my own way, and loaf along with no interferin'. So if you don't
want a gun bent on you, just mind what I tell you."

Potter looked at his enemy. "I ain't got a gun on me, Scratchy," he said. "Honest, I ain't." He was stiffening and steadying, but yet somewhere at the back of his mind a vision of the Pullman floated; the sea-green figured velvet, the shining brass, silver, and glass, the wood that gleamed as darkly brilliant as the surface of a pool of oil—all the glory of the marriage, the environment of the new estate. "You know I fight when it comes to fighting, Scratchy Wilson; but I ain't got a gun on me. You'll have to do all the shootin' yourself."

His enemy's face went livid. He stepped forward and lashed his weapon to and fro before Potter's chest. "Don't you tell me you ain't got no gun on you, you whelp. Don't tell me no lie like that. There ain't a man in Texas ever seen you without no gun. Don't take me for no kid." His eyes blazed with light, and his throat worked like a pump.

"I ain't takin' you for no kid," answered Potter. His heels had not moved an inch backward. "I'm takin' you for a damn fool. I tell you I ain't got a gun, and I ain't. If you're goin' to shoot me up, you better begin now; you'll never get a chance like this again."

So much enforced reasoning had told on Wilson's rage; he was calmer. "If you ain't got a gun, why ain't you got a gun?" he sneered. "Been to Sunday school?"

"I ain't got a gun because I've just come from San Anton' with my wife. I'm married," said Potter. "And if I'd thought there was going to be any galoots like you prowling around when I brought my wife home, I'd had a gun, and don't you forget it."

"Married!" said Scratchy, not at all comprehending.

"Yes, married. I'm married," said Potter, distinctly.

"Married?" said Scratchy. Seemingly for the first time, he saw the drooping, drowning woman at the other man's side. "No!" he said. He was like a creature allowed a glimpse of another world. He moved a pace backward, and his arm, with the revolver, dropped to his side. "Is this the lady?" he asked.

"Yes, this is the lady," answered Potter.

There was another period of silence.

"Well," said Wilson at last, slowly, "I s'pose it's all off now."

"It's all off if you say so, Scratchy. You know I didn't make the trouble." Potter lifted his valise.

"Well, I 'low it's off, Jack," said Wilson. He was looking at the ground. "Married!" He was not a student of chivalry; it was merely that in the presence of this foreign condition he was a simple child of the earlier plains. He picked up his starboard revolver, and, placing both weapons in their holsters, he went away. His feet made funnel-shape tracks in the heavy sand.

Check Your Reading

1. What scenes are taking place simultaneously? Where do they occur?

2. What relationship have Scratchy Wilson and Jack Potter maintained in the past? Why do the townspeople respect Jack?

3. What people observe the bride and bridegroom on the train and in the station? How do the newlyweds reveal their nervousness?

4. Which character fails to understand the seriousness of Scratchy's periodic bouts of drunkenness? Who explains it to him?

5. How does the author use color to make each scene vivid? Why do Jack's hands seem "brick-red"?

Further Exploration

1. Why is Scratchy unable to understand the change in Jack? What does the author mean by the statement, "He was not a student of chivalry"?

2. What might Jack's new wife say as Scratchy walks away? Describe how she will fit into the society of her new home.

3. How will the townspeople react to the arrival of the bride? Why has Jack not told them to expect her? Was he wise to keep his plans a secret?

4. Compare the types of tension felt by the characters in the saloon and the characters in the train. Which scene contains more humor?

5. How might the confrontation between Jack and his old enemy have been staged for a TV western? How would the falling action change in the televised version?

Jack London (1876–1916)

Jack London lived adventures of his own—on the Oakland waterfront; during a sealing cruise to Japan; as a war correspondent; throughout myriad experiences in jail; as an oyster pirate; and prospecting for gold on the Alaskan frontier. These experiences became the nuclei of his writing. Although he was born in poverty and received only a grammar school education, he filled in the gaps with travel and reading at the public libraries.

His intense study of the theme of survival against the brutal forces of nature resulted in successful novels, including *The Call of the Wild* (1903), *The Sea-Wolf* (1904), and *White Fang* (1906). His most popular story, "To Build a Fire," stresses the impersonal fierceness of the Alaskan cold and its effect on two beings—a man and a dog.

To Build a Fire
Jack London

Day had broken cold and gray, exceedingly cold and gray, when the man turned aside from the main Yukon trail and climbed the high earth bank, where a dim and little-traveled trail led eastward through the fat spruce timberland. It was a steep bank, and he paused for breath at the top, excusing the act to himself by looking at his watch. It was nine o'clock. There was no sun or hint of sun, though there was not a cloud in the sky. It was a clear day, and yet there seemed an intangible pall over the face of things, a subtle gloom that made the day dark, and that was due to the absence of sun. This fact did not worry the man. He was used to the lack of sun. It had been days since he had seen the sun, and he knew that a few more days must pass before that cheerful orb, due south, would just peep above the skyline and dip immediately from view.

The man flung a look back along the way he had come. The Yukon lay a mile wide and hidden under three feet of ice. On top of this ice were as many feet of snow. It was all pure white, rolling in gentle undulations where the ice jams of the freeze-up had formed. North and south, as far as his eye could see, it was unbroken white, save for a dark hairline that curved and twisted from around the spruce-covered island to the south, and that curved and twisted away into the north, where it disappeared behind another spruce-covered island. This dark hairline was the trail—the main trail—that led south five hundred miles to the Chilkoot pass, Dyea, and salt water; and that led north seventy miles to Dawson, and still on to the north a thousand miles to Nulato, and finally to St. Michael on the Bering Sea, a thousand miles and half a thousand more.

But all this—the mysterious, far-reaching hairline trail, the absence of sun from the sky, the tremendous cold, and the strangeness and weirdness of it all—made no impression on the man. It was not because he was long used to it. He was a newcomer in the land, a cheechako, and this was his first winter. The trouble with him was that he was without imagination. He was quick and alert in the things of life, but only in the things, and not in the significances. Fifty degrees below zero meant eighty-odd degrees of frost. Such fact impressed him as being cold and uncomfortable, and that was all. It did not lead him to meditate upon his frailty as a creature of temperature, and upon man's frailty in general, able only to live within certain narrow limits of heat and cold, and from there on it did not lead him to the conjectural field of immortality and man's place in the universe. Fifty degrees below zero stood for a bite of frost that hurt and that must be guarded against by the use of mittens, ear flaps, warm moccasins, and thick socks. Fifty degrees below zero was to him just precisely fifty degrees below zero. That there should be anything more to it than that was a thought that never entered his head.

As he turned to go on, he spat speculatively. There was a sharp, explosive crackle that startled him. He spat again. And again, in the air, before it could fall to the snow, the spittle crackled. He knew that at fifty below, spittle crackled on the snow, but this spittle had crackled in the air. Undoubtedly it was colder than fifty below—how much colder he did not know. But the temperature did not matter. He was bound for the old claim on the left fork of Henderson Creek, where the boys were already. They had come over across the divide from the Indian Creek country, while he had come the roundabout way to take a look at the possibilities of getting out logs in the spring from the islands in the Yukon. He would be into camp by six o'clock; a bit after dark, it was true, but the boys would be there, a fire would be going, and a hot supper would be ready. As for lunch, he pressed his hand against the protruding bundle under his jacket. It was also under his shirt, wrapped up in a handkerchief and lying against the naked skin. It was the only way to keep the biscuits from freezing. He smiled agreeably to himself as he thought of those biscuits, each cut open and sopped in bacon grease, and each enclosing a generous slice of fried bacon.

He plunged in among the big spruce trees. The trail was faint. A foot of snow had fallen since the last sled had passed over, and he was glad he was without a sled, traveling light. In fact, he carried nothing but the lunch wrapped in the handkerchief. He was surprised, however, at the cold. It certainly was cold, he concluded, as he rubbed his numb nose and cheekbones with his mittened hand. He was a warm-whiskered man, but the hair on his face did not protect the high cheekbones and the eager nose that thrust itself aggressively into the frosty air.

At the man's heels trotted a dog, a big native husky, the proper wolf dog, gray-coated and without any visible or temperamental difference from its brother, the wild wolf. The animal was depressed by the tremendous cold. It knew that it was no time for traveling. Its instinct told it a truer tale than was told to the man by the man's judgment. In reality, it was not merely colder than fifty below zero; it was colder than sixty below, than seventy below. It was seventy-five below zero. Since the freezing point is thirty-two above zero, it meant that one hundred and seven degrees of frost obtained. The dog did not know anything about thermometers. Possibly in its brain there was no sharp consciousness of a condition of very cold such as was in the man's brain. But the brute had its instinct. It experienced a vague but menacing apprehension that subdued it and made it slink along at the man's heels and that made it question eagerly every unwonted movement of the man, as if expecting him to go into camp or to seek shelter somewhere and build a fire. The dog had learned fire, and it wanted fire, or else to burrow under the snow and cuddle its warmth away from the air.

The frozen moisture of its breathing had settled on its fur in a fine powder of frost, and especially were its jowls, muzzle, and eyelashes whitened by its crystaled breath. The man's red beard and mustache were likewise frosted, but more solidly, the deposit taking the form of ice and increasing with every warm, moist breath he exhaled. Also, the man was chewing tobacco, and the muzzle of ice held his lips so rigidly that he was unable to clear his chin when he expelled the juice. The result was that a crystal beard of the color and solidity of amber was increasing its length on his chin. If he fell down it would shatter itself, like glass, into brittle fragments. But he did not mind the appendage. It was the penalty all tobacco chewers paid in that country, and he had been out before in two cold snaps. They had not been so cold as this, he knew, but by the spirit thermometer at Sixty Mile he knew they had been registered at fifty below and at fifty-five.

He held on through the level stretch of woods for several miles, crossed a wide flat, and dropped down a bank to the frozen bed of a small stream. This was Henderson Creek, and he knew he was ten miles from the forks. He looked at his watch. It was ten o'clock. He was making four miles an hour, and he calculated that he would arrive at the forks at half-past twelve. He decided to celebrate that event by eating his lunch there.

The dog dropped in again at his heels, with a tail drooping discouragement, as the man swung along the creek bed. The furrow of the old sled trail was plainly visible, but a dozen inches of snow covered the marks of the last runners. In a month no man had come up or down that silent creek. The man held steadily on. He was not much given to thinking, and just then particularly he had nothing to think about save that he would eat lunch at the forks and that at six o'clock he would be in camp with the boys. There was nobody to talk to, and had there been, speech would have been impossible because of the ice muzzle on his mouth. So he continued monotonously to chew tobacco and to increase the length of his amber beard.

Once in a while the thought reiterated itself that it was very cold and that he had never experienced such cold. As he walked along he rubbed his cheekbones and nose with the back of his mittened hand, He did this automatically, now and again changing hands. But rub as he would, the instant he stopped his cheekbones went numb, and the following instant the end of his nose went numb. He was sure to frost his cheeks; he knew that, and experienced a pang of regret that he had not devised a nose strap of the sort Bud wore in cold snaps. Such a strap passed across the cheeks, as well, and saved them. But it didn't matter much, after all. What were frosted cheeks? A bit painful, that was all; they were never serious.

Empty as the man's mind was of thought, he was keenly observant, and he noticed the changes in the creek, the curves and bends and timber jams, and always he sharply noted where he placed his feet. Once, coming around a bend, he shied abruptly, like a startled horse, curved away from the place where he had been walking, and retreated several paces back along the trail. The creek, he knew, was frozen clear to the bottom—no creek could contain water in that arctic winter—but he knew also that there were springs that bubbled out from the hillsides and ran along under the snow and on top of the ice of the creek. He knew that the coldest snaps never froze these springs, and he knew likewise their danger. They were traps. They hid pools of water under the snow that might be three inches deep, or three feet. Sometimes a skin of ice half an inch thick covered them, and in turn was covered by the snow. Sometimes there were alternate layers of water and ice skin, so that when one broke through he kept on breaking through for a while, sometimes wetting himself to the waist.

That was why he had shied in such panic. He had felt the give under his feet and heard the crackle of a snow-hidden ice skin. And to get his feet wet in such a temperature meant trouble and danger. At the very least it meant delay, for he would be forced to stop and build a fire, and under its protection to bare his feet while he dried his socks and moccasins. He stood and studied the creek bed and its banks, and decided that the flow of water came from the right. He reflected a while, rubbing his nose and cheeks, then skirted to the left, stepping gingerly and testing the footing for each step. Once clear of the danger, he took a fresh chew of tobacco and swung along at his four-mile gait.

In the course of the next two hours he came upon several similar traps. Usually the snow above the hidden pools had a sunken, candied appearance that advertised the danger. Once again, however, he had a close call; and once, suspecting danger, he compelled the dog to go on in front. The dog did not want to go. It hung back until the man shoved it forward, and then it went quickly across the white, unbroken surface. Suddenly it broke through, floundered to one side, and got away to firmer footing. It had wet its forefeet and legs, and almost immediately the water that clung to it turned to ice. It made quick efforts to lick the ice off its legs, then dropped down in the snow and began to bite out the ice that had formed between the toes. This was a matter of instinct. To permit the ice to remain would mean sore feet. It did not know this. It merely obeyed the mysterious prompting that arose from the deep crypts of its being. But the man knew, having achieved a judgment on the subject, and he removed the mitten from his right hand and helped tear out the ice particles. He did not expose his fingers more than a minute, and was astonished at the swift numbness that smote them. It certainly was cold. He pulled on the mitten hastily, and beat the hand savagely across his chest.

At twelve o'clock the day was at its brightest. Yet the sun was too far south on its winter journey to clear the horizon. The bulge of the earth intervened between it and Henderson Creek, where the man walked under a clear sky at noon and cast no shadow. At half-past twelve, to the minute, he arrived at the forks of the creek. He was pleased at the speed he had made. If he kept it up, he would certainly be with the boys by six. He unbuttoned his jacket and shirt and drew forth his lunch. The action consumed no more than a quarter of a minute, yet in that brief moment the numbness laid hold of the exposed fingers. He did not put the mitten on, but instead struck the fingers a dozen sharp smashes against his leg. Then he sat down on a snow-covered log to eat. The sting that followed upon the striking of his fingers against his leg ceased so quickly that he was startled. He had had no chance to take a bite of biscuit. He struck the fingers repeatedly and returned them to the mitten, baring the other hand for the purpose of eating. He tried to take a mouthful, but the ice muzzle prevented. He had forgotten to build a fire and thaw out. He chuckled at his foolishness, and as he chuckled he noted the numbness creeping into the exposed fingers. Also, he noted that the stinging which had first come to his toes when he sat down was already passing away. He wondered whether the toes were warm or numb. He moved them inside the moccasins and decided that they were numb.

He pulled the mitten on hurriedly and stood up. He was a bit frightened. He stamped up and down until the stinging returned into the feet. It certainly was cold, was his thought. That man from Sulfur Creek had spoken the truth when telling how cold it sometimes got in the country. And he had laughed at him at the time! That showed one must not be too sure of things. There was no mistake about it, it was cold. He strode up and down, stamping his feet and threshing his arms, until reassured by the returning warmth. Then he got out matches and proceeded to make a fire. From the undergrowth, where high water of the previous spring had lodged a supply of seasoned twigs, he got his firewood. Working carefully from a small beginning, he soon had a roaring fire, over which he thawed the ice from his face and in the protection of which he ate his biscuits. For the moment the cold of space was outwitted. The dog took satisfaction in the fire, stretching out close enough for warmth and far enough away to escape being singed.

When the man had finished, he filled his pipe and took his comfortable time over a smoke. Then he pulled on his mittens, settled the ear flaps of his cap firmly about his ears, and took the creek trail up the left fork. The dog was disappointed and yearned back toward the fire. This man did not know cold. Possibly all the generations of his ancestry had been ignorant of cold, of real cold, of cold one hundred and seven degrees below freezing point. But the dog knew; all its ancestry knew, and it had inherited the knowledge. And it knew that it was not good to walk abroad in such fearful cold. It was the time to lie snug in a hole in the snow and wait for a curtain of cloud to be drawn across the face of outer space whence this cold came. On the other hand, there was no keen intimacy between the dog and the man. The one was the toil-slave of the other, and the only caresses it had ever received were the caresses of the whiplash and of harsh and menacing throat sounds that threatened the whiplash. So the dog made no effort to communicate its apprehension to the man. It was not concerned in the welfare of the man; it was for its own sake that it yearned back toward the fire. But the man whistled, and spoke to it with the sound of whiplashes, and the dog swung in at the man's heels and followed after.

The man took a chew of tobacco and proceeded to start a new amber beard. Also, his moist breath quickly powdered with white his mustache, eyebrows, and lashes. There did not seem to be so many springs on the left fork of the Henderson, and for half an hour the man saw no signs of any. And then it happened. At a place where there were no signs, where the soft, unbroken snow seemed to advertise solidity beneath, the man broke through. It was not deep. He wet himself halfway to the knees before he floundered out to the firm crust.

He was angry, and cursed his luck aloud. He had hoped to get into camp with the boys at six o'clock, and this would delay him an hour, for he would have to build a fire and dry out his footgear. This was imperative at that low temperature—he knew that much; and he turned aside to the bank, which he climbed. On top, tangled in the underbrush about the trunks of several small spruce trees, was a highwater deposit of dry firewood—sticks and twigs, principally, but also larger portions of seasoned branches and fine, dry, last year's grasses. He threw down several large pieces on top of the snow. This served for a foundation and prevented the young flame from drowning itself in the snow it otherwise would melt. The flame he got by touching a match to a small shred of birch bark that he took from his pocket. This burned even more readily than paper. Placing it on the foundation, he fed the young flame with wisps of dry grass and with the tiniest dry twigs.

He worked slowly and carefully, keenly aware of his danger. Gradually, as the flame grew stronger, he increased the size of the twigs with which he fed it. He squatted in the snow, pulling the twigs out from their entanglement in the brush and feeding directly to the flame. He knew there must be no failure. When it is seventy-five below zero, a man must not fail in his first attempt to build a fire—that is, if his feet are wet. If his feet are dry, and he fails, he can run along the trail for a half a mile and restore his circulation. But the circulation of wet and freezing feet cannot be restored by running, when it is seventy-five below. No matter how fast he runs, the wet feet will freeze the harder.

All this the man knew. The old-timer on Sulfur Creek had told him about it the previous fall, and now he was appreciating the advice. Already all sensation had gone out of his feet. To build the fire, he had been forced to remove his mittens, and the fingers had quickly gone numb. His pace of four miles an hour had kept his heart pumping blood to the surface of his body and to all the extremities. But the instant he stopped, the action of the pump eased down. The cold of space smote the unprotected tip of the planet, and he, being on that unprotected tip, received the full force of the blow. The blood of his body recoiled before it. The blood was alive, like the dog, and like the dog it wanted to hide away and cover itself up from the fearful cold. So long as he walked four miles an hour, he pumped that blood, willy-nilly, to the surface; but now it ebbed away and sank down into the recesses of his body. The extremities were the first to feel its absence. His wet feet froze the faster, and his exposed fingers numbed the faster, though they had not yet begun to freeze. Nose and cheeks were already freezing, while the skin of all his body chilled as it lost its blood.

But he was safe. Toes and nose and cheeks would be only touched by the frost, for the fire was beginning to burn with strength. He was feeding it with twigs the size of his finger. In another minute he would be able to feed it with branches the size of his wrist, and then he could remove his wet footgear, and, while it dried he could keep his naked feet warm by the fire, rubbing them at first, of course, with snow. The fire was a success. He was safe. He remembered the advice of the old-timer on Sulfur Creek, and smiled. The old-timer had been very serious in laying down the law that no man must travel alone in the Klondike after fifty below. Well, here he was; he had had the accident; he was alone; and he had saved himself. Those old-timers were rather womanish, some of them, he thought. All a man had to do was to keep his head and he was all right. Any man who was a man could travel alone. But it was surprising, the rapidity with which his cheeks and nose were freezing. And he had not thought his fingers could go lifeless in so short a time. Lifeless they were, for he could scarcely make them move together to grip a twig, and they seemed remote from his body and from him. When he touched a twig he had to look and see whether or not he had hold of it. The wires were pretty well down between him and his finger ends.

All of which counted for a little. There was the fire, snapping and crackling and promising life with every dancing flame. He started to untie his moccasins. They were coated with ice; the thick German socks were like sheaths of iron halfway to the knees; and the moccasins strings were like rods of steel all twisted and knotted as by some conflagration. For a moment he tugged with his numb fingers, then, realizing the folly of it, he drew his sheath knife.

But before he could cut the strings it happened. It was his own fault, or, rather, his mistake. He should not have built the fire under the spruce tree. He should have built it in the open. But it had been easier to pull the twigs from the bush and drop them directly on the fire. Now the tree under which he had done this carried a weight of snow on it boughs. No wind had blown for weeks, and each bough was fully freighted. Each time he had pulled a twig he had communicated a slight agitation to the tree—an imperceptible agitation, so far as he was concerned, but an agitation sufficient to bring about the disaster. High up in the tree one bough capsized its load of snow. This fell on the boughs beneath, capsizing them. This process continued, spreading out and involving the whole tree. It grew like an avalanche, and it descended without warning upon the man and the fire, and the fire was blotted out! Where it had burned was a mantle of fresh and disordered snow.

The man was shocked. It was as though he had just heard his own sentence of death. For a moment he sat and stared at the spot where the fire had been. Then he grew very calm. Perhaps the old-timer on Sulfur Creek was right. If he had only had a trailmate, he would have been in no danger now. The trailmate could have built the fire. Well, it was up to him to build the fire over again, and this second time there must be no failure. Even if he succeeded, he would most likely lose some toes. His feet must be badly frozen by now, and there would be some time before the second fire was ready.

Such were his thoughts, but he did not sit and think them. He was busy all the time they were passing through his mind. He made a new foundation for a fire, this time in the open, where no treacherous tree could blot it out. Next he gathered dry grasses and tiny twigs from the high-water flotsam. He could not bring his fingers together to pull them out, but he was able to gather them by the handful. In this way he got many rotten twigs and bits of green moss that were undesirable, but it was the best he could do. He worked methodically, even collecting an armful of the larger branches to be used later when the fire gathered strength. And all the while the dog sat and watched him, a certain yearning wistfulness in its eyes, for it looked upon him as the fire provider, and the fire was slow in coming.

When all was ready, the man reached in his pocket for a second piece of birch bark. He knew the bark was there, and, though he could not feel it with his fingers, he could hear its crisp rustling as he fumbled for it. Try as he would, he could not clutch hold of it. And all the time, in his consciousness, was the knowledge that each instant his feet were freezing. This thought tended to put him in a panic, but he fought against it and kept calm. He pulled on his mittens with his teeth, and threshed his arms back and forth, beating his hands with all his might against his sides. He did this sitting down, and he stood up to do it;

and all the while the dog sat in the snow, its wolf brush of a tail curled around warmly over its forefeet, its sharp wolf ears pricked forward intently as it watched the man. And the man, as he beat and threshed with his arms and hands, felt a great surge of envy as he regarded the creature that was warm and secure in its natural covering.

After a time he was aware of the faraway signals of sensation in his beaten fingers. The faint tingling grew stronger till it evolved into a stinging ache that was excruciating but which the man hailed with satisfaction. He stripped the mitten from his right hand and fetched forth the birch bark. The exposed fingers were quickly going numb again. Next he brought out his bunch of sulfur matches. But the tremendous cold had already driven the life out of his fingers. In his effort to separate one match from the others the whole bunch fell in the snow. He tried to pick it out of the snow, but failed. The dead fingers could neither touch nor clutch. He was very careful. He drove the thought of his freezing feet, and nose, and cheeks, out of his mind, devoting his whole soul to the matches. He watched, using the sense of vision in place of that of touch and when he saw his fingers on each side of the bunch, he closed them—that is, he willed to close them, for the wires were down, and the fingers did not obey. He pulled the mitten on the right hand, and beat it fiercely against his knee. Then, with both mittened hands, he scooped the bunch of matches, along with much snow, into his lap. Yet he was no better off.

After some manipulation he managed to get the bunch between the heels of his mittened hands. In this fashion he carried it to his mouth. The ice crackled and snapped when by a violent effort he opened his mouth. He drew the lower jaw in, curled the upper lip out of the way, and scraped the bunch with his upper teeth in order to separate a match. He succeeded in getting one, which he dropped on his lap. He was no better off. He could not pick it up. Then he devised a way. He picked it up in his teeth and scratched it on his leg. Twenty times he scratched before he succeeded in lighting it. As it flamed he held it with his teeth to the birch bark. But the burning brimstone went up his nostrils and into his lungs, causing him to cough spasmodically. The match fell into the snow and went out.

The old-timer on Sulfur Creek was right, he thought in the moment of controlled despair that ensued: after fifty below, a man should travel with a partner. He beat his hands, but failed in exciting any sensation. Suddenly he bared both hands, removing the mittens with his teeth. He caught the whole bunch between the heels of his hands. His arm muscles, not being frozen, enabled him to press the hand heels tightly against the matches. Then he scratched the bunch along his leg. It flared into flame, seventy sulfur matches at once! There was no wind to blow them out. He kept his head to one side to escape the strangling fumes, and held the blazing bunch to the birch bark. As he so held it, he became aware of sensation in his hand. His flesh was burning. He could smell it. Deep down below the surface he could feel it. The sensation developed into pain that grew acute. And still he endured it, holding the flame of the matches clumsily to the bark that would not light readily because his own burning hands were in the way, absorbing most of the flame.

At last, when he could endure no more, he jerked his hands apart. The blazing matches fell sizzling into the snow, but the birch bark was alight. He began laying dry grass and the tiniest twigs on the flame. He could not pick and choose, for he had to lift the fuel between the heels of his hands. Small pieces of rotten wood and green moss clung to the twigs, and he bit them off as well as he could with his teeth. He cherished the flame carefully and awkwardly. It meant life, and it must not perish. The withdrawal of blood from the surface of his body now made him begin to shiver, and he grew more awkward. A large piece of green moss fell squarely on the little fire. He tried to poke it out with his fingers, but his shivering frame made him poke too far, and he disrupted the nucleus of the little fire, the burning grasses and tiny twigs separating and scattering. He tried to poke them together again, but in spite of the tenseness of the effort, his shivering got away with him, and the twigs were hopelessly scattered. Each twig gushed a puff of smoke and went out. The fire provider had failed. As he looked apathetically about him, his eyes chanced on the dog, sitting across the ruins of the fire from him, in the snow, making restless, hunching movements, slightly lifting one forefoot and then the other, shifting its weight back and forth on them with wistful eagerness.

The sight of the dog put a wild idea into his head. He remembered the tale of the man, caught in a blizzard, who killed a steer and crawled inside the carcass, and so was saved. He would kill the dog and bury his hands in the warm body until the numbness went out of them. Then he could build another fire. He spoke to the dog, calling it to him; but in his voice was a strange note of fear that frightened the animal, who had never known the man to speak in such a way before. Something was the matter, and its suspicious nature sensed danger—it knew not what danger, but somewhere, somehow, in its brain arose an apprehension of the man. It flattened its ears down at the sound of the man's voice, and its restless, hunching movements and the liftings and shiftings of its forefeet became more pronounced; but it would not come to the man. He got on his hands and knees and crawled toward the dog. This unusual posture again excited suspicion, and the animal sidled mincingly away.

The man sat up in the snow for a moment and struggled for calmness. Then he pulled on his mittens, by means of his teeth, and got up on his feet. He glanced down at first in order to assure himself that he was really standing up, for the absence of sensation in his feet left him unrelated to the earth. His erect position in itself started to drive the webs of suspicion from the dog's mind; and when he spoke peremptorily with the sound of whiplashes in his voice, the dog rendered its customary allegiance and came to him. As it came within reaching distance, the man lost his control. His arms flashed out to the dog, and he experienced genuine surprise when he discovered that his hands could not clutch, that there was neither bend nor feeling in the fingers. He had forgotten for the moment that they were frozen and that they were freezing more and more. All this happened quickly, and before the animal could get away, he encircled its body with his arms. He sat down in the snow, and in this fashion held the dog, while it snarled and whined and struggled.

But it was all he could do, hold its body encircled in his arms and sit there. He realized that he could not kill the dog. There was no way to do it. With his helpless hands he could neither draw nor hold his sheath knife nor throttle the animal. He released it, and it plunged wildly away, its tail between its legs and still snarling. It halted forty feet away and surveyed him curiously, with ears sharply pricked forward. The man looked down at his hands in order to locate them, and found them hanging on the ends of his arms. It struck him as curious that one should have to use his eyes in order to find out where his hands were. He began threshing his arms back and forth, beating the mittened hands against his sides. He did this for five minutes, violently, and his heart pumped enough blood up to the surface to put a stop to his shivering. But no sensation was aroused in his hands. He had an impression that they hung like weights on the ends of his arms, but when he tried to run the impression down, he could not find it.

A certain fear of death, dull and oppressive, came to him. This fear quickly became poignant as he realized that it was no longer a mere matter of freezing his fingers and toes, or of losing his hands and feet, but that it was a matter of life and death, with the chances against him. This threw him into a panic, and he turned and ran up the creek bed along the old, dim trail. The dog joined in behind and kept up with him. He ran blindly, without intention, in fear such as he had never known in his life. Slowly, as he plowed and floundered through the snow, he began to see things again—the banks of the creek, the old timber jams, the leafless aspens, and the sky. The running made him feel better. He did not shiver. Maybe, if he ran on, his feet would thaw out; and, anyway, if he ran far enough, he would reach the camp and the boys. Without doubt he would lose some fingers and toes and some of his face; but the boys would take care of him, and save the rest of him when he got there. And at the same time there was another thought in his mind that said he would never get to the camp and the boys; that it was too many miles away, that the freezing had too great a start on him, and that he would soon be stiff and dead. This thought he kept in the background and refused to consider. Sometimes it pushed itself forward and demanded to be heard, but he thrust it back and strove to think of other things.

It struck him as curious that he could run at all on feet so frozen that he could not feel them when they struck the earth and took the weight of his body. He seemed to himself to skim along above the surface, and to have no connection with the earth. Somewhere he had once seen a winged Mercury, and he wondered if Mercury felt as he felt when skimming over the earth.

His theory of running until he reached camp and the boys had one flaw in it: he lacked the endurance. Several times he stumbled, and finally he tottered crumpled up, and fell. When he tried to rise, he failed. He must sit and rest, he decided, and next time he would merely walk and keep on going. As he sat and regained his breath, he noted that he was feeling quite warm and comfortable. He was not shivering, and it even seemed that a warm glow had come to his chest and trunk. And yet, when he touched his nose or cheeks, there was no sensation. Running would not thaw them out. Nor would it thaw out his hands and feet. Then the thought came to him that the frozen portions of his body must be extending. He tried to keep this thought down, to forget it, to think of something else; he was aware of the panicky feeling that he caused, and he was afraid of the panic. But the thought asserted itself, and persisted, until it produced a vision of his body totally frozen. This was too much, and he made another wild run along the trail. Once he slowed down to a walk, but the thought of the freezing extending itself made him run again.

And all the time the dog ran with him, at his heels. When he fell down a second time, it curled its tail over its forefeet and sat in front of him, facing him, curiously eager and intent. The warmth and security of the animal angered him, and he cursed it till it flattened down its ears appeasingly. This time the shivering came more quickly upon the man. He was losing in his battle with the frost. It was creeping into his body from all sides. The thought of it drove him on, but he ran no more than a hundred feet when he staggered and pitched headlong. It was his last panic. When he had recovered his breath and control, he sat up and entertained in his mind the conception of meeting death with dignity. However, the conception did not come to him in such terms. His idea of it was that he had been making a fool of himself, running around like a chicken with its head cut off—such was the simile that occurred to him. Well, he was bound to freeze anyway, and he might as well take it decently. With this new-found peace of mind came the first glimmerings of drowsiness. A good idea, he thought, to sleep off to death. It was like taking an anesthetic. Freezing was not so bad as people thought. There were lots worse ways to die.

He pictured the boys finding his body next day. Suddenly he found himself with them, coming along the trail and looking for himself. And, still with them, he came around a turn in the trail and found himself lying in the snow. He did not belong with himself any more, for even then he was out of himself, standing with the boys and looking at himself in the snow. It certainly was cold, was his thought. When he got back to the States, he could tell the folks what real cold was. He drifted on from this to a vision of the old-timer on Sulfur Creek. He could see him quite clearly, warm and comfortable, and smoking a pipe.

"You were right, old hoss; you were right," the man mumbled to the old-timer of Sulfur Creek.

Then the man drowsed off into what seemed to him the most comfortable and satisfying sleep he had ever known. The dog sat facing him and waiting. The brief day drew to a close in a long, slow twilight. There were no signs of a fire to be made, and, besides, never in the dog's experience had it known a man to sit like that in the snow and make no fire. As the twilight drew on, its eager yearning for the fire mastered it, and with a great lifting and shifting of forefeet, it whined softly, then flattened its ears down in anticipation of being chidden by the man. But the man remained silent. Later, the dog whined loudly. And still later it crept close to the man and caught the scent of death. This made the animal bristle and back away. A little longer it delayed, howling under the stars that leaped and danced and shone brightly in the cold sky. Then it turned and trotted up the trail in the direction of the camp it knew, where were the other food providers and fire providers.

Check Your Reading

1. What is the temperature in the Yukon during the story? How has the man ignored warnings about the dangers of traveling alone in the cold?

2. What supplies does the man carry with him and how are they useful?

3. What hints are given that this trip will end in disaster?

4. What vision does the man have of the next day and how does it make him feel?

5. When and why does the dog decide to leave the man?

Further Exploration

1. What is the effect of reading about a man and a dog who have no names?

2. Is the man responsible for causing his own death or is nature at fault?

3. Does the author want you to assume that nature is an enemy of mankind?

4. Explain the man's last words. To whom is he speaking? Does what he says change your attitude about him?

5. Give examples of other situations in which animals are protected by instinct. Do people possess similar protective instincts?

William Melvin Kelley (1937–)

An all-around student and leader in New York's Fieldston School, William Kelley excelled in academics, track, and the student council. During his sophomore year, along the way to a Harvard law degree, Kelly discovered satisfaction in writing under the guidance of novelist John Hawkes. That experience, plus another rewarding course taught by Archibald MacLeish, brought about his decision to become a writer.

Without completing his degree, Kelley left Harvard and began publishing novels, including *A Different Drummer* (1962), *A Drop of Patience* (1965), *Dem* (1967), and *Dunsfords Travels Everywheres* (1970). He also published a collection of short stories, *Dancers on the Shore* (1964). He has taught at the New School for Social Research and the State University College in Geneseo, New York. "Enemy Territory" reflects Kelley's experiences in the diverse and sometimes violent neighborhoods of Bronx, New York.

Enemy Territory
William Melvin Kelley

I peered over a rotting tree stump and saw him moving, without a helmet, in the bushes. I got his forehead in my sights, squeezed the trigger, and imagined I saw the bullet puncture his head and blood trickle out. "I got you, Jerome. I got you!"

"Awh, you did not."

"I got you; you're dead."

I must have sounded very definite because he compromised. "You only wounded me."

"Tommy? Tommy! Come here." Her voice came from high above me.

I scrambled to my knees. "What, Ma?" She was on the porch of our house, next to the vacant lot where we were playing.

"Come here a minute, dear. I want you to do something for me." She was wearing a yellow dress. The porch was red brick.

I hopped up and ran to the foot of our steps. She came to the top. "Mister Bixby left his hat."

As I had waited in ambush for Jerome, I had seen Mister Bixby climb and, an hour later, chug down the steps. He was one of my father's poker-playing friends. It was only after she mentioned it that I remembered Mister Bixby had been wearing, when he arrived, a white, wide-brimmed panama hat with a black band.

Entering my parents' room on the second floor, I saw it on their bed. My mother picked it up. "Walk it around to his house. Now walk, I say. Don't run because you'll probably drop it and ruin it." It was so white a speck of dirt would have shone like a black star in a white sky. "So walk! Let me see your hands."

I extended them palms up and she immediately sent me to the

bathroom to wash. Then she gave me the hat. I did not really grip it; rather, with my finger in the crown, I balanced it, as if about to twirl it.

When I stepped onto the porch again, I saw them playing on their corner—Valentine's Gang. Well, in this day of street gangs organized like armies, I cannot rightly call Joey Valentine, who was eight, and his acquaintances, who ranged in aged from five to seven, a gang. It was simply that they lived on the next block, and since my friends and I were just at the age when we were allowed to cross the street, but were not yet used to this new freedom, we still stood on opposite sides of the asphalt strip that divided us and called each other names. It was not until I got onto the porch that I realized, with a sense of dread that only a six-year-old can conjure up, that Mister Bixby lived one block beyond Valentine's Territory.

Still, with faith that the adult nature of my mission would give me unmolested passage, I approached the corner, which was guarded by a red fire-alarm box, looked both ways for the cars that seldom came, and, swallowing, began to cross over.

They were playing with toy soldiers and tin tanks in the border of dry yellow dirt that separated the flagstones from the gutter. I was in the middle of the street when they first realized I was invading; they were shocked. At the time, I can remember thinking they must have been awed that I should have the unequaled courage to cross into their territory. But looking back, I realize it probably had little to do with me. It was the hat, a white panama hat. A more natural target for abuse has never existed.

I was two steps from the curb when Joey Valentine moved into my path. "Hey, what you got?"

Since he was obviously asking the question to show off, I bit my lips and did not answer. I saw myself as one of my radio heroes resisting Japanese interrogation. I was aloof. However, the white panama hat was not at all aloof. Before I knew it, Joey Valentine reached out a mud-caked hand and knocked the hat off my finger to a resounding chorus of cheers and laughter.

I scooped up the hat before any of them, retreated at a run across the street, and stopped beside the red alarm box. Wanting to save some small amount of my dignity, I screamed at them: "I'll get you guys! I'll get you. I'm not really an American. I'm an African and Africans are friends of the Japs and I'll get them to *bomb your house!*"

But even as I ranted at them I could see I was doing so vain. Across the way, Valentine's Gang lounged with the calm of movie Marines listening to Japanese propaganda on the radio. I turned toward my house, inspecting the hat for smudges. There were none; it was as blinding white as ever. Already I felt tears inching down my cheeks.

Not until I was halfway up the porch steps did I see my grandmother sitting in her red iron chair. But before I could say anything, before I could appeal for understanding and comfort, she lifted herself out of the chair and disappeared into the house. She had seen it all—I knew that—and she was too ashamed to face me.

Suddenly, she was coming back, holding a broom handle. She had never before lifted a hand to me, but in my state, I felt sure that many things would change. I closed my eyes and waited.

Instead of the crunch of hard wood on bone, I heard her chair creak. I opened my eyes and found the end of the broom handle under my nose.

"You know if you don't go back and deliver that hat, you'll feel pretty bad tonight."

I nodded.

"Well, take this. We don't like you fighting. But sometimes you have to. So now you march down there and tell those boys if they don't let you alone, you'll have to hit them with this. Here." She pushed the broom handle at me.

I took it, but was not very happy about it. I studied her; she looked the same, her white hair bunned at her neck, her blue eyes large behind glasses, her skin the color of unvarnished wood. But something inside must have changed for her actually to tell me to hit someone. I had been in fights, fits and starts of temper that burned out in a second. But to walk deliberately down to the corner, threaten someone, and hit him if he did not move aside, this was completely different, and, as my parents and grandmother had raised me, downright evil. She must have realized what I was thinking.

"You know who Teddy Roosevelt was?"

I nodded.

"Well, he once said: *Speak softly and carry a big stick; you will go far.*"

I understood her, but to do something like this was still alien to my nature. I held back.

"Come on." She stood abruptly and took my hand. We went into the house, down the hall, and into her bedroom. "I have to see to the mulatto rice. You sit on my bed and look at the picture on the wall." She went on to the kitchen. I was still holding the broom handle and now put it down across the bed, and climbed up beside it, surrounded by her room, an old woman's room with its fifty years of perfume, powder, and sweet soap. I felt a long way from the corner and Valentine's Gang.

There were three pictures on the wall and I was not certain which she wanted me to study. The smallest was of my granduncle Wilfred, who lived on Long Island and came to Thanksgiving dinner. The largest was of Jesus, the fingers of His right hand crossed and held up, His left hand baring His chest, in the middle of which was His heart, red and dripping blood. In the cool darkness of the room, He looked at me with gentle eyes, a slight smile on His lips. The third was my grandmother's husband, who had died so long before that I had never known him and had no feeling for him as my grandfather. He was light, like my grandmother, but more like some of the short, sallow Italian men who lived on the block. His black hair was parted in the middle. He wore a big mustache which hid his mouth. His jaw was square and dimpled. With black eyes, he seemed to look at something just above my head.

"Well, all right now." My grandmother came in, sweating from standing over the stove, and sat in a small armchair beside the bed. "Did you look at the picture?"

"I didn't know which one." I looked at Jesus again.

"No, not Him this time. This one." She indicated her husband. "I meant him."

Now Pablo Cortés, your grandfather—she started—was just like you, as gentle as a milkweed flower settling into honey, and as friendly as ninety-seven puppy dogs. He was from Cuba, which is an island in the Atlantic Ocean.

He was so kind that he'd meet every boat coming in from Cuba and talk to all of the people getting off, and if he found that one of them didn't have a place to stay, and no money for food, he'd bring him home. He'd lead his new friend into the kitchen and say: "Jennie, this is a countryman. He got no place to sleep, and he's hungry." And I'd sigh and say: "All right. Dinner'll be ready in ten minutes." They'd go into the living room and sing and roll cigars.

That's what he did for a living, roll cigars, working at home. The leaves were spread out all over the floor like a rug and I never did like cigars because I know somebody's been walking all over the leaves, sometimes in bare feet like your mother did when she was a little girl.

Pablo was so friendly he gave a party every day while I was at work. I'd come home and open the door and the cigar smoke would tumble out, and through the haze I would see twenty drunken Cubans, most with guitars, others rolling cigars, and all of them howling songs.

So now fifty years ago, I'd come from down South to stay with my brother Wilfred, and I was so dumb that the first time I saw snow I thought somebody upstairs'd broken open a pillow out the window. So my brother Wilfred had to explain a lot of things to me. And the first thing was about the neighborhoods. The Italians lived in one neighborhood, and the Polish in another, and the Negroes and Cubans someplace else. After Pablo and I got married, we lived with the Negroes. And if you walked two blocks one way, you'd come to the Irish neighborhood, and if you were smart, you'd turn around and come back because if the Irish caught you, they'd do something terrible to you.

I don't know if Pablo knew this or not, or if he just thought he was so friendly that everybody would just naturally be friendly right back. But one day he went for a walk. He got over into the Irish neighborhood and got a little thirsty—which he did pretty often—so he went into an Irish bar and asked for a drink. I guess they thought he was new in this country because the bartender gave him his drink. So Pablo, smiling all the time, and waiting for them to smile back, stood there in that Irish bar and drank slow. When he was finished, the bartender took the glass, and instead of washing it, he smashed it down on the floor and stepped on it and crushed the pieces under his heel. What he meant was that it was pretty bad to be a Cuban and no Irishman would want to touch a glass a Cuban had drunk from.

I don't know if Pablo knew that either. He asked for another drink. And he got it. And after he finished this one, the bartender smashed it in the sink and glared at him.

Pablo was still thirsty and ordered again.

The bartender came and stood in front of him. He was a big man, with a face as red as watermelon. "Say, buddy, can't you take a hint?"

Pablo smiled. "What hint?"

The bartender was getting pretty mad. "Why you think I'm breaking them glasses?"

"I thought you like to break glasses. You must got a high bill on glasses."

The bartender got an ax handle from under the bar. "Get out of here, Cuban!"

So now Pablo knew the bartender didn't want him in the bar. "Now, let me get this straight. If I ask you for drink, and you give me drink, you would break that glass too?"

"That's right. But you better not order again."

Pablo sighed. He was sad. "Well, then we will pretend I got drunk in this bar." And the next thing anybody knew Pablo was behind the bar, breaking all the glasses he could reach.

"And we will pretend that I look at myself in your mirror." He picked up a bottle and cracked the big mirror they had.

By now there was a regular riot going on with all the men in the bar trying to catch and hold him, and Pablo running around, breaking chairs and tables. Finally, just before they caught and tied him up, he tipped over their piano. "We will pretend I played a Cuban song on this piano!"

They called the police and held him until the wagon came. And the next time I saw him was in court the next morning, where the judge kept looking at Pablo like he really didn't believe that a man who seemed so kind and gentle could do such things. But it was plain Pablo had wrecked the Irishman's bar. The judge sentenced him to thirty days in the city jail, and fifty dollars damages, which Pablo couldn't pay. So the judge gave him thirty extra days.

I didn't see Pablo for the next two months. When he came home, he was changed. He wasn't smiling at all, and you remember that he used to smile all the time. As soon as he came in the house he told me he was going out again. I knew where and I got mad. "Do you want to spend another two months in jail? Is that what you want?"

He didn't understand me. "Why you ask me that?"

"Why! You're going over there to that white man's bar and get into a fight and go on back to jail. Did you like it that much? Did jail change you so much?"

"Jennie, don't you see? I try not to change." He picked up five boxes of cigars he'd made before he went to jail and put them into a brown paper bag, and tucked the bag under his arm.

I watched him go out the door and then started to cry. I loved him, you see, and didn't want him back in jail. And I cried because I didn't understand him now and was afraid of that.

When the Irishmen saw him coming into their bar, they were stunned. Their mouths dropped open and they all got quiet. Pablo didn't pay them any mind, just walked up to bar and put his foot on the brass rail.

The bartender picked up his ax handle. "What you want here Cuban? Ain't you had enough?"

"No." Pablo didn't smile. He took the brown paper bag and put it gently on the counter. Cigars, he said, are delicate and shouldn't be tossed around.

The bartender looked at the bag. "What you got there?"

"Maybe you find out." He touched the box with his fingers. "I like a drink."

The bartender stared at him for a second and then at the paper bag for a long time. He started to sweat. "All right." He set the drink down in front of Pablo.

For a minute, Pablo just looked at it. Then he lifted it to his lips and drank it down and pushed it across the bar to the bartender.

The bartender picked it up and studied it. Finally, he looked at Pablo again. "What the . . . ! I had to close up for a week after you was here the first time." He took the glass to the sink, washed it with soap and water, and put it with the other clean glasses. Then he looked at Pablo again. "Satisfied?"

"Not yet." Pablo grabbed the paper bag and started to open it.

"Watch out, fellows!" the bartender yelled in his ear. When Pablo looked up, all the men in the bar were lying on their stomachs covering their heads. The bartender was behind the bar on his knees, his hands over his ears.

Pablo took a cigar box out of the bag, opened it, pulled himself up and across the bar, and reached the box down to the bartender. "Hey, you want fine, hand made Havana cigar?" He was smiling.

"Are you going back down to that corner?" My grandmother took my hand.

I looked into her face and then at the picture of her husband. He was still studying something just above my head. "I guess so." I did not really want to do it.

"You may not even have to use that." She pointed at the broom handle. "But you should know you can."

I knew this was true, and climbed off the bed and picked up the white hat and the broom handle. "Okay."

"I'll be waiting on the porch for you." She smiled, got up, and, sighing, went out to the kitchen.

For a while, I listened to pots knocking and being filled with water. Then I stood in her room and practiced what I would say to Valentine's Gang: "If you guys don't let me go by, I'll have to hit you with this." There was a quake in my voice the first time I said it out loud, but, if I had to, I thought I would actually be able to say it and then use the stick. I went down the hall, onto the porch, and looked down toward the corner.

It was empty. The mothers of the members of Valentine's Gang had summoned them home to supper.

Check Your Reading

1. Which former president does the grandmother quote?

2. Why does Tommy not have to use the broomstick on his second trip?

3. What does Pablo Cortés do for a living?

4. Why does Tommy's grandmother dislike cigars?

5. What does Pablo do to show the Irish bartender his willingness to make peace?

Further Exploration

1. Explain your own understanding of "Speak softly and carry a big stick." Do you think the advice would benefit a child as young as Tommy? Is there any other way for Tommy to avoid a confrontation with the Valentine gang? If there is a way, explain what it is.

2. How does the bartender's breaking of glasses show contempt for Cubans? Why does Pablo break more glasses, smash the mirror, and overturn the piano? How do the bar patrons reveal their fear of Pablo? Is Pablo's violent behavior justified?

3. Describe Tommy's feelings as he gazes at the three pictures. Why does he feel secure in his grandmother's room? What does he learn from her?

4. What two images does Jennie use to describe her husband at the start of her story and how does she link them to Tommy?

5. Why would a story about courage in one's own family be comforting? Relate an incident about a member of your family who displayed a quality you admire and might want to develop in yourself.

Facing Conflict

Thinking It Over

These activities offer opportunities for you to consider how the stories in Part One relate to one another and to the theme of *Facing Conflict*.

1. In which story is the conflict most complicated? Is there more than one way the conflict could be resolved? Describe several alternatives.

2. Chose a character you admire from one of the stories and explain why he or she deserves your respect. Compare the character to a real person who has faced a similar struggle.

3. Compose a newspaper account of either "To Build a Fire" or "The Bride Comes to Yellow Sky." Follow the journalistic formula of who, what, where, when, why, and how.

4. Write a dialogue between two characters from different stories in which the characters discuss their reactions to conflict. Include their second thoughts about how they might react differently if confronted by a similar situation.

5. Advice from an outside source often helps people resolve their conflicts. Which character from these four stories receives the best advice? Explain how the character benefits from another person's wisdom.

6. Discuss the use of violence in one of the stories. Is violence a suitable answer to that character's conflict? Is violence ever beneficial?

PART TWO

Adjusting to Life

We all suffer "growing pains," both real and imaginary, as a natural part of the maturing process. Physically, our bodies sometimes suffer from growing too fast. Psychologically, we experience a variety of conflicts as our perceptions of who we are go through periods of change and adaptation. Of course, these experiences are not limited to youth because growth is a lifelong process.

The pain of accepting responsibility for our actions, although sharp in our first encounter, often becomes less troublesome as we become accustomed to the demands of adulthood. But similar feelings recur throughout life. The pain of leaving home for the first time to visit grandparents or to go to summer camp might be repeated when a young person leaves to begin college or a new job. Disappointments can also trouble us. Even when these disappointments are trivial, they seem serious at the time. Learning to cope with disappointments in ourselves and in others is a significant part of maturity.

Literature can help us realize that growing pains are universal; everyone suffers some adjustment problems, but rarely are the results fatal. The stories in this Part describe young people who must face responsibility, separation, and disappointment. Even though the endings do not always work out in the best interest of the characters, these stories will offer insight and solace to anyone who undergoes similar growing pains.

John Updike (1932–)

Updike has been described as a writer who "reaches out the front door and grabs a couple of people and pulls them inside for inspection." He grew up in a middle class family in Shillington, Pennsylvania, and pursued an English major at Harvard University. Updike showed early promise by becoming president of the Harvard *Lampoon* and graduating *summa cum laude*.

With a year of studies at Oxford, England and several years' work for *The New Yorker*, Updike was suitably prepared for success. His best novels include *Rabbit Run* (1960), *The Centaur* (1963), and *Couples* (1968). A book of poetry, *The Carpentered Hen and Other Tame Creatures* (1958), was followed by four collections of short stories, *Pigeon Feathers and Other Stories* (1959), *The Same Door* (1959), *The Music School* (1962), and *Museums and Women* (1972). In intervening years Updike published a series of novels, including a book of poetry, *Facing Nature: Poems* (1985).

A major figure in contemporary American literature, Updike succeeds by taking commonplace people and events and weaving them into compelling narratives. "A & P" gives ample evidence of his keen wit and clever understanding of a character who experiences a sudden revelation about his place in an unfair world.

A & P

John Updike

In walks these three girls in nothing but bathing suits. I'm in the third checkout slot, with my back to the door, so I don't see them until they're over by the bread. The one that caught my eye first was the one in the plaid green two-piece. She was a chunky kid, with a good tan and a sweet broad soft-looking can with those two crescents of white just under it, where the sun never seems to hit, at the top of the backs of her legs. I stood there with my hand on a box of HiHo crackers trying to remember if I rang it up or not. I ring it up again and the customer starts giving me hell. She's one of these cash-register-watchers, a witch about fifty with rouge on her cheekbones and no eyebrows, and I know it made her day to trip me up. She'd been watching cash registers for fifty years and probably never seen a mistake before.

By the time I got her feathers smoothed and her goodies into a bag—she gives me a little snort in passing, if she'd been born at the right time they would have burned her over in Salem—by the time I get her on her way the girls had circled around the bread and were coming back, without a pushcart, back my way along the counters, in the aisle between the checkouts and the Special bins. They didn't even have shoes on. There was this chunky one, with the two-piece—it was bright green and the seams on the bra were still sharp and her belly was still pretty pale so I guessed she just got it (the suit)—there was this one, with one of those chubby berry-faces, the lips all bunched together under her nose, this one, and a tall one, with black hair that hadn't quite frizzed right, and one of these sunburns right across under the eyes, and a chin that was too long—you know, the kind of girl other girls think is very "striking" and "attractive" but never quite makes it, as they very well know, which is why they like her so much—and then the third one, that wasn't quite so tall. She was the queen. She kind of led them, the other two peeking around and making their shoulders round. She didn't look around, not this queen, she just walked straight on slowly, on these long white prima-donna legs. She came down a little hard on her heels, as if she didn't walk in her bare feet that much, putting down her heels and then letting the weight move along to her toes as if she was testing the floor with every step, putting a little deliberate extra action into it. You never know for sure how girls' minds work (do you really think it's a mind in there or just a little buzz like a bee in a glass jar?) but you got the idea she had talked the other two into coming in here with her, and now she was showing them how to do it, walk slow and hold yourself straight.

She had on a kind of dirty-pink—beige maybe, I don't know—bathing suit with a little nubble all over it and, what got me, the straps were down. They were off her shoulders looped loose around the cool tops of her arms, and I guess as a result the suit had slipped a little on her, so all around the top of the cloth there was this shining rim. If it hadn't been there you wouldn't have known there could have been anything whiter than those shoulders. With the straps pushed off, there was nothing between the top of the suit and the top of her head except just *her*, this clean bare plane of the top of her chest down from the shoulder bones like a dented sheet of metal tilted in the light. I mean, it was more than pretty.

She had sort of oaky hair that the sun and salt had bleached, done up in a bun that was unravelling, and a kind of prim face. Walking into the A & P with your straps down, I suppose it's the only kind of face you *can* have. She held her head so high her neck, coming up out of those white shoulders, looked kind of stretched, but I didn't mind. The longer her neck was, the more of her there was.

She must have felt in the corner of her eye me and over my shoulder Stokesie in the second slot watching, but she didn't tip. Not this queen. She kept her eyes moving across the racks, and stopped, and turned so slow it made my stomach rub the inside of my apron, and buzzed to the other two, who kind of huddled against her for relief, and then they all three of them went up the cat-and-dog-food-breakfast-cereal-macaroni-rice-raisins-seasoning-spreads-spaghetti- soft-drinks-crackers-and-cookies aisle. From the third slot I look straight up this aisle to the meat counter, and I watched them all the way. The fat one with the tan sort of fumbled with the cookies, but on second thought she put the package back. The sheep pushing their carts down the aisle—the girls were walking against the usual traffic (not that we have one-way signs or anything)—were pretty hilarious. You could see them, when Queenie's white shoulders dawned on them, kind of jerk, or hop, or hiccup, but their eyes snapped back to their own baskets and on they pushed. I bet you could set off dynamite in an A & P and the people would by and large keep reaching and checking oatmeal off their lists and muttering "Let me see, there was a third thing, began with A, asparagus, no, ah, yes, apple-sauce!" or whatever it is they do mutter. But there was no doubt, this jiggled them. A few houseslaves in pin curlers even looked around after pushing their carts past to make sure what they had seen was correct.

You know, it's one thing to have a girl in a bathing suit down on the beach, where what with the glare nobody can look at each other much anyway, and another thing in the cool of the A & P, under the fluorescent lights, against all those stacked packages, with her feet paddling along naked over our checkerboard green-and-cream rubber-tile floor.

"Oh Daddy," Stokesie said beside me. "I feel so faint."

"Darling," I said. "Hold me tight." Stokesie's married, with two babies chalked up on his fuselage already, but as far as I can tell that's the only difference. He's twenty-two, and I was nineteen this April.

"Is it done?" he asks, the responsible married man finding his voice. I forgot to say he thinks he's going to be manager some sunny day, maybe in 1990 when it's called the Great Alexandrov and Petrooshki Tea Company or something.

What he meant was, our town is five miles from a beach, with a big summer colony out on the point, but we're right in the middle of town, and the women generally put on a shirt or shorts or something before they get out of the car into the street. And anyway these are usually women with six children and varicose veins mapping their legs and nobody, including them, could care less. As I say, we're right in the middle of town, and if you stand at our front doors you can see two banks and the Congregational church and the newspaper store and three real-estate offices and about twenty-seven old freeloaders tearing up Central Street because the sewer broke again. It's not as if we're on the Cape; we're north of Boston and there's people in this town haven't seen the ocean for twenty years.

The girls had reached the meat counter and were asking McMahon something. He pointed, they pointed, and they shuffled out of sight behind a pyramid of Diet Delight peaches. All that was left for us to see was old McMahon patting his mouth and looking after them sizing up their joints. Poor kids, I began to feel sorry for them, they couldn't help it.

Now here comes the sad part of the story, at least my family says it's sad, but I don't think it's so sad myself. The store's pretty empty, it being Thursday afternoon, so there was nothing much to do except lean on the register and wait for the girls to show up again. The whole store was like a pinball machine and I didn't know which tunnel they'd come out of. After a while they come around out of the far aisle, around the light bulbs, records at discount of the Caribbean Six or Tony Martin Sings or some such gunk you wonder they waste the wax on, sixpacks of candy bars, and plastic toys done up in cellophane that fall apart when a kid looks at them anyway. Around they come, Queenie still leading the way, and holding a little gray jar in her hand. Slots Three through Seven are unmanned and I could see her wondering between Stokes and me, but Stokesie with his usual luck draws an old party in baggy gray pants who stumbles up with four giant cans of pineapple juice (what do these bums *do* with all that pineapple juice? I've often asked myself) so the girls come to me. Queenie puts down the jar and I take it into my fingers icy cold. Kingfish Fancy Herring Snacks in pure Sour Cream: 49¢. Now her hands are empty, not a ring or a bracelet, bare as God made them, and I wonder where the money's coming from. Still with that prim look she lifts a folded dollar bill out of the hollow at the center of her nubbled pink top. The jar went heavy in my hand. Really, I thought that was so cute.

Then everybody's luck begins to run out. Lengel comes in from haggling with a truck full of cabbages on the lot and is about to scuttle into that door marked MANAGER behind which he hides all day when the girls touch his eye. Lengel's pretty dreary, teaches Sunday school and the rest, but he doesn't miss that much. He comes over and says, "Girls, this isn't the beach."

Queenie blushes, though maybe it's just a brush of sunburn I was noticing for the first time, now that she was so close. "My mother asked me to pick up a jar of herring snacks." Her voice kind of startled me, the way voices do when you see the people first, coming out so flat and dumb yet kind of tony, too, the way it tickled over "pick up" and "snacks." All of a sudden I slid right down her voice into her living room. Her father and the other men were standing around in ice-cream coats and bow ties and the women were in sandals picking up herring snacks on toothpicks off a big glass plate and they were all holding drinks the color of water with olives and sprigs of mint in them. When my parents have somebody over they get lemonade and if it's a real racy affair Schlitz in tall glasses with "They'll Do It Every Time" cartoons stencilled on.

"That's all right," Lengel said. "But this isn't the beach." His repeating this struck me as funny, as if it had just occurred to him, and he had been thinking all these years the A & P was a great big dune and he was the head lifeguard. He didn't like my smiling—as I say he doesn't miss much—but he concentrates on giving the girls that sad Sunday-school-superintendent stare.

Queenie's blush is no sunburn now, and the plump one in plaid, that I like better from the back—a really sweet can—pipes up, "We weren't doing any shopping. We just came in for the one thing."

"That makes no difference," Lengel tells her, and I could see from the way his eyes went that he hadn't noticed she was wearing a two-piece before. "We want you decently dressed when you come in here."

"We *are* decent," Queenie says suddenly, her lower lip pushing, getting sore now that she remembers her place, a place from which the crowd that runs the A & P must look pretty crummy. Fancy Herring Snacks flashed in her very blue eyes.

"Girls, I didn't want to argue with you. After this come in here with your shoulders covered. It's our policy." He turns his back. That's policy for you. Policy is what the kingpins want. What the others want is juvenile delinquency.

All this while, the customers had been showing up with their carts but, you know, sheep, seeing a scene, they had all bunched up on Stokesie, who shook open a paper bag as gently as peeling a peach, not wanting to miss a word. I could feel in the silence everybody getting nervous, most of all Lengel, who asks me, "Sammy, have you rung up their purchase?"

I thought and said "No" but it wasn't about that I was thinking. I go through the punches, 4, 9, GROC, ToT—it's more complicated than you think, and after you do it often enough, it begins to make a little song, that you hear words to, in my case "Hello (*bing*) there, you (*gung*) hap-py *pee*-pul (*splat*)!—the *splat* being the drawer flying out. I uncrease the bill, tenderly as you may imagine, it just having come from between the two smoothest scoops of vanilla I had ever known were there, and pass a half and a penny into her narrow pink palm, and nestled the herrings in a bag and twist its neck and hand it over, all the time thinking.

The girls, and who'd blame them, are in a hurry to get out, so I say "I quit" to Lengel quick enough for them to hear, hoping they'll stop and watch me, their unsuspected hero. They keep right on going, into the electric eye; the door flies open and they flicker across the lot to their car, Queenie and Plaid and Big Tall Goony-Goony (not that as raw material she was so bad), leaving me with Lengel and a kink in his eyebrow.

"Did you say something, Sammy?"

"I said I quit."

"I thought you did."

"You didn't have to embarrass them."

"It was they who were embarrassing us."

I started to say something that came out "Fiddle-de-doo." It's a saying of my grandmother's, and I know she would have been pleased.

"I don't think you know what you're saying," Lengel said.

"I know you don't," I said. "But I do." I pull the bow at the back of my apron and start shrugging it off my shoulders. A couple customers that had been heading for my slot begin to knock against each other, like scared pigs in a chute.

Lengel sighs and begins to look very patient and old and gray. He's been a friend of my parents for years. "Sammy, you don't want to do this to your Mom and Dad," he tells me. It's true, I don't. But it seems to me that once you begin a gesture it's fatal not to go through with it. I fold the apron, "Sammy" stitched in red on the pocket, and put it on the counter, and drop the bow tie on top of it. The bow tie is theirs, if you've ever wondered. "You'll feel this for the rest of your life," Lengel says, and I know that's true, too, but remembering how he made that pretty girl blush makes me so scrunchy inside I punch the No Sale tab and the machine whirs "pee-pul" and the drawer splats out. One advantage to this scene taking place in summer, I can follow this up with a clean exit, there's no fumbling around getting your coat and galoshes, I just saunter into the electric eye in my white shirt that mother ironed the night before, and the door heaves itself open, and outside the sunshine is skating around on the asphalt.

I look around for my girls, but they're gone, of course. There wasn't anybody but some young married screaming with her children about some candy they didn't get by the door of a powder-blue Falcon station wagon. Looking back in the big windows, over the bags of peat moss and aluminum lawn furniture stacked on the pavement, I could see Lengel in my place in the slot, checking the sheep through. His face was dark gray and his back stiff, as if he'd just had an injection of iron, and my stomach kind of fell as I felt how hard the world was going to be to me hereafter.

Check Your Reading

1. What causes Sammy to focus his attention on Queenie?

2. Why does Sammy think of customers as sheep?

3. What is Lengel's reaction to the girls' style of dress?

4. What does Sammy envision when the girls make their purchase at the A & P?

5. What details in the story suggest that working in a grocery store is boring?

Further Exploration

1. How does the author use humor to describe Stokesie and McMahon's reactions to the three girls?

2. Describe the differences in reactions that the following people will have to Sammy's quitting his job: his parents? Lengel? Stokesie? The girls?

3. What does Sammy's punching of the "no sale" key symbolize?

4. What might Queenie's parents say to Lengel if Queenie complains about being embarrassed in public? How might Lengel have spared the girls from public humiliation?

5. In your opinion, under what circumstances are dress codes necessary and justified?

Shirley Jackson (1919–1965)

Shirley Jackson, herself the mother of four, once said, "Mothers are harried creatures . . . [who are] called upon, from time to time, to endure periods of such unnerving strain that only a heroine could meet them." Born in San Francisco, she married Stanley E. Hyman, literary critic, and moved to a quiet Vermont community to raise her family and write in an array of genre, including juvenile novels, adult novels, fictionalized autobiographies, essays, and short stories.

She wrote Gothic horror tales entitled *The Haunting of Hill House* (1959) and *We Have Always Lived in the Castle* (1962). Her most famous story, "The Lottery," became an instant classic. The subject of parenthood is the focus of her humorous book, *Life Among the Savages*, which, like "Charles," details the hectic and often unpredictable escapades of growing children.

Charles
Shirley Jackson

The day my son Laurie started kindergarten he renounced corduroy overalls with bibs and began wearing blue jeans with a belt; I watched him go off the first morning with the older girl next door, seeing clearly that an era of my life was ended, my sweet-voiced nursery-school tot replaced by a long-trousered, swaggering character who forgot to stop at the corner and wave good-bye to me.

He came home the same way, the front door slamming open, his cap on the floor, and the voice suddenly become raucous shouting, "Isn't anybody *here?*"

At lunch he spoke insolently to his father, spilled his baby sister's milk, and remarked that his teacher said we were not to take the name of the Lord in vain.

"How *was* school today?" I asked, elaborately casual.

"All right," he said.

"Did you learn anything?" his father asked.

Laurie regarded his father coldly. "I didn't learn nothing," he said.

"Anything," I said. "Didn't learn anything."

"The teacher spanked a boy, though," Laurie said, addressing his bread and butter. "For being fresh." he added, with his mouth full.

"What did he do?" I asked. "Who was it?"

Laurie thought. "It was Charles," he said. "He was fresh. The teacher spanked him and made him stand in a corner. He was awfully fresh."

"What did he do?" I asked again, but Laurie slid off his chair, took a cookie, and left, while his father was still saying, "See here, young man."

The next day Laurie remarked at lunch, as soon as he sat down, "Well, Charles was bad again today." He grinned enormously and said,

"Today Charles hit the teacher."

"Good heavens," I said, mindful of the Lord's name, "I suppose he got spanked again?"

"He sure did," Laurie said. "Look up," he said to his father.

"What?" his father said, looking up.

"Look down," Laurie said. "Look at my thumb. Gee, you're dumb." He began to laugh insanely.

"Why did Charles hit the teacher?" I asked quickly.

"Because she tried to make him color with red crayons," Laurie said. "Charles wanted to color with green crayons so he hit the teacher and she spanked him and said nobody play with Charles but everybody did."

The third day—it was Wednesday of the first week—Charles bounced a see-saw on to the head of a little girl and made her bleed, and the teacher made him stay inside all during recess. Thursday Charles had to stand in a corner during story-time because he kept pounding his feet on the floor. Friday Charles was deprived of blackboard privileges because he threw chalk.

On Saturday I remarked to my husband, "Do you think kindergarten is too unsettling for Laurie? All this toughness, and bad grammar, and this Charles boy sounds like such a bad influence."

"It'll be all right," my husband said reassuringly. "Bound to be people like Charles in the world. Might as well meet them now as later."

On Monday Laurie came home late, full of news. "Charles," he shouted as he came up the hill; I was waiting anxiously on the front steps. "Charles," Laurie yelled all the way up the hill, "Charles was bad again."

"Come right in," I said, as soon as he came close enough. "Lunch is waiting."

"You know what Charles did?" he demanded, following me through the door. "Charles yelled so in school they sent a boy in from first grade to tell the teacher she had to make Charles keep quiet, and so Charles had to stay after school. And so all the children stayed to watch him."

"What did he do?" I asked.

"He just sat there," Laurie said, climbing into his chair at the table. "Hi, Pop, y'old dust mop."

"Charles had to stay after school today," I told my husband. "Everyone stayed with him."

"What does this Charles look like?" my husband asked Laurie. "What's his other name?"

"He's bigger than me," Laurie said. "And he doesn't have any rubbers and he doesn't ever wear a jacket."

Monday night was the first Parent-Teachers meeting, and only the fact that the baby had a cold kept me from going; I wanted passionately to meet Charles's mother. On Tuesday Laurie remarked suddenly, "Our teacher had a friend come to see her in school today."

"Charles's mother?" my husband and I asked simultaneously.

"Naaah," Laurie said scornfully. "It was a man who came and made us do exercises, we had to touch our toes. Look." He climbed down from his chair and squatted down and touched his toes. "Like this," he said. He got solemnly back into his chair and said, picking up his fork, "Charles didn't even *do* exercises."

"That's fine, I said heartily. "Didn't Charles want to do exercises?"

"Naaah," Laurie said. "Charles was so fresh to the teacher's friend he wasn't *let* do exercises."

"Fresh again?" I said.

"He kicked the teacher's friend," Laurie said. "The teacher's friend told Charles to touch his toes like I just did and Charles kicked him."

"What are they going to do about Charles, do you suppose?" Laurie's father asked him.

Laurie shrugged elaborately. "Throw him out of school, I guess," he said.

Wednesday and Thursday were routine; Charles yelled during story hour and hit a boy in the stomach and made him cry. On Friday Charles stayed after school again and so did all the other children.

With the third week of kindergarten Charles was an institution in our family; the baby was being a Charles when she cried all afternoon; Laurie did a Charles when he filled his wagon full of mud and pulled it through the kitchen; even my husband, when he caught his elbow in the telephone cord and pulled telephone, ashtray, and a bowl of flowers off the table, said, after the first minute, "Looks like Charles."

During the third and fourth weeks it looked like a reformation in Charles; Laurie reported grimly at lunch on Thursday of the third week, "Charles was so good today the teacher gave him an apple."

"What?" I said, and my husband added warily, "You mean Charles?"

"Charles," Laurie said. "He gave the crayons around and he picked up the books afterward and the teacher said he was her helper."

"What happened?" I asked incredulously.

"He was her helper, that's all," Laurie said, and shrugged.

"Can this be true, about Charles?" I asked my husband that night. "Can something like this happen?"

"Wait and see," my husband said cynically. "When you've got a Charles to deal with, this may mean he's only plotting."

He seemed to be wrong. For over a week Charles was the teacher's helper; each day he handed things out and he picked things up; no one had to stay after school.

"The P.T.A. meeting's next week again," I told my husband one evening. "I'm going to find Charles's mother there."

"Ask her what happened to Charles," my husband said. "I'd like to know."

"I'd like to know myself," I said.

On Friday of that week things were back to normal. "You know what Charles did today?" Laurie demanded at the lunch table, in a voice slightly awed. "He told a little girl to say a word and she said it and the teacher washed her mouth out with soap and Charles laughed."

"What word?" his father asked unwisely, and Laurie said, "I'll have to whisper it to you, it's so bad." He got down off his chair and went around to his father. His father bent his head down and Laurie whispered joyfully. His father's eyes widened.

"Did Charles tell the little girl to say *that?*" he asked respectfully.

"She said it *twice,*" Laurie said. "Charles told her to say it *twice.*"

"What happened to Charles?" my husband asked.

"Nothing," Laurie said. "He was passing out the crayons."

Monday morning Charles abandoned the little girl and said the evil word himself three or four times, getting his mouth washed out with soap each time. He also threw chalk.

My husband came to the door with me that evening as I set out for the P.T.A. meeting. "Invite her over for a cup of tea after the meeting," he said. "I want to get a look at her."

"If only she's there," I said prayerfully.

"She'll be there," my husband said. "I don't see how they could hold a P.T.A. meeting without Charles's mother."

At the meeting I sat restlessly, scanning each comfortable matronly face, trying to determine which one hid the secret of Charles. None of them looked to me haggard enough. No one stood up in the meeting and apologized for the way her son had been acting. No one mentioned Charles.

After the meeting I identified and sought out Laurie's kindergarten teacher. She had a plate with a cup of tea and a piece of chocolate cake; I had a plate with a cup of tea and a piece of marshmallow cake. We maneuvered up to one another cautiously, and smiled.

"I've been so anxious to meet you," I said. "I'm Laurie's mother."

"We're all so interested in Laurie," she said.

"Well, he certainly likes kindergarten," I said. "He talks about it all the time."

"We had a little trouble adjusting, the first week or so," she said primly, "but now he's a fine little helper. With occasional lapses, of course."

"Laurie usually adjusts very quickly," I said. "I suppose this time it's Charles's influence."

"Charles?"

"Yes," I said, laughing, "you must have your hands full in that kindergarten, with Charles."

"Charles?" she said. "We don't have any Charles in the kindergarten."

Check Your Reading

1. How does Laurie show his delight in Charles's misbehavior?

2. Why does Laurie's mother fail to locate Charles's mother at the P.T.A. meeting?

3. How does Charles get the little girl in trouble?

4. At what point in the opening weeks of kindergarten does Charles begin to show improvement?

5. How do Laurie's parents reflect differences of opinion about the rearing of children?

Further Exploration

1. Explain why Laurie would find it necessary to create a person like Charles.

2. Why would a mischievous child suddenly start being helpful?

3. If you were a kindergarten teacher, how would you approach the parents of a child who misbehaves?

4. What type of discipline would work best on a student like Charles?

5. Describe the scene at Laurie's home when Laurie's mother returns from the P.T.A. meeting.

Toni Cade Bambara (1959–)

A native New Yorker with a background in social work and recreation, Toni Cade Bambara reflects keen observations of dialect and human motivation in her three collection of short stories, *Gorilla, My Love*; *The Sea Birds Are Still Alive*, and *Tales and Stories for Black Folks*. Poet Lucille Clifton sums up Bambara's skill: "She has captured it all, how we really talk, how we really are; and done it with love and respect. I laughed until I cried, then laughed again."

Bambara taught English and served as visiting professor at Drake University, Stephens College, Emory University, and Spelman College. "Happy Birthday" reveals her understanding of young people by evoking our empathy for Ollie's disappointment with a boring day that should have been a special occasion.

Happy Birthday
Toni Cade Bambara

Ollie spent the whole morning waiting. First she tried shaking Grand-daddy Larkins, who just wouldn't wake up. She thought he was just playing, but he was out. His teeth weren't even in the glass and there was a bottle on the bedstand. He'd be asleep for days. Then she waited on the cellar steps for Chalky, the building superintendent, to get through hauling garbage and come talk. But he was too busy. And then Ollie sat on the stairs waiting for Wilma. But it was Saturday and Wilma'd be holed up somewhere stuffing herself with potato chips and crunching down on jawbreakers, too greedy to cool it and eat 'em slow. Wilma'd come by tomorrow, though, and lie her behind off. "I went to Bear Mountain yesterday on a big boat with my brother Chestnut and his wife," she'd say, "and that's why I didn't come by for you 'cause we left so early in the morning that my mother even had to get me up when it was still dark out and we had a great time and I shot bows and arrows when we got there, and do you like my new dress?" Wilma always had some jive tale and always in one breath.

Ollie tried to figure out why she was even friends with Wilma. Wilma was going to grow up to be a lady and marry a doctor and live in New York, Wilma's mother said. But Ollie, poor orphan, was going to grow up and marry a drinking man if she didn't get killed first, Wilma's mother said. Ollie never told Granddaddy Larkins what Wilma's mother was all the time saying. She just hated her in private.

Ollie spent the early afternoon sitting on the rail in front of The Chicken Shack Restaurant, watching the cooks sling the wire baskets of chicken in and out of the frying fat. They were too sweaty and tired to tell her to move from in front. "Ruining the business," the owner used to fuss. Later she stood between the laundry and shoe store, watching some men pitch pennies against the building. She waited for a while, squeezing a rubber ball in her hand. If I can just get the wall for a minute, she thought, maybe somebody'll come along and we'll have us a good game of handball. But the men went right on pitching while other ones were waiting their turn. They'd be there for hours, so Ollie left.

She knocked on Mrs. Robinson's door to see if she wanted her dog walked. It was cool in the hallway at least. No one was home, not even the loud-mouth dog that usually slammed itself against the door like he was big and bad instead of being just a sorry little mutt. Then Ollie took the stairs two at a time, swinging up past the fourth floor to the roof. There was rice all over. Ronnie must have already fed his pigeons. The door to the roof was unlocked, and that meant that the big boys were on the roof. She planted her behind against the door and pushed. She kicked at a cluster of rice. Some grains bounced onto the soft tar of the roof and sank. When Ollie moved onto the roof, the blinding sun made her squint. And there they were, the big boys, jammed between the skylight and the chimney like dummies in a window, just doing nothing and looking half-asleep.

Peter Proper, as always, was dressed to the teeth. "I naturally stays clean," he was always saying. Today he said nothing, just sitting. Marbles, a kid from the projects, had an open book on his knees. James was there, too, staring at a fingernail. And Ferman, the nut from crosstown, and Frenchie, the athlete. A flurry of cinders floated down from the chimney and settled into their hair like gray snow.

"Why don't you just sit in the incinerator? You can get even dirtier that way," Ollie yelled. No one moved or said anything. She expected Frenchie to at least say, "Here comes Miss Freshmouth," or for Peter to send her to the store for eighteen cents' worth of American cheese. It was always eighteen cents' worth, and he always handed her a quarter and a nickel. Big Time. "Don't none of you want nothing from the store today?" She squinted with her hands on her hips, waiting for the store dummies to start acting like Marbles, Peter, James, and so forth.

Ferman straightened out a leg against the skylight. "Ollie, when are you going to learn how to play with dolls?"

"Ya want anything from the store, Ferman Fruitcake? I'm too big for dolls." Ollie hitched up her jeans.

Ferman started to say something, but his audience was nearly asleep. Frenchie's head was nodding. James was staring into space. The pages of the open book on Marbles' knees were turning backward, three at a time, by themselves. Peter Proper was sitting very straight, back against the chimney with his eyes closed to the sun.

Ollie turned, looking over the edge of the roof. There was no one down in the park today. There was hardly anyone on the block. She propped a sticky foot against the roof railing and scraped off the tar. Everything below was gray as if the chimney had snowed on the whole block.

Chalky, the superintendent, was rolling a mattress onto a cart. Maybe he'd play cards with her. Just last Friday he had, but sometimes he wouldn't even remember her and would run and hide thinking she was King Kong come down just to hit him in the head or something. Ollie looked past the swings to the track. Empty. Frenchie should be out there trotting, she thought, looking back at him. He was dipping his head. Sometimes she'd trot beside Frenchie, taking big jumps to keep up. He'd smile at her but never teased her about them silly little jumps. He'd tell her for the hundredth time how he was going to enter the Olympics and walk off with a cup full of money.

"Go away, little girl!" Ferman had just yelled at her as if he had forgotten her name or didn't know her any more. He's as crazy as Chalky, thought Ollie, slamming the big roof door behind her and running down the stairs to the street. They must be brothers.

It was now four o'clock by the bank clock. Ollie remembered the bar-b-que place that had burned down. But she'd already rummaged through the ruins and found nothing. No use messing up her sneakers any further. She turned around to look the block over. Empty. Everyone was either at camp or at work or was sleeping like the boys on the roof or dead or just plain gone off. She perched on top of the fire hydrant with one foot, balancing with her arms. She could almost see into the high windows of Mount Zion A.M.E. Church. "This time I'm going to fly off and kill myself," she yelled, flapping her arms. A lady with bundles turned the corner and gave Ollie a look, crossed against the traffic, looking over her shoulder and shaking her head at what the kids of today had come to. Reverend Hall came out of the church basement, mopping his head with a big handkerchief.

"You go play somewhere else," he said, frowning into the sun.

"Where?" Ollie asked.

"Well, go to the park and play."

"With who?" she demanded. "I've got nobody to play with."

Reverend Hall just stood there trying to control his temper. He was always chasing the kids. That's why he's got no choir, Granddaddy Larkins was always saying. He always chases kids and dogs and pigeons and drunks.

"Little girl, you can't act up here in front of the church. Have you no—"

"How come you always calling me little girl, but you sure know my name when I'm walking with my grandfather?" Ollie said.

"Tell'm all about his sanctified self," said Miss Hazel, laughing out her window. But when the Reverend looked up to scowl, she ducked back in. He marched back into the church, shooing the pigeons off the steps.

"Wish me happy birthday," Ollie whispered to the pigeons. They hurried off toward the curb. "Better wish me happy birthday," she yelled, "or somebody around here is gonna get wasted."

Miss Hazel leaned out the window again. "What's with you, Ollie? You sick or something?"

"You should never have a birthday in the summertime," Ollie yelled, "cause nobody's around to wish you happy birthday or give you a party."

"Well, don't cry, sugar. When you get as old as me, you'll be glad to forget all about—"

"I'm not crying." Ollie stamped her foot, but the tears kept coming and before she could stop herself she was howling, right there in the middle of the street and not even caring who saw her. And she howled so loudly that even Miss Hazel's great-grandmother had to come to the window to see who was dying and with so much noise and on such a lovely day.

"What's the matter with the Larkins child?" asked the old woman.

"Beats me." Miss Hazel shook her head and watched Ollie for a minute. "I don't understand kids sometimes," she sighed, and closed the window so she could hear the television good.

Check Your Reading

1. Why can't Ollie awaken Granddaddy Larkins?

2. Compare Wilma's mother's predictions for Ollie and Wilma.

3. Why is Miss Hazel's attempt at comfort a failure?

4. How is Reverend Hall's treatment of Ollie different on days when she walks with her grandfather?

5. To whom does Ollie whisper, "Wish me a happy birthday"?

Further Exploration

1. How would you respond to Ollie's threat to "fly off and kill myself"?

2. Why is Ollie indignant about Ferman's remark about playing with dolls and what does this suggest about her maturity?

3. Describe the neighborhood in which Ollie lives. Why does Ollie choose the Chicken Shack Restaurant and the roof when she looks for companions?

4. How has Ollie earned the name "Miss Freshmouth"? What is her reaction to it?

5. Why do people often feel disappointment at special times, such as Christmas, birthdays, and vacations? Have you ever felt this way on a special occasion? Relate your experience in terms of Ollie's experience.

Robert Cormier (1925–)

Robert Cormier, a journalist and author of novels and short stories, has been accused of using too many unhappy endings in his works. His reply reveals his personal philosophy about the underlying emotion of writing: "As long as what I write is true and believable, why should I have to create happy endings?" The story "The Moustache," which Cormier derived from a visit his son Peter made to his maternal grandmother, reveals a poignant moment in the life of a normal teenage boy. Its ending captures a boy's understanding of the complex nature of adult love.

Cormier's works appear in current periodicals, including *McCall's, Woman's Day,* and *The Saturday Evening Post.* Three of his novels have won the *New York Times's* Outstanding Book of the Year Award: *The Chocolate War* (1974), *I Am the Cheese* (1977), and *After the First Death* (1979).

The Moustache
Robert Cormier

At the last minute Annie couldn't go. She was invaded by one of those twenty-four-hour flu bugs that sent her to bed with a fever, moaning about the fact that she'd also have to break her date with Handsome Harry Arnold that night. We call him Handsome Harry because he's actually handsome, but he's also a nice guy, cool, and he doesn't treat me like Annie's kid brother, which I am, but like a regular person. Anyway, I had to go to Lawnrest alone that afternoon. But first of all I had to stand inspection. My mother lined me up against the wall. She stood there like a one-man firing squad, which is kind of funny because she's not like a man at all, she's very feminine, and we have this great relationship—I mean, I feel as if she really likes me. I realize that sounds strange, but I know guys whose mothers love them and cook special stuff for them and worry about them and all but there's something missing in their relationship.

Anyway. She frowned and started the routine.

"That hair," she said. Then admitted: "Well, at least you combed it."

I sighed. I have discovered that it's better to sigh than argue.

"And that moustache." She shook her head. "I still say a seventeen-year-old has no business wearing a moustache."

"It's an experiment," I said. "I just wanted to see if I could grow one." To tell the truth, I had proved my point about being able to grow a decent moustache, but I also had learned to like it.

"It's costing you money, Mike," she said.

"I know, I know."

The money was a reference to the movies. The Downtown Cinema has a special Friday night offer—half-price admission for high school couples, seventeen or younger. But the woman in the box office took one look at my moustache and charged me full price. Even when I showed her my driver's license. She charged full admission for Cindy's ticket, too, which left me practically broke and unable to take Cindy out for a hamburger with the crowd afterward. That didn't help matters, because Cindy has been getting impatient recently about things like the fact that I don't own my own car and have to concentrate on my studies if I want to win that college scholarship, for instance. Cindy wasn't exactly crazy about the moustache, either.

Now it was my mother's turn to sigh.

"Look," I said, to cheer her up. "I'm thinking about shaving it off." Even though I wasn't. Another discovery: You can build a way of life on postponement.

"Your grandmother probably won't even recognize you," she said. And I saw the shadow fall across her face.

Let me tell you what the visit to Lawnrest was all about. My grandmother is seventy-three years old. She is a resident—which is supposed to be a better word than *patient*—at the Lawnrest Nursing Home. She used to make the greatest turkey dressing in the world and was a nut about baseball and could even quote batting averages, for crying out loud. She always rooted for the losers. She was in love with the Mets until they started to win. Now she has arteriosclerosis, which the dictionary says is "a chronic disease characterized by abnormal thickening and hardening of the arterial walls." Which really means that she can't live at home anymore or even with us, and her memory has betrayed her as well as her body. She used to wander off and sometimes didn't recognize people. My mother visits her all the time, driving the thirty miles to Lawnrest almost every day. Because Annie was home for a semester break from college, we had decided to make a special Saturday visit. Now Annie was in bed, groaning theatrically—she's a drama major—but I told my mother I'd go, anyway. I hadn't seen my grandmother since she'd been admitted to Lawnrest. Besides, the place is located on the Southwest Turnpike, which meant I could barrel along in my father's new Le Mans. My ambition was to see the speedometer hit seventy-five. Ordinarily, I used the old station wagon, which can barely stagger up to fifty.

Frankly, I wasn't too crazy about visiting a nursing home. They reminded me of hospitals and hospitals turn me off. I mean, the smell of ether makes me nauseous, and I feel faint at the sight of blood. And as I approached Lawnrest—which is a terrible cemetery kind of name, to begin with—I was sorry I hadn't avoided the trip. Then I felt guilty about it. I'm loaded with guilt complexes. Like driving like a madman after promising my father to be careful. Like sitting in the parking lot, looking at the nursing home with dread and thinking how I'd rather be with Cindy. Then I thought of all the Christmas and birthday gifts my grandmother had given me and I got out of the car, guilty, as usual.

Inside, I was surprised by the lack of hospital smell, although there was another odor or maybe the absence of an odor. The air was antiseptic, sterile. As if there was no atmosphere at all or I'd caught a cold suddenly and couldn't taste or smell.

A nurse at the reception desk gave me directions—my grandmother was in East Three. I made my way down the tiled corridor and was glad to see that the walls were painted with cheerful colors like yellow and pink. A wheelchair suddenly shot around a corner, self-propelled by an old man, white-haired and toothless, who cackled merrily as he barely missed me. I jumped aside—here I was, almost getting wiped out by a two-mile-an-hour wheelchair after doing seventy-five on the pike. As I walked through the corridor seeking East Three, I couldn't help glancing into the rooms, and it was like some kind of wax museum—all these figures in various stances and attitudes, sitting in beds or chairs, standing at windows, as if they were frozen forever in these postures. To tell the truth, I began to hurry because I was getting depressed. Finally, I saw a beautiful girl approaching, dressed in white, a nurse or an attendant, and I was so happy to see someone young, someone walking and acting normally, that I gave her a wide smile and a big hello and I must have looked like a kind of nut. Anyway, she looked right through me as if I were a window, which is about par for the course whenever I meet beautiful girls.

I finally found the room and saw my grandmother in bed. My grand-mother looks like Ethel Barrymore. I never knew who Ethel Barrymore was until I saw a terrific movie, *None But the Lonely Heart,* on TV, starring Ethel Barrymore and Cary Grant. Both my grandmother and Ethel Barrymore have these great craggy faces like the side of a mountain and wonderful voices like syrup being poured. Slowly. She was propped up in bed, pillows puffed behind her. Her hair had been combed out and fell upon her shoulders. For some reason, this flowing hair gave her an almost girlish appearance, despite its whiteness.

She saw me and smiled. Her eyes lit up and her eyebrows arched and she reached out her hands to me in greeting. "Mike, Mike," she said. And I breathed a sigh of relief. This was one of her good days. My mother had warned me that she might not know who I was at first.

I took her hands in mine. They were fragile. I could actually feel her bones, and it seemed as if they would break if I pressed too hard. Her skin was smooth, almost slippery, as if the years had worn away all the roughness the way the wind wears away the surfaces of stones.

"Mike, Mike, I didn't think you'd come," she said, so happy, and she was still Ethel Barrymore, that voice like a caress. "I've been waiting all this time." Before I could reply, she looked away, out the window. "See the birds? I've been watching them at the feeder. I love to see them come. Even the blue jays. The blue jays are like hawks—they take the food that the small birds should have. But the small birds, the chickadees, watch the blue jays and at least learn where the feeder is."

She lapsed into silence, and I looked out the window. There was no feeder. No birds. There was only the parking lot and the sun glinting on car windshields.

She turned to me again, eyes bright. Radiant, really. Or was it a medicine brightness? "Ah, Mike. You look so grand, so grand. Is that a new coat?"

"Not really," I said. I'd been wearing my Uncle Jerry's old army-fatigue jacket for months, practically living in it, my mother said. But she insisted that I wear my raincoat for the visit. It was about a year old but looked new because I didn't wear it much. Nobody was wearing raincoats lately.

"You always loved clothes, didn't you, Mike?" she said. I was beginning to feel uneasy because she regarded me with such intensity. Those bright eyes. I wondered—are old people in places like this so lonesome, so abandoned that they go wild when someone visits? Or was she so happy because she was suddenly lucid and everything was sharp and clear? My mother had described those moments when my grandmother suddenly emerged from the fog that so often obscured her mind. I didn't know the answers, but it felt kind of spooky, getting such an emotional welcome from her.

"I remember the time you bought the new coat—the Chesterfield," she said, looking away again, as if watching the birds that weren't there. "That lovely coat with the velvet collar. Black, it was. Stylish. Remember that, Mike? It was hard times, but you could never resist the glitter."

I was about to protest—I had never heard of a Chesterfield, for crying out loud. But I stopped. Be patient with her, my mother had said. Humor her. Be gentle.

We were interrupted by an attendant who pushed a wheeled cart into the room. "Time for juices, dear," the woman said. She was the standard forty- or fifty-year-old woman: glasses, nothing hair, plump cheeks. Her manner was cheerful but a businesslike kind of cheerfulness. I'd hate to be called "dear" by someone getting paid to do it. "Orange or grape or cranberry, dear? Cranberry is good for the bones, you know."

My grandmother ignored the interruption. She didn't even bother to answer, having turned away at the woman's arrival, as if angry about her appearance.

The woman looked at me and winked. A conspiratorial kind of wink. It was kind of horrible. I didn't think people winked like that anymore. In fact, I hadn't seen a wink in years.

"She doesn't care much for juices," the woman said, talking to me as if my grandmother weren't even there. "But she loves her coffee. With lots of cream and two lumps of sugar. But this is juice time, not coffee time." Addressing my grandmother again, she said, "Orange or grape or cranberry, dear?"

"Tell her I want no juices, Mike," my grandmother commanded regally, her eyes still watching invisible birds.

The woman smiled, patience like a label on her face. "That's all right, dear. I'll just leave some cranberry for you. Drink it at your leisure. It's good for the bones."

She wheeled herself out of the room. My grandmother was still absorbed in the view. Somewhere a toilet flushed. A wheelchair passed the doorway—probably that same old driver fleeing a hit-run accident. A television set exploded with sound somewhere, soap-opera voices filling the air. You can always tell soap-opera voices.

I turned back to find my grandmother staring at me. Her hands cupped her face, her index fingers curled around her cheeks like parenthesis marks.

"But you know, Mike, looking back, I think you were right," she said, continuing our conversation as if there had been no interruption. "You always said, 'It's the things of the spirit that count, Meg.' The spirit! And so you bought the baby-grand piano—a baby grand in the middle of the Depression. A knock came on the door and it was the deliveryman. It took five of them to get it into the house." She leaned back, closing her eyes. "How I loved that piano, Mike. I was never that fine a player, but you loved to sit there in the parlor, on Sunday evenings, Ellie on your lap, listening to me play and sing." She hummed a bit, a fragment of melody I didn't recognize. Then she drifted into silence. Maybe she'd fallen asleep. My mother's name is Ellen, but everyone always calls her Ellie. "Take my hand, Mike," my grandmother said suddenly. Then I remembered—my grandfather's name was Michael. I had been named for him.

"Ah, Mike," she said, pressing my hands with all her feeble strength. "I thought I'd lost you forever. And here you are, back with me again. . . ."

Her expression scared me. I don't mean scared as if I were in danger but scared because of what could happen to her when she realized the mistake she had made. My mother always said I favored her side of the family. Thinking back to the pictures in the old family albums, I recalled my grandfather as tall and thin. Like me. But the resemblance ended there. He was thirty-five when he died, almost forty years ago. And he wore a moustache. I brought my hand to my face. I also wore a moustache now, of course.

"I sit here these days, Mike," she said, her voice a lullaby, her hand still holding mine, "and I drift and dream. The days are fuzzy sometimes, merging together. Sometimes it's like I'm not here at all but somewhere else altogether. And I always think of you. Those years we had. Not enough years, Mike, not enough. . . ."

Her voice was so sad, so mournful that I made sounds of sympathy, not words exactly but the kind of soothings that mothers murmur to their children when they awaken from bad dreams.

"And I think of that terrible night, Mike, that terrible night. Have you ever really forgiven me for that night?"

"Listen . . ." I began. I wanted to say: "Nana, this is Mike your grandson, not Mike your husband."

"Sh . . . sh . . ." she whispered, placing a finger as long and cold as a candle against my lips. "Don't say anything. I've waited so long for this moment. To be here. With you. I wondered what I would say if suddenly you walked in that door like other people have done. I've thought and thought about it. And I finally made up my mind—I'd ask you to forgive me. I was too proud to ask before." Her fingers tried to mask her face. "But I'm not proud anymore, Mike." That great voice quivered and then grew strong again. "I hate you to see me this way—you always said I was beautiful. I didn't believe it. The Charity Ball when we led the grand march and you said I was the most beautiful girl there . . ."

"Nana," I said. I couldn't keep up the pretense longer, adding one more burden to my load of guilt, leading her on this way, playing a pathetic game of make-believe with an old woman clinging to memories. She didn't seem to hear me.

"But that other night, Mike. The terrible one. The terrible accusations I made. Even Ellie woke up and began to cry. I went to her and rocked her in my arms and you came into the room and said I was wrong. You were whispering, an awful whisper, not wanting to upset little Ellie but wanting to make me see the truth. And I didn't answer you, Mike. I was too proud. I've even forgotten the name of the girl. I sit here, wondering now—was it Laura or Evelyn? I can't remember. Later, I learned that you were telling the truth all the time, Mike. That I'd been wrong . . ." Her eyes were brighter than ever as she looked at me now, but tear-bright, the tears gathering. "It was never the same after that night, was it, Mike? The glitter was gone. From you. From us. And then the accident . . . and I never had the chance to ask you to forgive me . . ."

My grandmother. My poor, poor grandmother. Old people aren't supposed to have those kinds of memories. You see their pictures in the family albums and that's what they are: pictures. They're not supposed to come to life. You drive out in your father's Le Mans doing seventy-five on the pike and all you're doing is visiting an old lady in a nursing home. A duty call. And then you find out that she's a person. She's *somebody*. She's my grandmother, all right, but she's also herself. Like my own mother and father. They exist outside of their relationship to me. I was scared again. I wanted to get out of there.

"Mike, Mike," my grandmother said. "Say it, Mike."

I felt as if my cheeks would crack if I uttered a word.

"Say you forgive me, Mike. I've waited all these years . . ."

I was surprised at how strong her fingers were.

"Say '*I forgive you, Meg.*' "

I said it. My voice sounded funny, as if I were talking in a huge tunnel. "I forgive you, Meg."

Her eyes studied me. Her hands pressed mine. For the first time in my life, I saw love at work. Not movie love. Not Cindy's sparkling eyes when I tell her that we're going to the beach on a Sunday afternoon. But love like something alive and tender, asking nothing in return. She raised her face, and I knew what she wanted me to do. I bent and brushed my lips against her cheek. Her flesh was like a leaf in autumn, crisp and dry.

She closed her eyes and I stood up. The sun wasn't glinting on the cars any longer. Somebody had turned on another television set, and the voices were the show-off voices of the panel shows. At the same time you could still hear the soap-opera dialogue on the other television set.

I waited awhile. She seemed to be sleeping, her breathing serene and regular. I buttoned my raincoat. Suddenly she opened her eyes again and looked at me. Her eyes were still bright, but they merely stared at me. Without recognition or curiosity. Empty eyes. I smiled at her, but she didn't smile back. She made a kind of moaning sound and turned away on the bed, pulling the blankets around her.

I counted to twenty-five and then to fifty and did it all over again. I cleared my throat and coughed tentatively. She didn't move; she didn't respond. I wanted to say, "Nana, it's me." But I didn't. I thought of saying, "Meg, it's me." But I couldn't.

Finally I left. Just like that. I didn't say goodbye or anything. I stalked through the corridors, looking neither to the right nor the left, not caring whether that wild old man with the wheelchair ran me down or not.

On the Southwest Turnpike I did seventy-five—no, eighty—most of the way. I turned the radio up as loud as it could go. Rock music—anything to fill the air. When I got home, my mother was vacuuming the living-room rug. She shut off the cleaner, and the silence was deafening. "Well, how was your grandmother?" she asked.

I told her she was fine. I told her a lot of things. How great Nana looked and how she seemed happy and had called me Mike. I wanted to ask her—hey, Mom, you and Dad really love each other, don't you? I mean—there's nothing to forgive between you, is there? But I didn't.

Instead I went upstairs and took out the electric razor Annie had given me for Christmas and shaved off my moustache.

Check Your Reading

1. What are Mike's grandparents' names?

2. Why doesn't Annie accompany her brother on the visit to Lawnrest?

3. What part of the journey appeals to Mike?

4. What is Mike's first clue that his grandmother is not rational?

5. How does wearing a moustache cost Mike money?

Further Exploration

1. Explain how Mike makes use of sighs and postponements.

2. Why does Mike shave his moustache? How do you think he explained his action to his mother? How do you think she responded?

3. How does Mike relieve his grandmother's mental unrest? Does he understand why his grandmother regrets "that terrible night"?

4. Does Mike deceive his grandmother by letting her think of him as his grandfather? Who do you think has received the greatest benefit from his visit, Mike or his grandmother? Why?

5. Do you think that Mike will grow his moustache back? Why or why not?

Maureen Daly (1921–)

Despite her birth in Castle Caufield, County Tyrone, Ireland, Maureen Daly reflects the typical upbringing of an American teenager. She wrote "Sixteen" for *Scholastic Magazine*'s annual writing competition when she was sixteen. The first prize she won, added to the honor of being the first high school student to have a story included in the *O'Henry Memorial Award Prize Stories of 1938*, was an auspicious beginning for her career. Daly worked as a reporter for the *Chicago Tribune* and assistant editor at *The Ladies' Home Journal*. She also served as a women's editor for *The Saturday Evening Post* for nine years.

Daly, married to writer William P. McGivern and mother of two, possesses the ability to convey the ideas, thoughts, and emotions of teenagers. "Sixteen" is an example of writing that has survived the changes in styles and manners of five decades and is still able to address the needs of young readers. Her highly successful novel, *Seventeenth Summer*, has been reprinted many times and translated into thirteen languages. In 1986, forty-four years after its publication, Daly published another novel directed at the young adult reader. *Acts of Love* is an autobiographical and fictional story of Daly's daughter and her first love. Some of Daly's stories and novels have been made into movies.

Sixteen
Maureen Daly

Now don't get me wrong. I mean, I want you to understand from the beginning that I'm not really so dumb. I know what a girl should do and what she shouldn't. I get around. I read. I listen to the radio. And I have two older sisters. So you see, I know what the score is. I know it's smart to wear tweedish skirts and shaggy sweaters with the sleeves pushed up and pearls and ankle socks and saddle shoes that look as if they've seen the world. And I know that your hair should be long, almost to your shoulders, and sleek as a wet seal, just a little fluffed on the ends, and you should wear a campus hat or a dink or else a peasant hankie if you've that sort of face. Properly, a peasant hankie should make you think of edelweiss, mist and sunny mountains, yodeling and Swiss cheese. You know, that kind of peasant. Now, me, I never wear a hankie. It makes my face seem wide and Slavic and I look like a picture always in one of those magazine articles that run—"And Stalin says the future of Russia lies in its women. In its women who have tilled its soil, raised its children—" Well, anyway. I'm not exactly too small-town either. I read Winchell's column. You get to know what New York boy is that way about some pineapple princess on the West Coast and what Paradise pretty is currently the prettiest, and why someone, eventually, will play Scarlett O'Hara. It gives you that cosmopolitan feeling. And I know that anyone who orders a strawberry sundae in a drugstore instead of a lemon coke would probably be dumb enough to wear colored ankle socks with high-heeled pumps or use Evening in Paris with a tweed suit. But I'm sort of drifting. This isn't what I wanted to tell you. I just wanted to give you the general idea of how I'm not so dumb. It's important that you understand that.

You see, it was funny how I met him. It was a winter night like any other winter night. And I didn't have my Latin done, either. But the way the moon tinseled the twigs and silverplated the snowdrifts, I just couldn't stay inside. The skating rink isn't far from our house—you can make it in five minutes if the sidewalks aren't slippery—so I went skating. I remember it took me a long time to get ready that night because I had to darn my skating socks first. I don't know why they always wear out so fast—just in the toes, too. Maybe it's because I have metal protectors on the toes of my skates. That probably is why. And then I brushed my hair—hard, so hard it clung to my hand and stood up around my head in a hazy halo.

My skates were hanging by the back door all nice and shiny, for I'd just got them for Christmas and they smelled so queer—just like fresh-smoked ham. My dog walked with me as far as the corner. She's a red chow, very polite and well mannered, and she kept pretending it was me she liked when all the time I knew it was the ham smell. She panted along beside me and her hot breath made a frosty little balloon balancing on the end of her nose. My skates thumped me good-naturedly on my back as I walked and the night was breathlessly quiet and the stars winked down like a million flirting eyes. It was all so lovely.

It was all so lovely I ran most of the way and it was lucky the sidewalks had ashes on them or I'd have slipped surely. The ashes crunched like crackerjack and I could feel their cindery shape through the thinness of my shoes. I always wear old shoes when I go skating.

I had to cut across someone's back garden to get to the rink and last summer's grass stuck through the thin ice, brown and discouraged. Not many people came through this way and the crusted snow broke through the little hollows between corn stubbles frozen hard in the ground. I was out of breath when I got to the shanty—out of breath with running and with the loveliness of the night. Shanties are always such friendly places. The floor all hacked to wet splinters from skate runners and the wooden wall frescoed with symbols of dead romance. There was a smell of singed wool as someone got too near the glowing isinglass grin of the iron stove. Girls burst through the door laughing, with snow on their hair, and tripped over shoes scattered on the floor. A pimply-faced boy grabbed the hat from the frizzled head of an eighth-grade blonde and stuffed it into an empty galosh to prove his love and then hastily bent to examine his skate strap with innocent unconcern.

It didn't take me long to get my own skates on and I stuck my shoes under the bench—far back where they wouldn't get knocked around and would be easy to find when I wanted to go home. I walked out on my toes and the shiny runners of my new skates dug deep into the sodden floor.

It was snowing a little outside—quick, eager little Luxlike flakes that melted as soon as they touched your hand. I don't know where the snow came from, for there were stars out. Or maybe the stars were in my eyes and I just kept seeing them every time I looked up into the darkness. I waited a moment. You know, to start to skate at a crowded rink is like jumping on a moving merry-go-round. The skaters go skimming round in a colored blur like gaudy painted horses and the shrill musical jabber re-echoes in the night from a hundred human calliopes. Once in I went all right. At least after I found out exactly where that rough ice was. It was "round, round, jump the rut, round, round, round, jump the rut, round, round—"

And then he came. All of a sudden his arm was around my waist so warm and tight and he said very casually, "Mind if I skate with you?" and then he took my other hand. That's all there was to it. Just that and then we were skating. It wasn't that I'd never skated with a boy before. Don't be silly. I told you before I get around. But this was different. He was a smoothie! He was a big shot up at school and he went to all the big dances and he was the best dancer in town except Harold Wright, who didn't count because he'd been to college in New York for two years! Don't you see? This was different.

I can't remember what we talked about at first; I can't even remember if we talked at all. We just skated and skated and laughed every time we came to that rough spot and pretty soon we were laughing all the time at nothing at all. It was all so lovely.

Then we sat on the big snowbank at the edge of the rink and just watched. It was cold at first even with my skating pants on, sitting on that hard heap of snow, but pretty soon I got warm all over. He threw a handful of snow at me and it fell in a little white shower on my hair and he leaned over to brush it off. I held my breath. The night stood still.

The moon hung just over the warming shanty like a big quarter slice of muskmelon and the smoke from the pipe chimney floated up in a sooty fog. One by one the houses around the rink twinkled out their lights and somebody's hound wailed a mournful apology to a star as he curled up for the night. It was all so lovely.

Then he sat up straight and said, "We'd better start home." Not "Shall I take you home?" or "Do you live far?" but "We'd better start home." See, that's how I know he wanted to take me home. Not because he *had* to but because he *wanted* to. He went to the shanty to get my shoes. "Black ones," I told him. "Same size as Garbo's." And he laughed again. He was still smiling when he came back and took off my skates and tied the wet skate strings in a soggy knot and put them over his shoulder. Then he held out his hand and I slid off the snowbank and brushed off the seat of my pants and we were ready.

It was snowing harder now. Big, quiet flakes that clung to twiggy bushes and snuggled in little drifts against the tree trunks. The night was an etching in black and white. It was all so lovely I was sorry I lived only a few blocks away. He talked softly as we walked, as if every little word were a secret. "Did I like Wayne King, and did I plan to go to college next year, and had I a cousin who lived in Appleton and knew his brother?" A very respectable Emily Post sort of conversation, and then finally "how nice I looked with snow in my hair and had I ever seen the moon so—close?" For the moon was following us as we walked and ducking playfully behind a chimney every time I turned to look at it. And then we were home.

The porch light was on. My mother always puts the porch light on when I go away at night. And we stood there a moment by the front steps and the snow turned pinkish in the glow of the colored light and a few feathery flakes settled on his hair. Then he took my skates and put them over my shoulder and said, "Good night now. I'll call you."

"I'll call you," he said.

I went inside then and in a moment he was gone. I watched him from my window as he went down the street. He was whistling softly and I waited until the sound faded away so I couldn't tell if it was he or my heart whistling out there in the night. And then he was gone, completely gone.

I shivered. Somehow the darkness seemed changed. The stars were little hard chips of light far up in the sky and the moon stared down with a sullen yellow glare. The air was tense with sudden cold and a gust of wind swirled his footprints into white oblivion. Everything was quiet.

But he'd said, "I'll call you." That's what he said—"I'll call you." I couldn't sleep all night.

And that was last Thursday. Tonight is Tuesday. Tonight is Tuesday and my homework's done, and I darned some stockings that didn't really need it, and I worked a crossword puzzle, and I listened to the radio, and now I'm just sitting. I'm just sitting because I can't think of anything else to do. I can't think of anything, anything but snowflakes and ice skates and yellow moons and Thursday night. The telephone is sitting on the corner table with its old black face turned to the wall so I can't see its leer. I don't even jump when it rings any more. My heart still prays, but my mind just laughs. Outside the night is still, so still I think I'll go crazy, and the white snow's all dirtied and smoked into grayness and the wind is blowing the arc light so it throws weird, waving shadows from the trees onto the lawn—like thin, starved arms begging for I don't know what. And so I'm just sitting here and I'm not feeling anything; I'm not even sad, because all of a sudden I know. All of a sudden I know. I can sit here now forever and laugh and laugh and laugh while the tears run salty in the corners of my mouth. For all of a sudden I know, I know what the stars knew all the time—he'll never, never call—never.

Check Your Reading

1. How does the girl reveal her interest in movies?

2. Why does her chow take an interest in her departure?

3. What is a "smoothie"?

4. What proof does she give that she's "not so dumb"?

5. How does the boy show his good manners?

Further Exploration

1. Find evidence of personification in the narrator's description of the telephone, moon, and trees.

2. What clues in the story tell you that it is set in an earlier period? Have modern young people changed in how they spend their leisure time? What characteristics of the story would you change in order to bring it up to date?

3. How does a snowy landscape add to the romance of a chance meeting? Would a rainy night have been different? Would the meeting seem different in daytime?

4. Describe the girl's reaction to her disappointment. How is it possible for her to feel humor and sorrow at the same time? How do you think she will react the next time a boy says, "I'll call you."?

5. Do you think the narrator is sorry that it all happened? Have you ever had a similar experience?

Adjusting to Life

Thinking It Over

These activities offer opportunities for you to consider how the stories in Part Two relate to one another and to the theme of *Adjusting to Life*.

1. Growing up always involves disappointments, sometimes in yourself and sometimes in others. Write a composition about a time when you were disappointed and show how you coped with your discouragement.

2. At one time or another, nearly everyone has created an imaginary friend or playmate. Recall a time in your life when you created a friend. In an essay, describe your imaginary friend and include as many details as you can remember.

3. People must learn to accept the consequences of their actions regardless of how painful they might be. Write an essay about the first time you had to accept the consequences of your actions.

4. One aspect of growing up is a willingness to take risks. Choose one character who risks being laughed at, punished, or hurt by his or her own actions; explain why the character dares to become vulnerable. Emphasize what he or she might gain.

5. A sense of self-esteem is often the result of maturity. Which character from these stories show the strongest awareness of self-worth? How is this displayed to its best advantage?

PART THREE

Encountering the Unexpected

Since the beginning of recorded history, human beings have sought answers to questions about life on this planet and beyond. Their interest in strange, bizarre, and exotic occurrences can be found in the earliest literature. Homer's *Iliad* and *Odyssey*, for example, are filled with incidents involving the supernatural, such as advice from the gods, visits to the underworld, and conversations with the dead. Ghost stories and horror tales have thrilled and perplexed people in all lands for centuries.

Some writers have shown their interest in the supernatural by compiling and retelling legends and myths from distant lands. Others have produced their own versions of folk tales as ways of providing answers for the unknown. Still other have created unique science fiction stories in which strange happenings occur and have no apparent rational explanations. The stories by Poe and Jacobs in this Part are examples of the third type—unusual tales of bizarre, supernatural occurrences.

One particular kind of story about the unexplained can be labeled prophecy. In such a tale the writer creates situations that take place in the future. Using some well known person, event, or place from the present or immediate past as a model, the writer proposes a land of the future. In that fictional landscape, a current trend takes on new meaning, such as Mr. Stendahl's house of horrors, which he builds on Mars in a futile effort to escape bureaucratic regulations against fantasy, or Harrison Bergeron's rebellion against an oppressive society. Both Ray Bradbury and Kurt Vonnegut have used this method to comment on present lifestyles and values and to urge us to guard our freedoms from external control.

Science fiction, which focuses on suspense and mystery, can grip our attention, but at the same time offer challenging thoughts about universal matters, such as loneliness, survival, love, loyalty, or courage. All the stories in this Part pose, in one way or another, the question "what if." When we tease our minds by exploring the realm of the unexplained and the unexpected, we are usually compelled to look back on the real world.

As we ponder mysterious or fantastic tales of science fiction and the supernatural, we can scrutinize more clearly our past experiences and our ability to cope with everyday challenges. By escaping from the realistic, we are better able to return to the dragons and demons that haunt us each day. By emulating the fearless challengers of the unknown, our own battles become, by comparison, much easier.

Edgar Allan Poe (1809–1849)

A master of two types of short fiction, the detective story and the horror tale, Poe achieved an enviable position in the annals of American literature. Despite unfortunate events in his early childhood which left him an orphan, he received ample opportunity from his foster parents to educate himself. But Poe's inclination toward gambling and drinking ended his stays at the University of Virginia and West Point. He was already writing poetry during his college years and published three volumes by 1831. He married his thirteen-year-old cousin, Virginia Clemm, and settled in the Baltimore area.

Poe received recognition for "MS Found in a Bottle," his first published short story, and pursued the writing and editing of short fiction in magazines such as the *Southern Literary Messenger*, the *Evening Mirror*, and the *American Review*. He established a reputation for his emphasis on mood as a means of heightening suspense. Although he received acclaim at home and abroad, his personal life was filled with misfortune, including his wife's death in her mid-twenties from tuberculosis, his own pitiable addiction to drugs and alcohol, and his death at the age of forty.

Poe's legacy to American literature includes literary criticism, such as memorable poems as "The Raven" and "Annabel Lee," and an enthralling collection of classic short stories, including "The Pit and the Pendulum," "The Murders in the Rue Morgue," "The Tell-Tale Heart," "The Black Cat," "The Cask of Amontillado," "The Gold Bug," "The Masque of the Red Death," and "The Fall of the House of Usher."

Poe's narration of "The Fall of the House of Usher" occupies a special place among the twenty-two short stories of this book and in all science fiction. For the terrified narrator, Madeline's premature burial and the decaying dynasty of Roderick Usher become ghastly realities.

The Fall of The House of Usher

Edgar Allan Poe

> His heart is a suspended lute;
> As soon as it's touched it resonates.
>
> —De Béranger

During the whole of a dull, dark, and soundless day in the autumn of the year, when the clouds hung oppressively low in the heavens, I had been passing alone, on horseback, through a singularly dreary tract of country, and at length found myself, as the shades of the evening drew on, within view of the melancholy House of Usher. I know not how it was—but, with the first glimpse of the building, a sense of insufferable gloom pervaded my spirit. I say insufferable; for the feeling was unrelieved by any of that half-pleasurable, because poetic, sentiment with which the mind usually receives even the sternest natural images of the desolate or terrible. I looked upon the scene before me—upon the mere house, and the simple landscape features of the domain—upon the bleak walls—upon the vacant eye-like windows—upon a few rank sedges—and upon a few white trunks of decayed trees—with an utter depression of soul which I can compare to no earthly sensation more properly than to the after-dream of the reveller upon opium—the bitter lapse into every-day life—the hideous dropping off of the veil. There was an iciness, a sinking, a sickening of the heart—an unredeemed dreariness of thought which no goading of the imagination could torture into aught of the sublime. What was it—I paused to think—what was it that so unnerved me in the contemplation of the House of Usher? It was a mystery all insoluble; nor could I grapple with the shadowy fancies that crowded upon me as I pondered. I was forced to fall back upon the unsatisfactory conclusion, that while, beyond doubt, there *are* combinations of very simple natural objects which have the power of thus affecting us, still the analysis of this power lies among considerations beyond our depth. It was possible, I reflected, that a mere different arrangement of the particulars of the scene, of the details of the picture, would be sufficient to modify, or perhaps to annihilate its capacity for sorrowful impression; and, acting upon this idea, I reined my horse to the precipitous brink of a black and lurid tarn that lay in unruffled lustre by the dwelling and gazed down—but with a shudder even more thrilling than before—upon the remodelled and inverted images of the gray sedge, and the ghastly tree-stems, and the vacant and eye-like windows.

Nevertheless, in this mansion of gloom I now proposed to myself a sojourn of some weeks. Its proprietor, Roderick Usher, had been one of my boon companions in boyhood; but many years had elapsed since our last meeting. A letter, however, had lately reached me in a distant part of the country—a letter from him—which, in its wildly importunate nature, had admitted of no other than a personal reply. The MS. gave evidence of nervous agitation. The writer spoke of acute bodily illness—of a mental disorder which oppressed him—and of an earnest desire to see me, as his best and indeed his only personal friend, with a view of attempting, by the cheerfulness of my society, some alleviation of his malady. It was the manner in which all this, and much more, was said—it was the apparent *heart* that went with his request—which allowed me no room for hesitation; and I accordingly obeyed forthwith what I still considered a very singular summons.

Although, as boys, we had been even intimate associates, yet I really knew little of my friend. His reserve had been always excessive and habitual. I was aware, however, that his very ancient family had been noted, time out of mind, for a peculiar sensibility of temperament, displaying itself, through long ages, in many works of exalted art, and manifested, of late, in repeated deeds of munificent yet unobtrusive charity, as well as in a passionate devotion to the intricacies, perhaps even more than to the orthodox and easily recognizable beauties, of musical science. I had learned, too, the very remarkable fact, that the stem of the Usher race, all time-honored as it was, had put forth, at no period, any enduring branch; in other words, that the entire family lay in the direct line of descent, and had always, with very trifling and very temporary variation, so lain. It was this deficiency, I considered, while running over in thought the perfect keeping of the character of the premises with the accredited character of the people, and while speculating upon the possible influence which the one, in the long lapse of centuries, might have exercised upon the other—it was this deficiency, perhaps, of collateral issue, and the consequent undeviating transmission, from sire to son, of the patrimony with the name, which had, at length, so identified the two as to merge the original title of the estate in the quaint and equivocal appellation of the "House of Usher"—an appellation which seemed to include, in the minds of the peasantry who used it, both the family and the family mansion.

I have said that the sole effect of my somewhat childish experiment—that of looking down within the tarn—had been to deepen the first singular impression. There can be no doubt that the consciousness of the rapid increase of my superstition—for why should I not so term it?—served mainly to accelerate the increase itself. Such, I have long known, is the paradoxical law of all sentiments having terror as a basis. And it might have been for this reason only, that, when I again uplifted my eyes to the house itself, from its image in the pool, there grew in my mind a strange fancy—a fancy so ridiculous, indeed, that I but mention it to show the vivid force of the sensations which oppressed me. I had so worked upon my imagination as really to believe that about the whole mansion and domain there hung an atmosphere peculiar to themselves and their immediate vicinity—an atmosphere which had no affinity with the air of heaven, but which had reeked up from the decayed trees, and the gray wall, and the silent tarn—a pestilent and mystic vapor, dull, sluggish, faintly discernible, and leaden-hued.

Shaking off from my spirit what *must* have been a dream, I scanned more narrowly the real aspect of the building. Its principal feature seemed to be that of an excessive antiquity. The discoloration of ages had been great. Minute fungi overspread the whole exterior, hanging in a fine tangled webwork from the leaves. Yet all this was apart from any extraordinary dilapidation. No portion of the masonry had fallen; and there appeared to be a wild inconsistency between its still perfect adaptation of parts, and the crumbling condition of the individual stones. In this there was much that reminded me of the specious totality of old woodwork which has rotted for long years in some neglected vault, with no disturbance from the breath of the external air. Beyond this indication of extensive decay, however, the fabric gave little token of instability. Perhaps the eye of a scrutinizing observer might have discovered a barely perceptible fissure, which, extending from the roof of the building in front, made its way down the wall in a zigzag direction, until it became lost in the sullen waters of the tarn.

Noticing these things, I rode over a short causeway to the house. A servant in waiting took my horse, and I entered the Gothic archway of the hall. A valet, of stealthy step, thence conducted me, in silence, through many dark and intricate passages in my progress to the *studio* of his master. Much that I encountered on the way contributed, I know not how, to heighten the vague sentiments of which I have already spoken. While the objects around me—while the carvings of the ceilings, the sombre tapestries of the walls, the ebon blackness of the floors, and the phantasmagoric armorial trophies which rattled as I strode, were but matters to which, or to such as which, I had been accustomed from my infancy—while I hesitated not to acknowledge how familiar was all this—I still wondered to find how unfamiliar were the fancies which ordinary images were stirring up. On one of the staircases, I met the physician of the family. His countenance, I thought, wore a mingled expression of low cunning and perplexity. He accosted me with trepidation and passed on. The valet now threw open a door and ushered me into the presence of his master.

The room in which I found myself was very large and lofty. The windows were long, narrow, and pointed, and at so vast a distance from the black oaken floor as to be altogether inaccessible from within. Feeble gleams of encrimsoned light made their way through the trellissed panes, and served to render sufficiently distinct the more prominent objects around; the eye, however, struggled in vain to reach the remoter angles of the chamber, or the recesses of the vaulted and fretted ceiling. Dark draperies hung upon the walls. The general furniture was profuse, comfortless, antique, and tattered. Many books and musical instruments lay scattered about, but failed to give any vitality to the scene. I felt that I breathed an atmosphere of sorrow. An air of stern, deep, and irredeemable gloom hung over and pervaded all.

Upon my entrance, Usher arose from a sofa on which he had been lying at full length, and greeted me with a vivacious warmth which had much in it, I at first thought, of an overdone cordiality—of the constrained effort of the *ennuyé* man of the world. A glance, however, at his countenance convinced me of his perfect sincerity. We sat down; and for some moments, while he spoke not, I gazed upon him with a feeling half of pity, half of awe. Surely, man had never before so terribly altered, in so brief a period, as had Roderick Usher! It was with difficulty that I could bring myself to admit the identity of the wan being before me with the companion of my early boyhood. Yet the character of his face had been at all times remarkable. A cadaverousness of complexion; an eye large, liquid, and luminous beyond comparison; lips somewhat thin and very pallid, but of a surpassingly beautiful curve; a nose of a delicate Hebrew model, but with a breadth of nostril unusual in similar formations; a finely moulded chin, speaking, in its want of prominence, of a want of moral energy; hair of a more than web-like softness and tenuity;—these features, with an inordinate expansion above the regions of the temple, made up altogether a countenance not easily to be forgotten. And now in the mere exaggeration of the prevailing character of these features, and of the expression they were wont to convey, lay so much of change that I doubted to whom I spoke. The now ghastly pallor of the skin, and the now miraculous lustre of the eye, above all things startled and even awed me. The silken hair, too, had been suffered to grow all unheeded, and as, in its wild gossamer texture, it floated rather than fell about the face, I could not, even with effort, connect its Arabesque expression with any idea of simple humanity.

In the manner of my friend I was at once struck with an incoherence—an inconsistency; and I soon found this to arise from a series of feeble and futile struggles to overcome an habitual trepidancy—an excessive nervous agitation. For something of this nature I had indeed been prepared, no less by his letter, than by reminiscences of certain boyish traits, and by conclusions deduced from his peculiar physical conformation and temperament. His action was alternately vivacious and sullen. His voice varied rapidly from a tremulous indecision (when the animal spirits seemed utterly in abeyance) to that species of energetic concision—that abrupt, weighty, unhurried, and hollow-sounding enunciation—that leaden, self-balanced, and perfectly modulated guttural utterance, which may be observed in the lost drunkard, or the irreclaimable eater of opium, during the periods of his most intense excitement.

It was thus that he spoke of the object of my visit, of his earnest desire to see me, and of the solace he expected me to afford him. He entered, at some length, into what he conceived to be the nature of his malady. It was, he said, a constitutional and a family evil, and one for which he despaired to find a remedy—a mere nervous affection, he immediately added, which would undoubtedly soon pass off. It displayed itself in a host of unnatural sensations. Some of these, as he detailed them, interested and bewildered me; although, perhaps, the terms and the general manner of their narration had their weight. He suffered much from a morbid acuteness of the senses; the most insipid food was alone endurable; he could wear only garments of certain texture; the odors of all flowers were oppressive; his eyes were tortured by even a faint light; and there were but peculiar sounds, and these from stringed instruments, which did not inspire him with horror.

To an anomalous species of terror I found him a bounden slave. "I shall perish," said he, "I *must* perish in this deplorable folly. Thus, thus, and not otherwise, shall I be lost. I dread the events of the future not in themselves, but in their results. I shudder at the thought of any, even the most trivial, incident, which may operate upon this intolerable agitation of soul. I have, indeed, no abhorrence of danger, except in its absolute effect—in terror. In this unnerved, in this pitiable, condition I feel that the period will sooner or later arrive when I must abandon life and reason together, in some struggle with the grim phantasm, FEAR."

I learned, moreover, at intervals, and through broken and equivocal hints, another singular feature of his mental condition. He was enchained by certain superstitious impressions in regard to the dwelling which he tenanted, and whence, for many years, he had never ventured forth—in regard to an influence whose supposititious force was conveyed in terms too shadowy here to be re-stated—an influence which some peculiarities in the mere form and substance of his family mansion had, by dint of long sufferance, he said, obtained over his spirit—an effect which the *physique* of the gray walls and turrets, and of the dim tarn into which they all looked down, had, at length, brought about upon the *morale* of his existence.

He admitted, however, although with hesitation, that much of the peculiar gloom which thus afflicted him could be traced to a more natural and far more palpable origin—to the severe and long-continued illness—indeed to the evidently approaching dissolution—of a tenderly beloved sister, his sole companion for long years, his last and only relative on earth. "Her decease," he said, with a bitterness which I can never forget, "would leave him (him, the hopeless and the frail) the last of the ancient race of the Ushers." While he spoke, the lady Madeline (for so was she called) passed through a remote portion of the apartment, and, without having noticed my presence, disappeared. I regarded her with an utter astonishment not unmingled with dread; and yet I found it impossible to account for such feelings. A sensation of stupor oppressed me as my eyes followed her retreating steps. When a door, at length, closed upon her, my glance sought instinctively and eagerly the countenance of the brother; but he had buried his face in his hands, and I could only perceive that a far more than ordinary wanness had overspread the emaciated fingers through which trickled many passionate tears.

The disease of the lady Madeline had long baffled the skill of her physicians. A settled apathy, a gradual wasting away of the person, and frequent although transient affections of a partially cataleptical character

were the unusual diagnosis. Hitherto she had steadily borne up against
the pressure of her malady, and had not betaken herself finally to bed;
but on the closing in of the evening of my arrival at the house, she
succumbed (as her brother told me at night with inexpressible agitation)
to the prostrating power of the destroyer; and I learned that the glimpse
I had obtained of her person would thus probably be the last I should
obtain—that the lady, at least while living, would be seen by me no more.

For several days ensuing, her name was unmentioned by either Usher
or myself; and during this period I was busied in earnest endeavors to
alleviate the melancholy of my friend. We painted and read together,
or I listened, as if in a dream, to the wild improvisations of his speaking
guitar. And thus, as a closer and still closer intimacy admitted me more
unreservedly into the recesses of his spirit, the more bitterly did I perceive
the futility of all attempts at cheering a mind from which darkness, as
if an inherent positive quality, poured forth upon all objects of the
moral and physical universe in one unceasing radiation of gloom.

I shall ever bear about me a memory of the many solemn hours I
thus spent alone with the master of the House of Usher. Yet I should
fail in any attempt to convey an idea of the exact character of the
studies, or of the occupations, in which he involved me, or led me the
way. An excited and highly distempered ideality threw a sulphureous
lustre over all. His long improvised dirges will ring forever in my ears.
Among other things, I hold painfully in mind a certain singular perversion
and amplification of the wild air of the last waltz of Von Weber. From
the paintings over which his elaborate fancy brooded, and which grew,
touch by touch, into vaguenesses at which I shuddered the more thril-
lingly, because I shuddered knowing not why—from these paintings
(vivid as their images now are before me) I would in vain endeavor to
educe more-than a small portion which should lie within the compass
of merely written words. By the utter simplicity, by the nakedness of
his designs, he arrested and overawed attention. If ever mortal painted
an idea, that mortal was Roderick Usher. For me at least, in the
circumstances then surrounding me, there arose out of the pure abstrac-
tions which the hypochondriac contrived to throw upon his canvas, an
intensity of intolerable awe, no shadow of which felt I ever yet in the
contemplation of the certainly glowing yet too concrete reveries of Fuseli.

One of the phantasmagoric conceptions of my friend, partaking not
so rigidly of the spirit of abstraction, may be shadowed forth, although
feebly, in words. A small picture presented the interior of an immensely
long and rectangular vault or tunnel, with low walls, smooth, white,

and without interruption or device. Certain accessory points of the design served well to convey the idea that this excavation lay at an exceeding depth below the surface of the earth. No outlet was observed in any portion of its vast extent, and no torch or other artificial source of light was discernible; yet a flood of intense rays rolled throughout, and bathed the whole in a ghastly and inappropriate splendor.

I have just spoken of that morbid condition of the auditory nerve which rendered all music intolerable to to the sufferer, with the exception of certain effects of stringed instruments. It was, perhaps, the narrow limits to which he thus confined himself upon the guitar which gave birth, in great measure, to the fantastic character of his performances. But the fervid *facility* of his *impromptus* could not be so accounted for. They must have been, and were, in the notes, as well as in the words of his wild fantasies (for he not unfrequently accompanied himself with rhymed verbal improvisations), the result of that intense mental collectedness and concentration to which I have previously alluded as observable only in particular moments of the highest artificial excitement. The words of one of these rhapsodies I have easily remembered. I was, perhaps, the more forcibly impressed with it as he gave it, because, in the under or mystic current of its meaning, I fancied that I perceived, and for the first time, a full consciousness on the part of Usher of the tottering of his lofty reason upon her throne. The verses, which were entitled "The Haunted Palace," ran very nearly, if not accurately, thus:—

I.

In the greenest of our valleys,
   By good angels tenanted,
Once a fair and stately palace—
   Radiant palace—reared its head.
In the monarch Thought's dominion—
   It stood there!
Never seraph spread a pinion
   Over fabric half so fair.

II.

Banners yellow, glorious, golden,
   On its roof did float and flow
(This—all this—was in the olden
   Time long ago);
And every gentle air that dallied,
   In that sweet day,

Along the ramparts plumed and pallid,
  A winged odor went away.

III.

Wanderers in that happy valley
  Through two luminous windows saw
Spirits moving musically
  To a lute's well-tuned law;
Round about a throne, where sitting
  (Porphyrogene!)
In state his glory well befitting,
  The ruler of the realm was seen.

IV.

And all with pearl and ruby glowing
  Was the fair palace door,
Through which came flowing, flowing, flowing
  And sparkling evermore,
A troop of Echoes whose sweet duty
  Was but to sing,
In voices of surpassing beauty,
  The wit and wisdom of their king.

V.

But evil things, in robes of sorrow,
  Assailed the monarch's high estate;
(Ah, let us mourn, for never morrow
  Shall dawn upon him, desolate!)
And, round about his home, the glory
  That blushed and bloomed
Is but a dim-remembered story
  Of the old time entombed.

VI.

And travellers now within that valley,
  Through the red-litten windows see
Vast forms that move fantastically
  To a discordant melody;
While, like a rapid ghastly river,
  Through the pale door;

A hideous throng rush out forever,
And laugh—but smile no more.

I well remember that suggestions arising from this ballad led us into
a train of thought wherein there became manifest an opinion of Usher's
which I mention not so much on account of its novelty (for other men
have thought thus), as on account of the pertinacity with which he
maintained it. This opinion, in its general form, was that of the sentience
of all vegetable things. But, in his disordered fancy, the idea had assumed
a more daring character, and trespassed, under certain conditions, upon
the kingdom of inorganization. I lack words to express the full extent,
or the earnest *abandon* of his persuasion. The belief, however, was
connected (as I have previously hinted) with the gray stones of the
home of his forefathers. The conditions of the sentience had been here,
he imagined, fulfilled in the method of collocation of these stones—in
the order of their arrangement, as well as in that of the many *fungi*
which overspread them, and of the decayed trees which stood around—
above all, in the long undisturbed endurance of this arrangement, and
in its reduplication in the still waters of the tarn. Its evidence—the
evidence of the sentience—was to be seen, he said (and I here started
as he spoke), in the gradual yet certain condensation of an atmosphere
of their own about the waters and the walls. The result was discoverable,
he added, in that silent yet importunate and terrible influence which
for centuries had moulded the destinies of his family, and which made
him what I now saw him—what he was. Such opinions need no comment,
and I will make none.

Our books—the books which, for years, had formed no small portion
of the mental existence of the invalid—were, as might be supposed, in
strict keeping with this character of phantasm. We pored together over
such works as the "Ververt et Chartreuse" of Gresset; the "Belphegor"
of Machiavelli; the "Heaven and Hell" of Swedenborg; the "Subterranean
Voyage of Nicholas Klimm" of Holberg; the "Chiromancy" of Robert
Flud, of Jean D'Indaginé, and of Dela Chambre; the "Journey into the
Blue Distance" of Tieck; and the "City of the Sun" of Campanella. One
favorite volume was a small octavo edition of the "Directorium In-
quisitorium," by the Dominican Eymeric de Gironne; and there were
passages in Pomponius Mela, about the old African Satyrs and Œgipans,
over which Usher would sit dreaming for hours. His chief delight,
however, was found in the perusal of an exceedingly rare and curious
book in quarto Gothic—the manual of a forgotten church—the *Vigiliæ*

Mortuorum Secundum Chorum Ecclesiæ Maguntinæ.

I could not help thinking of the wild ritual of this work, and of its probable influence upon the hypochondriac, when, one evening, having informed me abruptly that the lady Madeline was no more, he stated his intention of preserving her corpse for a fortnight (previously to its final interment), in one of the numerous vaults within the main walls of the building. The worldly reason, however, assigned for this singular proceeding, was one which I did not feel at liberty to dispute. The brother had been led to his resolution (so he told me) by consideration of the unusual character of the malady of the deceased, of certain obtrusive and eager inquiries on the part of her medical men, and of the remote and exposed situation of the burial-ground of the family. I will not deny that when I called to mind the sinister countenance of the person whom I met upon the staircase, on the day of my arrival at the house, I had no desire to oppose what I regarded as at best but a harmless, and by no means an unnatural, precaution.

At the request of Usher, I personally aided him in the arrangements for the temporary entombment. The body having been encoffined, we two alone bore it to its rest. The vault in which we placed it (and which had been so long unopened that our torches, half smothered in its oppressive atmosphere, gave us little opportunity for investigation) was small, damp, and entirely without means of admission for light; lying, at great depth, immediately beneath that portion of the building in which was my own sleeping apartment. It had been used, apparently, in remote feudal times, for the worst purposes of a donjon-keep, and, in later days, as a place of deposit for powder, or some other highly combustible substance, as a portion of its floor, and the whole interior of a long archway through which we reached it, were carefully sheathed with copper. The door, of massive iron, had been, also, similarly protected. Its immense weight caused an unusually sharp, grating sound, as it moved upon its hinges.

Having deposited our mournful burden upon tressels within this region of horror, we partially turned aside the yet unscrewed lid of the coffin, and looked upon the face of the tenant. A striking similitude between the brother and sister now first arrested my attention; and Usher, divining, perhaps, my thoughts, murmured out some few words from which I learned that the deceased and himself had been twins, and that sympathies of a scarcely intelligible nature had always existed between them. Our glances, however, rested not long upon the dead—for we could not regard her unawed. The disease which had thus entombed the lady in the maturity of youth, had left, as usual in all maladies of a strictly cataleptical character, the mockery of a faint blush upon the bosom and the face, and that suspiciously lingering smile upon the lip which is so terrible in death. We replaced and screwed down the lid, and, having secured the door of iron, made our way, with toil, into the scarcely less gloomy apartments of the upper portion of the house.

And now, some days of bitter grief having elapsed, an observable change came over the features of the mental disorder of my friend. His ordinary manner had vanished. His ordinary occupations were neglected or forgotten. He roamed from chamber to chamber with hurried, unequal, and objectless step. The pallor of his countenance had assumed, if possible, a more ghastly hue—but the luminousness of his eye had utterly gone out. The once occasional huskiness of his tone was heard no more; and a tremendous quaver, as if of extreme terror, habitually characterized his utterance. There were times, indeed, when I thought his unceasingly agitated mind was laboring with some oppressive secret, to divulge which he struggled for the necessary courage. At times, again, I was obliged to resolve all into the mere inexplicable vagaries of madness, for I beheld him gazing upon vacancy for long hours, in an attitude of the profoundest attention, as if listening to some imaginary sound. It was no wonder that his condition terrified—that it infected me. I felt creeping upon me, by slow yet certain degrees, the wild influences of his own fantastic yet impressive superstitions.

It was, especially, upon retiring to bed late in the night of the seventh or eighth day after the placing of the lady Madeline within the donjon, that I experienced the full power of such feelings. Sleep came not near my couch—while the hours waned and waned away. I struggled to reason off the nervousness which had dominion over me. I endeavored to believe that much, if not all of what I felt, was due to the bewildering influence of the gloomy furniture of the room—of the dark and tattered draperies, which, tortured into motion by the breath of a rising tempest, swayed fitfully to and fro upon the walls, and rustled uneasily about the decorations of the bed. But my efforts were fruitless. An irrepressible tremor gradually pervaded my frame; and, at length, there sat upon my very heart an incubus of utterly causeless alarm. Shaking this off with a gasp and a struggle, I uplifted myself upon the pillows, and, peering earnestly within the intense darkness of the chamber, hearkened—I know not why, except that an instinctive spirit prompted me—to certain low and indefinite sounds which came, through the pauses of the storm, at long intervals, I knew not whence. Overpowered by an intense sentiment of horror, unaccountable yet unendurable, I threw on my clothes with haste (for I felt that I should sleep no more during the night), and endeavored to arouse myself from the pitiable condition into which I had fallen, by pacing rapidly to and fro through the apartment.

I had taken but few turns in this manner, when a light step on an adjoining staircase arrested my attention. I presently recognized it as that of Usher. In an instant afterward he rapped, with a gentle touch, at my door, and entered, bearing a lamp. His countenance was, as usual, cadaverously wan—but, moreover, there was a species of mad hilarity in his eyes—an evidently restrained *hysteria* in his whole demeanor. His air appalled me—but any thing was preferable to the solitude, which I had so long endured, and I even welcomed his presence as a relief.

"And you have not seen it?" he said abruptly, after having stared about him for some moments in silence—"you have not then seen it?—but, stay! you shall." Thus speaking, and having carefully shaded his lamp, he hurried to one of the casements, and threw it freely open to the storm.

The impetuous fury of the entering gust nearly lifted us from our feet. It was, indeed, a tempestuous yet sternly beautiful night, and one wildly singular in its terror and its beauty. A whirlwind had apparently collected its force in our vicinity; for there were frequent and violent alterations in the direction of the wind; and the exceeding density of the clouds (which hung so low as to press upon the turrets of the house) did not prevent our perceiving the life-like velocity with which they flew careering from all points against each other, without passing away into the distance. I say that even their exceeding density did not prevent our perceiving this—yet we had no glimpse of the moon or stars, nor was there any flashing forth of the lightning. But the under surfaces of the huge masses, of agitated vapor, as well as all terrestrial objects immediately around us, were glowing in the unnatural light of a faintly luminous and distinctly visible gaseous exhalation which hung about and enshrouded the mansion.

"You must not—you shall not behold this!" said I, shuddering, to Usher, as I led him, with a gentle violence, from the window to a seat. "These appearances, which bewilder you, are merely electrical phenomena not uncommon—or it may be that they have their ghastly origin in the rank miasma of the tarn. Let us close this casement;—the air is chilling and dangerous to your frame. Here is one of your favorite romances. I will read, and you shall listen:—and so we will pass away this terrible night together."

The antique volume which I had taken up was the "Mad Trist" of

Sir Launcelot Canning; but I had called it a favorite of Usher's more in sad jest than in earnest; for, in truth, there is little in its uncouth and unimaginative prolixity which could have had interest for the lofty and spiritual ideality of my friend. It was, however, the only book immediately at hand; and I indulged a vague hope that the excitement which now agitated the hypochondriac, might find relief (for the history of mental disorder is full of similar anomalies) even in the extremeness of the folly which I should read. Could I have judged, indeed, by the wild overstrained air of vivacity with which he hearkened, or apparently hearkened, to the words of the tale, I might well have congratulated myself upon the success of my design.

I had arrived at that well-known portion of the story where Ethelred, the hero of the Trist, having sought in vain for peaceable admission into the dwelling of the hermit, proceeds to make good an entrance by force. Here, it will be remembered, the words of the narrative run thus:

"And Ethelred, who was by nature of a doughty heart, and was now mighty withal, on account of the powerfulness of the wine which he had drunken, waited no longer to hold parley with the hermit, who, in sooth, was of an obstinate and maliceful turn, but, feeling the rain upon his shoulders and fearing the rising of the tempest, uplifted his mace outright, and, with blows, made quickly room in the plankings of the door for his gauntleted hand; and now pulling therewith sturdily, he so cracked, and ripped, and tore all asunder, that the noise of the dry and hollow-sounding wood alarumed and reverberated throughout the forest."

At the termination of this sentence I started and, for a moment, paused; for it appeared to me (although I at once concluded that my excited fancy had deceived me)—it appeared to me that, from some very remote portion of the mansion, there came, indistinctly to my ears, what might have been, in its exact similarity of character, the echo (but a stifled and dull one certainly) of the very cracking and ripping sound which Sir Launcelot had so particularly described. It was, beyond doubt, the coincidence alone which had arrested my attention; for, amid the rattling of the sashes of the casements, and the ordinary commingled noises of the still increasing storm, the sound, in itself, had nothing, surely, which should have interested or disturbed me. I continued the story:

"But the good champion Ethelred, now entering within the door, was sore enraged and amazed to perceive no signal of the maliceful hermit; but, in the stead thereof, a dragon of a scaly and prodigious demeanor,

and of a fiery tongue, which sate in guard before a palace of gold, with
a floor of silver; and upon the wall there hung a shield of shining brass
with this legend enwritten—

> *Who entereth herein, a conqueror hath bin;*
> *Who slayeth the dragon, the shield he shall win.*

And Ethelred uplifted his mace, and struck upon the head of the dragon,
which fell before him, and gave up his pesty breath, with a shriek so
horrid and harsh, and withal so piercing, that Ethelred had fain to close
his ears with his hands against the dreadful noise of it, the like whereof
was never before heard."

Here again I paused abruptly, and now with a feeling of wild amazement—for there could be no doubt whatever that, in this instance, I
did actually hear (although from what direction it proceeded I found it
impossible to say) a low and apparently distant, but harsh, protracted,
and most unusual screaming or grating sound—the exact counterpart of
what my fancy had already conjured up for the dragon's unnatural shriek
as described by the romancer.

Oppressed, as I certainly was, upon the occurrence of this second and
most extraordinary coincidence, by a thousand conflicting sensations,
in which wonder and extreme terror were predominant, I still retained
sufficient presence of mind to avoid exciting, by any observation, the
sensitive nervousness of my companion. I was by no means certain that
he had noticed the sounds in question; although, assuredly, a strange
alteration had, during the last few minutes, taken place in his demeanor.
From a position fronting my own, he had gradually brought round his
chair, so as to sit with his face to the door of the chamber; and thus I
could but partially perceive his features, although I saw that his lips
trembled as if he were murmuring inaudibly. His head had dropped upon
his breast—yet I knew that he was not asleep, from the wide and rigid
opening of the eye as I caught a glance of it in profile. The motion of
his body, too, was at variance with this idea—for he rocked from side
to side with a gentle yet constant and uniform sway. Having rapidly
taken notice of all this, I resumed the narrative of Sir Launcelot, which
thus proceeded:

"And now, the champion, having escaped from the terrible fury of
the dragon, bethinking himself of the brazen shield, and of the breaking
up of the enchantment which was upon it, removed the carcass from
out of the way before him, and approached valorously over the silver

pavement of the castle to where the shield was upon the wall; which in sooth tarried not for his full coming, but fell down at his feet upon the silver floor, with a mighty great and terrible ringing sound."

No sooner had these syllables passed my lips, than—as if a shield of brass had indeed, at the moment, fallen heavily upon a floor of silver—I became aware of a distinct, hollow, metallic, and clangorous, yet apparently muffled, reverberation. Completely unnerved, I leaped to my feet; but the measured rocking movement of Usher was undisturbed. I rushed to the chair in which he sat. His eyes were bent fixedly before him, and throughout his whole countenance there reigned a stony rigidity. But, as I placed my hand upon his shoulder, there came a strong shudder over his whole person; a sickly smile quivered about his lips; and I saw that he spoke in a low, hurried, and gibbering murmur, as if unconscious of my presence. Bending closely over him, I at length drank in the hideous import of his words.

"Now hear it?—yes, I hear it, and *have* heard it. Long—long—long— many minutes, many hours, many days, have I heard it—yet I dared not—oh, pity me, miserable wretch that I am!—I dared not—*I dared not speak! We have put her living in the tomb!* Said I not that my senses were acute? I *now* tell you that I heard her first feeble movements in the hollow coffin. I heard them—many, many days ago—yet I dared not—*I dared not speak!* And now—to-night—Ethelred—ha! ha!—the breaking of the hermit's door, and the death-cry of the dragon, and the clangor of the shield—say, rather, the rending of her coffin, and the grating of the iron hinges of her prison, and her struggles within the coppered archway of the vault! Oh! whither shall I fly? Will she not be here anon? Is she not hurrying to upbraid me for my haste? Have I not heard her footstep on the stair? Do I not distinguish that heavy and horrible beating of her heart? Madman!"—here he sprang furiously to his feet, and shrieked out his syllables, as if in the effort he were giving up his soul—"*Madman! I tell you that she now stands without the door!*"

As if in the superhuman energy of his utterance there had been found the potency of a spell, the huge antique panels to which the speaker pointed threw slowly back, upon the instant, their ponderous and ebony jaws. It was the work of the rushing gust—but then without those doors there *did* stand the lofty and enshrouded figure of the lady Madeline of Usher. There was blood upon her white robes, and the evidence of some bitter struggle upon every portion of her emaciated frame. For a moment she remained trembling and reeling to and fro upon the threshold—then, with a low moaning cry, fell heavily inward upon the person of her brother, and in her violent and now final death-agonies, bore him to the floor a corpse, and a victim to the terrors he had anticipated.

From that chamber, and from that mansion, I fled aghast. The storm was still abroad in all its wrath as I found myself crossing the old causeway. Suddenly there shot along the path a wild light, and I turned to see whence a gleam so unusual could have issued; for the vast house and its shadows were alone behind me. The radiance was that of the full, setting and blood-red moon, which now shone vividly through that once barely discernible fissure, of which I have before spoken as extending from the roof of the building, in a zigzag direction, to the base. While I gazed, this fissure rapidly widened—there came a fierce breath of the whirlwind—the entire orb of the satellite burst at once upon my sight— my brain reeled as I saw the mighty walls rushing asunder—there was a long tumultuous shouting sound like the voice of a thousand waters— and the deep and dank tarn at my feet closed sullenly and silently over the fragments of the *"House of Usher."*

Check Your Reading

1. Why does the narrator visit his old friend?

2. What activities and interests fill the life of Roderick Usher?

3. How do doctors diagnose Madeline's illness?

4. Why is the narrator unable to sleep after assisting Roderick with Madeline's burial?

5. What does the narrator do to take Roderick's mind off the storm?

Further Exploration

1. How does the setting heighten the effect of the story of Ethelred? Explain Roderick's interpretation of the sound that he hears.

2. How does the narrator react to his old friend after many years of separation? What could explain the change in Roderick?

3. Why does a stormy night cause people to imagine terrors that would never occur to them in daylight?

4. How does Poe's use of rich vocabulary increase your involvement in the suspenseful tale? Give examples of words that conjure up a frightening picture.

5. In what respect is the House of Usher doubly destroyed?

Ray Bradbury (1920–)

Inspired by comic strips, Ray Bradbury, an Illinois native who has lived most of his life in California, enjoys flights of fancy. During his early years he performed magic tricks and composed space stories at an astounding rate of two-thousand words per day.

Although completely earthbound by his refusal to fly in an airplane and slowed by his preference for bicycles over automobiles, Bradbury has loosened readers from the bonds of earth with a steady output of short stories that emphasize man's need to be free, including *The Martian Chronicles* (1950), *The Illustrated Man* (1951), *Medicine for Melancholy* (1959), and *I Sing the Body Electric* (1969).

His most famous novel, *Fahrenheit 451* (1953), which describes a book-burning society of the future, cautions readers to guard freedom of the press. Another work, *Something Wicked This Way Comes* (1962), utilizes a carnival setting to warn the innocent of the lurking, enticing ways of evil. His steady outpouring of motion picture and television screenplays, novels, and short stories explores social, racial, religious, and cultural issues, urging society to rebel against dependence on machines.

Usher II
Ray Bradbury

During the whole of a dull, dark, and soundless day in the autumn of the year, when the clouds hung oppressively low in the heavens, I had been passing alone, on horseback, through a singularly dreary tract of country, and at length found myself, as the shades of evening drew on, within view of the melancholy House of Usher. . . .'"

Mr. William Stendahl paused in his quotation. There, upon a low black hill, stood the House, its cornerstone bearing the inscription 2005 A.D.

Mr. Bigelow, the architect, said, "It's completed. Here's the key, Mr. Stendahl."

The two men stood together silently in the quiet autumn afternoon. Blueprints rustled on the raven grass at their feet.

"The House of Usher," said Mr. Stendahl with pleasure. "Planned, built, bought, paid for. Wouldn't Mr. Poe be *delighted?*"

Mr. Bigelow squinted. "Is it everything you wanted, sir?"

"Yes!"

"Is the color right? Is it *desolate* and *terrible?*"

"*Very* desolate, *very* terrible!"

"The walls are—*bleak?*"

"Amazingly so!"

"The tarn, is it 'black and lurid' enough?"

"Most incredibly black and lurid."

"And the sedge—we've dyed it, you know—is it the proper gray and ebon?"

"Hideous!"

Mr. Bigelow consulted his architectural plans. From these he quoted in part: "Does the whole structure cause an 'iciness, a sickening of the heart, a dreariness of thought'? The House, the lake, the land; Mr. Stendahl?"

"Mr. Bigelow, it's worth every penny! . . . It's beautiful!"

"Thank you. I had to work in total ignorance. Thank the Lord you had your own private rockets or we'd never have been allowed to bring most of the equipment through. You notice, it's always twilight here, this land, always October, barren, sterile, dead. It took a bit of doing. We killed everything. Ten thousand tons of DDT. Not a snake, frog, or Martian fly left! Twilight always, Mr. Stendahl; I'm proud of that. There are machines hidden, which blot out the sun. It's always properly 'dreary.' "

Stendahl drank it in, the dreariness, the oppression, the fetid vapors, the whole "atmosphere," so delicately contrived and fitted. And that House! That crumbling horror, that evil lake, the fungi, the extensive decay! Plastic or otherwise, who could guess?

He looked at the autumn sky. Somewhere above, beyond, far off, was the sun. Somewhere it was the month of April on the planet Mars, a yellow month with a blue sky. Somewhere above, the rockets burned down to civilize a beautifully dead planet. The sound of their screaming passage was muffled by this dim, soundproofed world, this ancient autumn world.

"Now that my job's done," said Mr. Bigelow uneasily, "I feel free to ask what you're going to do with all this."

"With Usher? Haven't you guessed?"

"No."

"Does the name Usher mean nothing to you?"

"Nothing."

"Well, what about this name: Edgar Allan Poe?"

Mr. Bigelow shook his head.

"Of course." Stendahl snorted delicately, a combination of dismay and contempt. "How could I expect you to know blessed Mr. Poe? He died a long while ago, before Lincoln. All of his books were burned in the Great Fire. That's thirty years ago—1975."

"Ah," said Mr. Bigelow wisely. "One of *those!*"

"Yes, one of those, Bigelow. He and Lovecraft and Hawthorne and Ambrose Bierce and all the tales of terror and fantasy and horror and, for that matter, tales of the future were burned. Heartlessly. They passed a law. Oh, it started very small. In 1950 and '60 it was a grain of sand. They began by controlling books of cartoons and then detective books and, of course, films, one way or another, one group or another, political bias, religious prejudice, union pressures; there was always a minority afraid of something, and a great majority afraid of the dark, afraid of the future, afraid of the past, afraid of the present, afraid of themselves and shadows of themselves."

"I see."

"Afraid of the word 'politics' (which eventually became a synonym for Communism among the more reactionary elements, so I hear, and it was worth your life to use the word!), and with a screw tightened here, a bolt fastened there, a push, a pull, a yank, art and literature were soon like a great twine of taffy strung about, being twisted in braids and tied in knots and thrown in all directions, until there was no more resiliency and no more savor to it. Then the film cameras chopped short and the theaters turned dark, and the print presses trickled down from a great Niagara of reading matter to a mere innocuous dripping of 'pure' material. Oh, the word 'escape' was radical, too, I tell you!"

"Was it?"

"It was! Every man, they said, must face reality. Must face the Here and Now! Everything that was *not* so must go. All the beautiful literary lies and flights of fancy must be shot in mid-air. So they lined them up against a library wall one Sunday morning thirty years ago, in 1975; they lined them up, St. Nicholas and the Headless Horseman and Snow White and Rumpelstiltskin and Mother Goose—oh, what a wailing!— and shot them down, and burned the paper castles and the fairy frogs and old kings and the people who lived happily ever after (for of course it was a fact that *nobody* lived happily ever after!), and Once Upon A Time became No More! And they spread the ashes of the Phantom Rickshaw with the rubble of the Land of Oz; they filleted the bones of Glinda the Good and Ozma and shattered Polychrome in a spectroscope and served Jack Pumpkinhead with meringue at the Biologists' Ball! The Beanstalk died in a bramble of red tape! Sleeping Beauty awoke at the kiss of a scientist and expired at the fatal puncture of his syringe. And they made Alice drink something from a bottle which reduced her to a size where she could no longer cry 'Curiouser and curiouser,' and they gave the Looking Glass one hammer blow to smash it and every Red King and Oyster away!"

He clenched his fists. Lord, how immediate it was! His face was red and he was gasping for breath.

As for Mr. Bigelow, he was astounded at this long explosion. He blinked and at last said, "Sorry. Don't know what you're talking about. Just names to me. From what I hear, the Burning was a good thing."

"Get out!" screamed Stendahl. "You've done your job, now let me alone, you idiot!"

Mr. Bigelow summoned his carpenters and went away.

Mr. Stendahl stood alone before his House.

"Listen here," he said to the unseen rockets. "I came to Mars to get away from you Clean-Minded people, but you're flocking in thicker every day, like flies to offal. So I'm going to show you. I'm going to teach you a fine lesson for what you did to Mr. Poe on Earth. As of this day, beware. The House of Usher is open for business!"

He pushed a fist at the sky.

The rocket landed. A man stepped out jauntily. He glanced at the House, and his gray eyes were displeased and vexed. He strode across the moat to confront the small man there.

"Your name Stendahl?"

"Yes."

"I'm Garrett, Investigator of Moral Climates."

"So you finally got to Mars, you Moral Climate people? I wondered when you'd appear."

"We arrived last week. We'll soon have things as neat and tidy as Earth." The man waved an identification card irritably toward the House. "Suppose you tell me about that place, Stendahl?"

"It's a haunted castle, if you like."

"I don't like. Stendahl, I *don't* like. The sound of that word 'haunted.'"

"Simple enough. In this year of our Lord 2005 I have built a mechanical sanctuary. In it copper bats fly on electronic beams, brass rats scuttle in plastic cellars, robot skeletons dance; robot vampires, harlequins, wolves, and white phantoms, compounded of chemical and ingenuity, live here."

"That's what I was afraid of," said Garrett, smiling quietly. "I'm afraid we're going to have to tear your place down."

"I knew you'd come out as soon as you discovered what went on."

"I'd have come sooner, but we at Moral Climates wanted to be sure of your intentions before we moved in. We can have the Dismantlers and Burning Crew here by supper. By midnight your place will be razed to the cellar. Mr. Stendahl, I consider you somewhat of a fool, sir. Spending hard-earned money on a folly. Why, it must have cost you three million dollars——"

"Four million! But, Mr. Garrett, I inherited twenty-five million when very young. I can afford to throw it about. Seems a dreadful shame, though, to have the House finished only an hour and have you race out with your Dismantlers. Couldn't you possibly let me play with my Toy for just, well, twenty-four hours?"

"You know the law. Strict to the letter. No books, no houses, nothing to be produced which in any way suggests ghosts, vampires, fairies, or any creature of the imagination."

"You'll be burning Babbitts next!"

"You've caused us a lot of trouble, Mr. Stendahl. It's in the record. Twenty years ago. On Earth. You and your library."

"Yes, me and my library. And a few others like me. Oh, Poe's been forgotten for many years now, and Oz and the other creatures. But I had my little cache. We had our libraries, a few private citizens, until you sent your men around with torches and incinerators and tore my fifty thousand books up and burned them. Just as you put a stake through the heart of Halloween and told your film producers that if they made anything at all they would have to make and remake Ernest Hemingway. Good grief, how many times have I seen *For Whom the Bell Tolls* done! Thirty different versions. All realistic. Oh, realism! Oh, here, oh, now, . . . !"

"It doesn't pay to be bitter!"

"Mr. Garrett, you must turn in a full report, mustn't you?"

"Yes."

"Then, for curiosity's sake, you'd better come in and look around. It'll take only a minute."

"All right. Lead the way. And no tricks. I've a gun with me."

The door to the House of Usher creaked wide. A moist wind issued forth. There was an immense sighing and moaning, like a subterranean bellows breathing in the lost catacombs.

A rat pranced across the floor stones. Garrett, crying out, gave it a kick. It fell over, the rat did, and from its nylon fur streamed an incredible horde of metal fleas.

"Amazing!" Garrett bent to see.

An old witch sat in a niche, quivering her wax hands over some orange-and-blue tarot cards. She jerked her head and hissed through her toothless mouth at Garrett, tapping her greasy cards.

"Death!" she cried.

"Now *that's* the sort of thing I mean," said Garrett. "Deplorable!"

"I'll let you burn her personally."

"Will you, really?" Garrett was pleased. Then he frowned. "I must say you're taking this all so well."

"It was enough just to be able to create this place. To be able to say

I did it. To say I nurtured a medieval atmosphere in a modern, incredulous world."

"I've a somewhat reluctant admiration for your genius myself, sir." Garrett watched a mist drift by, whispering and whispering, shaped like a beautiful and nebulous woman. Down a moist corridor a machine whirled. Like the stuff from a cotton-candy centrifuge, mists sprang up and floated, murmuring, in the silent halls.

An ape appeared out of nowhere.

"Hold on!" cried Garrett.

"Don't be afraid." Stendahl tapped the animal's black chest. "A robot. Copper skeleton and all, like the witch. See?" He stroked the fur, and under it metal tubing came to light.

"Yes." Garrett put out a timid hand to pet the thing. "But why, Mr. Stendahl, why all *this*? What obsessed you?"

"Bureaucracy, Mr. Garrett. But I haven't time to explain. The government will discover soon enough." He nodded to the ape. "All right. Now."

The ape killed Mr. Garrett.

"Are we almost ready, Pikes?"

Pikes looked up from the table. "Yes, sir."

"You've done a splendid job."

"Well, I'm paid for it, Mr. Stendahl," said Pikes softly as he lifted the plastic eyelid of the robot and inserted the glass eyeball to fasten the rubberoid muscles neatly. "There."

"The spitting image of Mr. Garrett."

"What do we do with him, sir?" Pikes nodded at the slab where the real Mr. Garrett lay dead.

"Better burn him, Pikes. We wouldn't want two Mr. Garretts, would we?"

Pikes wheeled Mr. Garrett to the brick incinerator. "Goodby." He pushed Mr. Garrett in and slammed the door.

Stendahl confronted the robot Garrett. "You have your orders, Garrett?"

"Yes, sir." The robot sat up. "I'm to return to Moral Climates. I'll file a complimentary report. Delay action for at least forty-eight hours. Say I'm investigating more fully."

"Right, Garrett. Good-by."

The robot hurried out to Garrett's rocket, got in, and flew away.

Stendahl turned. "Now, Pikes, we send the remainder of the invitations for tonight. I think we'll have a jolly time, don't you?"

"Considering we waited twenty years, quite jolly!"

They winked at each other.

Seven o'clock. Stendahl studied his watch. Almost time. He twirled the sherry glass in his hand. He sat quietly. Above him, among the oaken beams, the bats, their delicate copper bodies hidden under rubber flesh, blinked at him and shrieked. He raised his glass to them. "To our success." Then he leaned back, closed his eyes, and considered the entire affair. How he would savor this in his old age. This paying back of the antiseptic government for its literary terrors and conflagrations. Oh, how the anger and hatred had grown in him through the years. Oh, how the plan had taken a slow shape in his numbed mind, until that day three years ago when he had met Pikes.

Ah yes, Pikes. Pikes with the bitterness in him as deep as a black, charred well of green acid. Who was Pikes? Only the greatest of them all! Pikes, the man of ten thousand faces, a fury, a smoke, a blue fog, a white rain, a bat, a gargoyle, a monster, that was Pikes! Better than Lon Chaney, the father? Stendahl ruminated. Night after night he had watched Chaney in the old, old films. Yes, better than Chaney. Better than that other ancient mummer? What was his name? Karloff? Far better! Lugosi? The comparison was odious! No, there was only one Pikes, and he was a man stripped of his fantasies now, no place on Earth to go, no one to show off to. Forbidden even to perform for himself before a mirror!

Poor impossible, defeated Pikes! How must it have felt, Pikes, the night they seized your films, like entrails yanked from the camera, out of your guts, clutching them in coils and wads to stuff them up a stove to burn away! Did it feel as bad as having some fifty thousand books annihilated with no recompense? Yes. Yes. Stendahl felt his hands grow cold with the senseless anger. So what more natural than they would one day talk over endless coffeepots into innumerable midnights, and out of all the talk and the bitter brewings would come—the House of Usher.

A great church bell rang. The guests were arriving.

Smiling, he went to greet them.

Full grown without memory, the robots waited. In green silks the color of forest pools, in silks the color of frog and fern, they waited. In yellow hair the color of the sun and sand, the robots waited. Oiled, with tube bones cut from bronze and sunk in gelatin, the robots lay. In coffins for the not dead and not alive, in planked boxes, the metronomes waited to be set in motion. There was a smell of lubrication and lathed brass. There was a silence of the tomb yard. Sexed but sexless, the robots. Named but unnamed, and borrowing from humans everything but humanity, the robots stared at the nailed lids of their labeled F.O.B. boxes, in a death that was not even a death, for there had never been a life. And now there was a vast screaming of yanked nails. Now there was a lifting of lids. Now there were shadows on the boxes and the pressure of a hand squirting oil from a can. Now one clock was set in motion, a faint ticking. Now another and another, until this was an immense clock shop, purring, The marble eyes rolled wide their rubber lids. The nostrils winked. The robots, clothed in hair of ape and white of rabbit, arose: Tweedledum following Tweedledee, Mock-Turtle, Dormouse, drowned bodies from the sea compounded of salt and whiteweed, swaying; hanging blue-throated men with turned-up, clam-flesh eyes, and creatures of ice and burning tinsel, loam-dwarfs and pepper-elves, Tik-tok, Ruggedo, St. Nicholas with a self-made snow flurry blowing on before him, Bluebeard with whiskers like acetylene flame, and sulphur clouds from which green fire snouts protruded, and, in scaly and gigantic serpentine, a dragon with a furnace in its belly reeled out the door with a scream, a tick, a bellow, a silence, a rush, a wind. Ten thousand lids fell back. The clock shop moved out into Usher. The night was enchanted.

A warm breeze came over the land. The guest rockets, burning the sky and turning the weather from autumn to spring, arrived.

The men stepped out in evening clothes and the women stepped out after them, their hair coiffed up in elaborate detail.

"So *that's* Usher!"

"But where's the door?"

At this moment Stendahl appeared. The women laughed and chattered. Mr. Stendahl raised a hand to quiet them. Turning, he looked up to a high castle window and called:

"Rapunzel, Rapunzel, let down your hair."

And from above, a beautiful maiden leaned out upon the night wind and let down her golden hair. And the hair twined and blew and became a ladder upon which the guests might ascend, laughing, into the House.

What eminent sociologists! What clever psychologists! What tremendously important politicians, bacteriologists, and neurologists! There they stood, within the dank walls.

"Welcome, all of you!"

Mr. Tryon, Mr. Owen, Mr. Dunne, Mr. Lang, Mr. Steffens, Mr.

Fletcher, and a double-dozen more.

"Come in, come in!"

Miss Gibbs, Miss Pope, Miss Churchil, Miss Blunt, Miss Drummond, and a score of other women, glittering.

Eminent, eminent people, one and all, members of the Society for the Prevention of Fantasy, advocators of the banishment of Halloween and Guy Fawkes, killers of bats, burners of books, bearers of torches; good clean citizens, every one, who had waited until the rough men had come up and buried the Martians and cleansed the cities and built the towns and repaired the highways and made everything safe. And then, with everything well on its way to Safety, the Spoil-Funs, the people with mercurochrome for blood and iodine-colored eyes, came now to set up their Moral Climates and dole out goodness to everyone. And they were his friends! Yes, carefully, carefully, he had met and befriended each of them on Earth in the last year!

"Welcome to the vasty halls of Death!" he cried.

"Hello, Stendahl, what is all this?"

"You'll see. Everyone off with their clothes. You'll find booths to one side there. Change into costumes you find there. Men on this side, women on that."

The people stood uneasily about.

"I don't know if we should stay," said Miss Pope, "I don't like the looks of this. It verges on — blasphemy."

"Nonsense, a *costume* ball!"

"Seems quite illegal." Mr. Steffens sniffed about.

"Come off it." Stendahl laughed. "Enjoy yourselves. Tomorrow it'll be a ruin. Get in the booths!"

The House blazed with life and color; harlequins rang by with belled caps and white mice danced miniature quadrilles to the music of dwarfs who tickled tiny fiddles with tiny bows, and flags rippled from scorched beams while bats flew in clouds about gargoyle mouths which spouted down wine, cool, wild, and foaming. A creek wandered through the seven rooms of the masked ball. Guests sipped and found it to be sherry. Guests poured from the booths, transformed from one age into another, their faces covered with dominoes, the very act of putting on a mask revoking all their licenses to pick a quarrel with fantasy and horror. The women swept about in red gowns, laughing. The men danced them attendance. And on the walls were shadows with no people to throw them, and here or there were mirrors in which no image showed. "All of us vampires!" laughed Mr. Fletcher. "Dead!"

There were seven rooms, each a different color, one blue, one purple, one green, one orange, another white, the sixth violet, and the seventh shrouded in black velvet. And in the black room was an ebony clock which struck the hour loud. And through these rooms the guests ran, drunk at last, among the robot fantasies, amid the Dormice and Mad Hatters, the Trolls and Giants, the Black Cats and White Queens, and under their dancing feet the floor gave off the massive pumping beat of a hidden and telltale heart.

"Mr. Stendahl!"

A whisper.

"Mr. Stendahl!"

A monster with the face of Death stood at his elbow. It was Pikes. "I must see you alone."

"What is it?"

"Here." Pikes held out a skeleton hand. In it were a few half-melted, charred wheels, nuts, cogs, bolts.

Stendahl looked at them for a long moment. Then he drew Pikes into a corridor. "Garrett?" he whispered.

Pikes nodded. "He sent a robot in his place. Cleaning out the incinerator a moment ago, I found these."

They both stared at the fateful cogs for a time.

"This means the police will be here any minute," said Pikes. "Our plan will be ruined."

"I don't know." Stendahl glanced in at the whirling yellow and blue and orange people. The music swept through the misting halls. "I should have guessed Garrett wouldn't be fool enough to come in person. But wait!"

"What's the matter?"

"Nothing. There's nothing the matter. Garrett sent a robot to us. Well, we sent one back. Unless he checks closely, he won't notice the switch."

"Of course!"

"Next time he'll come *himself.* Now that he thinks it's safe. Why, he might be at the door any minute, in *person!* More wine, Pikes!"

The great bell rang.

"There he is now, I'll bet you. Go let Mr. Garrett in."

Rapunzel let down her golden hair.

"Mr. Stendahl?"

"Mr. Garrett. The *real* Mr. Garrett?"

"The same." Garrett eyed the dank walls and the whirling people. "I thought I'd better come see for myself. You can't depend on robots. Other people's robots, especially. I also took the precaution of summoning the Dismantlers. They'll be here in one hour to knock the props out from under this horrible place."

Stendahl bowed. "Thanks for telling me." He waved his hand. "In the meantime, you might as well enjoy this. A little wine?"

"No, thank you. What's going on? How low can a man sink?"

"See for yourself, Mr. Garrett."

"Murder," said Garrett.

"Murder most foul," said Stendahl.

A woman screamed. Miss Pope ran up, her face the color of a cheese. "The most horrid thing just happened! I saw Miss Blunt strangled by an ape and stuffed up a chimney!"

They looked and saw the long yellow hair trailing down from the flue. Garrett cried out.

"Horrid!" sobbed Miss Pope, and then ceased crying.

She blinked and turned. "Miss Blunt!"

"Yes," said Miss Blunt, standing there.

"But I just saw you crammed up the flue!"

"No," laughed Miss Blunt. "A robot of myself. A clever facsimile!"

"But, but. . ."

"Don't cry, darling. I'm quite all right. Let me look at myself. Well, so there I *am*! Up the chimney. Like you said. Isn't that funny?"

Miss Blunt walked away, laughing.

"Have a drink, Garrett?"

"I believe I will. That unnerved me. What a place. This *does* deserve tearing down. For a moment there . . ."

Garrett drank.

Another scream. Mr. Steffens, borne upon the shoulders of four white rabbits, was carried down a flight of stairs which magically appeared in the floor. Into a pit went Mr. Steffens, where, bound and tied, he was left to face the advancing razor steel of a great pendulum which now whirled down, down, closer and closer to his outraged body.

"Is that me down there?" said Mr. Steffens, appearing at Garrett's elbow. He bent over the pit. "How strange, how odd, to see yourself die."

The pendulum made a final stroke.

"How realistic," said Mr. Steffens, turning away.

"Another drink, Mr. Garrett?"

"Yes, please."

"It won't be long. The Dismantlers will be here."

"Thank God!"

And for third time, a scream.

"What now?" said Garrett apprehensively.

"It's my turn," said Miss Drummond. "Look."

And a second Miss Drummond, shrieking, was nailed into a coffin and thrust into the raw earth under the floor.

"Why, I remember *that,*" gasped the Investigator of Moral Climates. "From the old forbidden books. The Premature Burial. And the others. The Pit, the Pendulum, and the ape, the chimney, the Murders in the Rue Morgue. In a book I burned, yes!"

"Another drink, Garrett. Here, hold your glass steady."

"My lord, you *have* an imagination, haven't you?"

They stood and watched five others die, one in the mouth of a dragon, the others thrown off into the black tarn, sinking and vanishing.

"Would you like to see what we have planned for you?" asked Stendahl.

"Certainly," said Garrett. " What's the difference? We'll blow the whole thing up, anyway. You're nasty."

"Come along then. This way."

And he led Garrett down into the floor, through numerous passages and down again upon spiral stairs into the earth, into the catacombs.

"What do you want to show me down here?" said Garrett.

"Yourself killed"

"A duplicate?"

"Yes. And also something else."

"What?"

"The Amontillado," said Stendahl, going ahead with a blazing lantern which he held high. Skeletons froze half out of coffin lids. Garrett held his hand to his nose, his face disgusted.

"The what?"

"Haven't you ever heard of the Amontillado?"

"No!"

"Don't you recognize this?" Stendahl pointed to a cell.

"Should I?"

"Or this?" Stendahl produced a trowel from under his cape smiling.

"What's that thing?"

"Come," said Stendahl.

They stepped into the cell. In the dark, Stendahl affixed the chains to the half-drunken man.

"For God's sake, what are you doing?" shouted Garrett, rattling about.

"I'm being ironic. Don't interrupt a man in the midst of being ironic, it's not polite. There!"

"You've locked me in chains!"

"So I have."

"What are you going to do?"

"Leave you here."

"You're joking."

"A very good joke."

"Where's my duplicate? Don't we see him killed?"

"There's no duplicate."

"But the *others?*"

"The others are dead. The ones you saw killed were the real people. The duplicates, the robots, stood by and watched."

Garrett said nothing.

"Now you're supposed to say, 'For the love of God, Montresor!'" said Stendahl. "And I will reply, 'Yes, for the love of God.' Won't you say it? Come on. *Say* it."

"You fool."

"Must I coax you? Say it. Say 'For the love of God, Montresor!'"

"I won't, you idiot. Get me out of here." He was sober now.

"Here. Put this on." Stendahl tossed in something that belled and rang.

"What is it?"

"A cap and bells. Put it on and I might let you out."

"Stendahl!"

"Put it on, I said!"

Garrett obeyed. The bells tinkled.

"Don't you have a feeling that this has all happened before?" inquired Stendahl, setting to work with trowel and mortar and brick now.

"What're you doing?"

"Walling you in. Here's one row. Here's another."

"You're insane!"

"I won't argue that point."

"You'll be prosecuted for this!"

He tapped a brick and placed it on the wet mortar, humming.

Now there was a thrashing and pounding and a crying out from within the darkening place. The bricks rose higher. "More thrashing, please," said Stendahl. "Let's make it a good show.'"

"Let me out, let me out!"

There was one last brick to shove into place. The screaming was continuous.

"Garrett?" called Stendahl softly. Garrett silenced himself. "Garrett," said Stendahl, "do you know why I've done this to you? Because you burned Mr. Poe's books without really reading them. You took other people's advice that they needed burning. Otherwise you'd have realized what I was going to do to you when we came down here a moment ago. Ignorance is fatal, Mr. Garrett."

Garrett was silent.

"I want this to be perfect," said Stendahl, holding his lantern up so its light penetrated in upon the slumped figure. "Jingle your bells softly." The bells rustled. "Now, if you'll please say, 'For the love of God, Montresor,' I might let you free."

The man's face came up in the light. There was a hesitation. Then grotesquely the man said, "For the love of God, Montresor."

"Ah," said Stendahl, eyes closed. He shoved the last brick into place and mortared it tight. "*Requiescat in pace,* dear friend."

He hastened from the catacomb.

In the seven rooms the sound of a midnight clock brought everything to a halt.

The Red Death appeared.

Stendahl turned for a moment at the door to watch. And then he ran out of the great House, across the moat, to where a helicopter waited.

"Ready, Pikes?"

"Ready."

"There it goes!"

They looked at the great House, smiling. It began to crack down the middle, as with an earthquake, and as Stendahl watched the magnificent sight he heard Pikes reciting behind him in a low, cadenced voice:

" '. . .my brain reeled as I saw the mighty walls rushing asunder—there was a long tumultuous shouting sound like the voice of a thousand waters—and the deep and dank tarn at my feet closed sullenly and silently over the fragments of the House of Usher.' "

The helicopter rose over the steaming lake and flew into the west.

Check Your Reading

1. What services do Pikes and Mr. Bigelow perform for William Stendahl?

2. What does Pikes learn about Mr. Garrett after Garrett's body is incinerated?

3. How does the application of DDT increase the overall effect of Stendahl's new house?

4. Why has Stendahl escaped to Mars?

5. Which society banishes Halloween and Guy Fawkes?

Further Exploration

1. This story, as suggested by the title, is a parody on the story by Poe that you read earlier. Explain how the opening and closing passages of "The Fall of the House of Usher" and "Usher II" are similar and different. What was actually destroyed in each story? Does either story end on a hopeful note? Defend your answer.

2. Why do people enjoy dressing in costumes and assuming new identities? How do people react to each other when wearing costumes and masks? If you were a guest at Stendahl's costume party, what identity would you assume?

3. Why is the destruction of books dangerous? How does the author express dissatisfaction with censorship by this fantasy set on Mars?

4. Give several examples of verbal irony used by the author to describe the people who make up the commission on Moral Climates.

5. Explain why a person should rebel against oppressive laws. Name some heroes who have refused to be governed by rules that are unjust.

Kurt Vonnegut (1922–)

Deeply affected by his experiences in World War II, including his imprisonment in an abandoned slaughterhouse and the subsequent fire-bombing of Dresden by British and American bombers, Kurt Vonnegut found a means of expressing his disillusionment with war in his novel *Slaughterhouse-Five*. Although he studied both biochemistry and anthropology during his years at Cornell University and the University of Chicago, Vonnegut chose writing for his life's work and has devoted himself to revealing the potential harm of man-made systems, whether political, religious, or scientific.

According to the author, humanity's insistence on inflicting catastrophes upon itself can be countered by only one human trait—the ability to laugh at its own folly. The humor found in Vonnegut's major works, *Cat's Cradle* (1962), *Breakfast of Champions* (1973), and *Welcome to the Monkey House* (1968), is often unsettling to readers who are lured by his playful tone only to find a gloomy view of mankind based on his lack of faith in science and technology. Another book that uses this theme is *Galapagos: A Novel* (1985). "Harrison Bergeron" reflects Vonnegut's characteristic theme that human beings must guard their creativity, sensitivity, and compassion from forces that would destroy all three.

Harrison Bergeron
Kurt Vonnegut

The year was 2081, and everybody was finally equal. They weren't only equal before God and the law. They were equal every which way. Nobody was smarter than anybody else. Nobody was better-looking than anybody else. Nobody was stronger or quicker than anybody else. All this equality was due to the 211th, 212th, and 213th Amendments to the Constitution, and to the unceasing vigilance of agents of the United States Handicapper General.

Some things about living still weren't quite right, though. April, for instance, still drove people crazy by not being springtime. And it was in that clammy month that the H-G men took George and Hazel Bergeron's fourteen-year-old son, Harrison, away.

It was tragic, all right, but George and Hazel couldn't think about it very hard. Hazel had a perfectly average intelligence, which meant she couldn't think about anything except in short bursts. And George, while his intelligence was way above normal, had a little mental handicap radio in his ear. He was required by law to wear it at all times. It was tuned to a government transmitter. Every twenty seconds or so, the transmitter would send out some sharp noise to keep people like George from taking unfair advantage of their brains

George and Hazel were watching television. There were tears on Hazel's cheek, but she'd forgotten for the moment what they were about.

On the television screen were ballerinas.

A buzzer sounded in George's head. His thought fled in panic, like bandits, from a burglar alarm.

"That was a real pretty dance, that dance they just did," said Hazel.

"Huh?" said George.

"That dance—it was nice," said Hazel.

"Yup," said George. He tried to think a little about the ballerinas. They weren't really very good—no better than anybody else would have been, anyway. They were burdened with sashweights and bags of birdshot, and their faces were masked, so that no one, seeing a free and graceful gesture or a pretty face, would feel like something the cat drug in. George was toying with the vague notion that maybe dancers shouldn't be handicapped. But he didn't get very far with it before another noise in his ear radio scattered his thoughts.

George winced. So did two out of the eight ballerinas.

Hazel saw him wince. Having no mental handicap herself, she had to ask George what the latest sound had been.

"Sounded like somebody hitting a milk bottle with a ball-peen hammer," said George.

"I'd think it would be real interesting, hearing all the diffent sounds," said Hazel, a little envious. "All the things they think up."

"Um," said George.

"Only, if I was Handicapper General, you know what I would do?" said Hazel. Hazel, as a matter of fact, bore a strong resemblance to the Handicapper General, a woman named Diana Moon Glampers. "If I was Diana Moon Glampers," said Hazel, "I'd have chimes on Sunday—just chimes. Kind of in honor of religion."

"I could think, if it was just chimes," said George.

"Well—maybe make 'em real loud," said Hazel. "I think I'd make a good Handicapper General."

"Good as anybody else," said George.

"Who knows better'n I do what normal is?" said Hazel.

"Right," said George. He began to think glimmeringly about his abnormal son who was now in jail, about Harrison, but a twenty-one-gun salute in his head stopped that.

"Boy!" said Hazel, "that was a doozy, wasn't it?"

It was such a doozy that George was white and trembling. and tears stood on the rims of his red eyes. Two of the eight ballerinas had collapsed to to the studio floor, were holding their temples.

"All of a sudden you look so tired," said Hazel. "Why don't you stretch out on the sofa, so's you can rest your handicap bag on the pillows, honeybunch." She was referring to the forty-seven pounds of birdshot in a canvas bag which was padlocked around George's neck. "Go on and rest the bag for a little while," she said. "I don't care if you're not equal to me for a while."

George weighed the bag with his hands. "I don't mind it," he said. "I don't notice it any more. It's just a part of me."

"You been so tired lately—kind of wore out," said Hazel. "If there was just some way we could make a little hole in the bottom of the bag, and just take out a few of them lead balls. Just a few."

"Two years in prison and two thousand dollars fine for every ball I took out," said George. "I don't call that a bargain."

"If you could just take a few out when you come home from work," said Hazel. "I mean—you don't compete with anybody around here. You just sit around."

"If I tried to get away with it," said George. "then other people'd get away with it—and pretty soon we'd be right back to the dark ages again, with everybody competing against everybody else. You wouldn't like that, would you?"

"I'd hate it," said Hazel.

"There you are," said George. "The minute people start cheating on laws, what do you think happens to society?"

If Hazel hadn't been able to come up with an answer to this question, George couldn't have supplied one. A siren was going off in his head.

"Reckon it'd fall all apart," said Hazel.

"What would?" said George blankly.

"Society," said Hazel uncertainly. "Wasn't that what you just said?"

"Who knows?" said George.

The television program was suddenly interrupted for a news bulletin, It wasn't clear at first as to what the bulletin was about, since the announcer, like all announcers, had a serious speech impediment. For about half a minute, and in a state of high excitement, the announcer tried to say, "Ladies and gentlemen—"

He finally gave up, handed the bulletin to a ballerina to read.

"That's all right—" Hazel said of the announcer, "he tried. That's the big thing. He tried to do the best he could with what God gave him. He should get a nice raise for trying so hard."

"Ladies and gentlemen—" said the ballerina, reading the bulletin. She must have been extraordinarily beautiful, because the mask she wore was hideous. And it was easy to see that she was the strongest and most graceful of all the dancers, for her handicap bags were as big as those worn by two-hundred-pound men.

And she had to apologize at once for her voice, which was a very unfair voice for a woman to use. Her voice was a warm, luminous, timeless melody. "Excuse me—" she said, and she began again, making her voice absolutely uncompetitive.

"Harrison Bergeron, age fourteen," she said in a grackle squawk, "has just escaped from jail, where he was held on suspicion of plotting to overthrow the government. He is a genius and an athlete, is under-handicapped, and should be regarded as extremely dangerous."

A police photograph of Harrison Bergeron was flashed on the screen—upside down, then sideways, upside down again, then right side up. The picture showed the full length of Harrison against a background calibrated in feet and inches. He was exactly seven feet tall.

The rest of Harrison's appearance was Halloween and hardware. Nobody had ever borne heavier handicaps. He had outgrown hindrances faster than the H-G men could think them up. Instead of a little ear radio for a mental handicap, he wore a tremendous pair of earphones, and spectacles with thick wavy lenses. The spectacles were intended to make him not only half blind, but to give him whanging headaches besides.

Scrap metal was hung all over him. Ordinarily, there was a certain symmetry, a military neatness to the handicaps issued to strong people, but Harrison looked like a walking junkyard. In the race of life, Harrison carried three hundred pounds.

And to offset his good looks, the H-G men required that he wear at all times a red rubber ball for a nose, keep his eyebrows shaved off, and cover his even white teeth with black caps at snaggle-tooth random.

"If you see this boy," said the ballerina, "do not—I repeat, do not—try to reason with him."

There was the shriek of a door being torn from its hinges. Screams and barking cries of consternation came from the television set. The photograph of Harrison Bergeron on the screen jumped again and again, as though dancing to the tune of an earthquake.

George Bergeron correctly identified the earthquake, and well he might have—for many was the time his own home had danced to the same crashing tune. "My God—" said George, "that must be Harrison!"

The realization was blasted form his mind instantly by the sound of an automobile collision in his head.

When George could open his eyes again, the photograph of Harrison was gone. A living, breathing Harrison filled the screen.

Clanking, clownish, and huge, Harrison stood in the center of the studio. The knob of the uprooted studio door was still in his hand. Ballerinas, technicians, musicians, and announcers cowered on their knees before him, expecting to die.

"I am the Emperor!" cried Harrison. "Do you hear? I am the Emperor! Everybody must do what I say at once!" He stamped his foot and the studio shook.

"Even as I stand here—" he bellowed, "cripped, hobbled, sickened—I am a greater ruler than any man who ever lived! Now watch me become what I *can* become!"

Harrison tore the straps of his handicap harness like wet tissue paper, tore straps guaranteed to support five thousand pounds.

Harrison's scrap-iron handicaps crashed to the floor.

Harrison thrust his thumbs under the bar of the padlock that secured his head harness. The bar snapped like celery. Harrison smashed his headphones and spectacles against the wall.

He flung away his rubber-ball nose, revealed a man that would have awed Thor, the god of thunder.

"I shall now select my Empress!" he said, looking down on the cowering people. "Let the first woman who dares rise to her feet claim her mate and her throne!"

A moment passed, and then a ballerina arose, swaying like a willow.

Harrison plucked the mental handicap from her ear, snapped off her physical handicaps with marvelous delicacy. Last of all, he removed her mask.

She was blindingly beautiful.

"Now—" said Harrison, taking her hand, "shall we show the people the meaning of the word *dance?* Music!" he commanded.

The musicians scrambled back into their chairs, and Harrison stripped them of their handicaps, too. "Play your best," he told them, "and I'll make you barons and dukes and earls."

The music began. It was normal at first—cheap, silly, false. But Harrison snatched two musicians from their chairs, waved them like batons as he sang the music as he wanted it played. He slammed them back into their chairs.

The music began again and was much improved.

Harrison and his Empress merely listened to the music for a while—listened gravely, as though synchronizing their heartbeats with it.

They shifted their weight to their toes.

Harrison placed his big hands on the girl's tiny waist, letting her sense the weightlessness that would soon be hers.

And then, in an explosion of joy and grace, into the air they sprang!

Not only were the laws of the land abandoned, but the law of gravity and the laws of motion as well.

They reeled, whirled, swiveled, flounced, capered, gamboled, and spun.

They leaped like deer on the moon.

The studio ceiling was thirty feet high, but each leap brought the dancers nearer to it.

It became their obvious intention to kiss the ceiling.

They kissed it.

And then, neutralizing gravity with love and pure will, they remained suspended in air inches below the ceiling, and they kissed each other for a long, long time.

It was then that Diana Moon Glampers, the Handicapper General, came into the studio with a double-barreled ten-gauge shotgun. She fired twice, and the Emperor and the Empress were dead before they hit the floor.

Diana Moon Glampers loaded the gun again. She aimed it at the musicians and told them that they had ten seconds to get their handicaps back on.

It was then that the Bergerons' television tube burned out.

Hazel turned to comment about the blackout to George. But George had gone out into the kitchen for a can of beer.

George came back in with the beer, paused while a handicap signal shook him up. And then he sat down again. "You been crying?" he said to Hazel.

"Yup," she said.

"What about?" he said.

"I forget," she said. "Something real sad on television."

"What was it?" he said.

"It's all kind of mixed-up in my mind," said Hazel.

"Forget sad things," said George.

"I always do," said Hazel.

"That's my girl," said George. He winced. There was the sound of a riveting gun in his head.

"Gee—I could tell that one was a doozy," said Hazel.

"You can say that again," said George.

"Gee—" said Hazel, "I could tell that one was a doozy."

Check Your Reading

1. What is the job of the Handicapper General?

2. What scene on the television screen causes Hazel to forget her grief?

3. What title does Harrison proclaim for himself?

4. How is Harrison's handsome face obscured from view?

5. How does Diana Moon Glampers end the dance?

Further Exploration

1. Why does George require greater handicapping than Hazel? What aspects of handicapping would you find most uncomfortable? How does Hazel offer to alleviate George's handicaps? Why does she not mind being unequal?

2. How does Harrison rebel against equalization? Is it likely that a rebellion against an oppressive society would be led by a young person? Can you think of examples of other young people who have led adults to rebel against unfairness or harmful governmental policies?

3. Why do Harrison's parents fail to grieve for him? Do you feel pity or disgust for the Bergerons?

4. The control of human behavior by psychological conditioning can result in a change in habits. Why do you think Vonnegut dwells on the evil aspects of conditioning? Describe some situations in our own society in which conditioning can be useful or beneficial.

5. "Harrison Bergeron" is a satire of contemporary society. Compare and contrast the two societies.

W.W. Jacobs (1863–1943)

In contrast to his mundane jobs in a government savings bank and a post office, William Wymark Jacobs created more interesting worlds through his writing of short stories. His life in London near the shipyards of the Thames River supplied him with background material, particularly in fiction featuring seafarers.

Jacobs excelled in two types of narrative—humor and stories of the macabre, which fill his three collections, *Many Cargoes* (1896), *The Skipper's Wooing* (1897), and *Night Watches* (1914). "The Monkey's Paw," which reflects the latter emphasis, hinges on a plot as old as fiction—the magical fulfillment of three wishes.

The Monkey's Paw
W. W. Jacobs

I

Without, the night was cold and wet, but in the small parlor of Lakesnam Villa the blinds were drawn and the fire burned brightly. Father and son were at chess, the former, who possessed ideas about the game involving radical changes, putting his king into such sharp and unnecessary perils that it even provoked comment from the white haired old lady knitting placidly by the fire.

"Hark at the wind," said Mr. White, who, having seen a fatal mistake after it was too late, was amiably desirous of preventing his son from seeing it.

"I'm listening," said the latter, grimly surveying the board as he stretched out his hand. "Check."

"I should hardly think that he'd come tonight," said his father, with his hand poised over the board.

"Mate," replied the son.

"That's the worst of living so far out," bawled Mr. White, with sudden and unlooked-for violence; "of all the beastly, slushy, out-of-the-way places to live in, this is the worst. Pathway's a bog, and the road's a torrent. I don't know what people are thinking about. I suppose because only two houses on the road are let, they think it doesn't matter."

"Never mind, dear," said his wife soothingly; "perhaps you'll win the next one."

Mr. White looked up sharply, just in time to intercept a knowing glance between mother and son. The words died away on his lips, and he hid a guilty grin in his thin gray beard.

"There he is," said Herbert White, as the gate banged to loudly and heavy footsteps came toward the door.

The old man rose with hospitable haste, and opening the door, was heard condoling with the new arrival. The new arrival also condoled with himself, so that Mrs. White said, "Tut, tut!" and coughed gently as her husband entered the room, followed by a tall burly man, beady of eye and rubicund of visage.

"Sergeant-Major Morris," he said, introducing him.

The sergeant-major shook hands, and taking the proffered seat by the fire, watched contentedly while his host got out whisky and tumblers and stood a small copper kettle on the fire.

At the third glass his eyes got brighter, and he began to talk, the little family circle regarding with eager interest this visitor from distant parts, as he squared his broad shoulders in the chair and spoke of strange scenes and doughty deeds, of wars and plagues and strange peoples.

"Twenty-one years of it," said Mr. White, nodding at his wife and son. "When he went away he was a slip of a youth in the warehouse. Now look at him."

"He don't look to have taken much harm," said Mrs. White politely.

"I'd like to go to India myself," said the old man, "just to look round a bit, you know."

"Better where you are," said the sergeant-major, shaking his head. He put down the empty glass and, sighing softly, shook it again.

"I should like to see those old temples and fakirs and jugglers," said the old man. "What was that you started telling me the other day about a monkey's paw or something, Morris?"

"Nothing," said the soldier hastily. "Leastways, nothing worth hearing."

"Monkey's paw?" said Mrs. White curiously.

"Well, it's just a bit of what you might call magic, perhaps," said the sergeant-major off-handedly.

His three listeners leaned forward eagerly. The visitor absent-mindedly put his empty glass to his lips and then set it down again. His host filled it for him.

"To look at," said the sergeant-major fumbling in his pocket, "it's just an ordinary little paw, dried to a mummy." He took something out of his pocket and proffered it. Mrs. White drew back with a grimace, but her son, taking it, examined it curiously.

"And what is there special about it?" inquired Mr. White, as he took it from his son and, having examined it, placed it upon the table.

"It had a spell put on it by an old fakir," said the sergeant-major, "a very holy man. He wanted to show that fate ruled people's lives, and that those who interfered with it did so to their sorrow. He put a spell on it so that three separate men could each have three wishes from it."

His manner was so impressive that his hearers were conscious that their light laughter jarred somewhat.

"Well, why don't you have three, sir?" said Herbert White cleverly.

The soldier regarded him in the way that middle age is wont to regard presumptuous youth. "I have," he said quietly, and his blotchy face whitened.

"And did you really have the three wishes granted?" asked Mrs. White.

"I did," said the sergeant-major, and his glass tapped against his strong teeth.

"And has anybody else wished?" inquired the old lady.

"The first man had his three wishes, yes," was the reply. "I don't know what the first two were, but the third was for death. That's how I got the paw."

His tones were so grave that a hush fell upon the group.

"If you've had your three wishes, it's no good to you now, then, Morris," said the old man at last. "What do you keep it for?"

The soldier shook his head. "Fancy, I suppose," he said slowly. "I did have some idea of selling it, but I don't think I will. It has caused enough mischief already. Besides, people won't buy. They think it's a fairy tale, some of them, and those who do think anything of it want to try it first and pay me afterward."

"If you could have another three wishes," said the old man, eyeing him keenly, "would you have them?"

"I don't know," said the other. "I don't know."

He took the paw, and dangling it between his front finger and thumb, suddenly threw it upon the fire. White, with a slight cry, stooped down and snatched it off.

"Better let it burn," said the soldier solemnly.

"If you don't want it Morris," said the old man, "give it to me."

"I won't" said his friend doggedly. "I threw it on the fire. If you keep it don't blame me for what happens. Pitch it on the fire again, like a sensible man."

The other shook his head and examined his new possession closely. "How do you do it?" he inquired.

"Hold it up in your right hand and wish aloud," said the sergeant-major, "but I warn you of the consequences."

"Sounds like the *Arabian Nights*," said Mrs. White, as she rose and began to set the supper. "Don't you think you might wish for four pairs of hands for me?"

Her husband drew the talisman from his pocket and then all three burst into laughter as the sergeant-major, with a look of alarm on his face, caught him by the arm.

"If you must wish," he said gruffly, "wish for something sensible."

Mr. White dropped it back into his pocket, and placing chairs, motioned his friend to the table. In the business of supper the talisman was partly forgotten, and afterward the three sat listening in an enthralled fashion to a second installment of the soldier's adventures in India.

"If the tale about the monkey paw is not more truthful than those he has been telling us," said Herbert, as the door closed behind their guest, just in time for him to catch the last train, "we shan't make much out of it."

"Did you give him anything for it, father?" inquired Mrs. White, regarding her husband closely.

"A trifle," said be, coloring slightly. "He didn't want it, but I made him take it. And he pressed me again to throw it away."

"Likely," said Herbert, with pretended horror. "Why, we're going to be rich, and famous, and happy. Wish to be an emperor, father, to begin with; then you can't be henpecked."

He darted round the table, pursued by the maligned Mrs. White armed with an antimacassar.

Mr. White took the paw from his pocket and eyed it dubiously. "I don't know what to wish for, and that's a fact," he said slowly. "It seems to me I've got all I want."

"If you only cleared the house, you'd be quite happy, wouldn't you?" said Herbert, with his hand on his shoulder. "Well, wish for two hundred pounds, then; that'll just do it."

His father, smiling shamefacedly at his own credulity, held up the talisman, as his son, with a solemn face somewhat marred by a wink at his mother, sat down at the piano and struck a few impressive chords.

"I wish for two hundred pounds," said the old man distinctly.

A fine crash from the piano greeted the words, interrupted by a shuddering cry from the old man. His wife and son ran toward him.

"It moved," he cried, with a glance of disgust at the object as it lay on the floor. "As I wished it twisted in my hands like a snake."

"Well, I don't see the money," said his son, as he picked it up and placed it on the table, "and I bet I never shall."

"It must have been your fancy, father," said his wife, regarding him anxiously.

He shook his head. "Never mind, though; there's no harm done, but it gave me a shock all the same."

They sat down by the fire again while the two men finished their pipes. Outside, the wind was higher than ever, and the old man started nervously at the sound of a door banging upstairs. A silence unusual and depressing settled upon all three, which lasted until the old couple rose to retire for the night

"I expect you'll find the cash tied up in a big bag in the middle of your bed," said Herbert, as he bade them good night, "and something horrible squatting up on top of the wardrobe watching you as you pocket your ill-gotten gains."

II

In the brightness of the wintry sun next morning as it streamed over the breakfast table Herbert laughed at his fears. There was an air of prosaic wholesomeness about the room which it had lacked on the previous night, and the dirty, shriveled little paw was pitched on the sideboard with a carelessness which betokened no great belief in its virtues.

"I suppose all old soldiers are the same," said Mrs. White. "The idea of our listening to such nonsense! How could wishes be granted in these days? And if they could, how could two hundred pounds hurt you, father?"

"Might drop on his head from the sky," said the frivolous Herbert.

"Morris said the things happened so naturally," said his father, "that you might if you so wished attribute it to coincidence."

"Well, don't break into the money before I come back," said Herbert, as he rose from the table. "I'm afraid it'll turn you into a mean, avaricious man, and we shall have to disown you."

His mother laughed, and following him to the door, watched him down the road, and returning to the breakfast table, was very happy at the expense of her husband's credulity. All of which did not prevent her from scurrying to the door at the postman's knock, nor prevent her from referring somewhat shortly to retired sergeant-majors of bibulous habits when she found that the post brought a tailor's bill.

"Herbert will have some more of his funny remarks, I expect, when he comes home," she said, as they sat at dinner.

"I dare say," said Mr. White, pouring himself out some beer; "but for all that, the thing moved in my hand; that I'll swear to."

"You thought it did," said the old lady soothingly.

"I say it did," replied the other. "There was no thought about it; I had just—What's the matter?"

His wife made no reply. She was watching the mysterious movements of a man outside, who, peering in an undecided fashion at the house, appeared to be trying to make up his mind to enter. In mental connection with the two hundred pounds, she noticed that the stranger was well dressed and wore a silk hat of glossy newness. Three times he paused at the gate, and then walked on again. The fourth time he stood with his hand upon it, and then with sudden resolution flung it open and walked up the path. Mrs. White at the same moment placed her hands behind her, and hurriedly unfastening the strings of her apron, put that useful article of apparel beneath the cushion of her chair.

She brought the stranger, who seemed ill at ease, into the room. He gazed furtively at Mrs. White, and listened in a preoccupied fashion as the old lady apologized for the appearance of the room, and her husband's coat, a garment which he usually reserved for the garden. She then waited as patiently as her sex would permit for him to broach his business, but he was at first strangely silent.

"I—was asked to call," he said at last, and stooped and picked a piece of cotton from his trousers. "I come from Maw and Meggins."

The old lady started. "Is anything the matter?" she asked breathlessly. "Has anything happened to Herbert? What is it? What is it?"

Her husband interposed. "There, there, mother," he said hastily. "Sit down, and don't jump to conclusions. You've not brought bad news, I'm sure, sir," and he eyed the other wistfully.

"I'm sorry—" began the visitor.

"Is he hurt?" demanded the mother.

The visitor bowed in assent. "Badly hurt," he said quietly, "but he is not in any pain."

"Oh, thank God!" said the old woman, clasping her hands. "Thank God for that! Thank—"

She broke off suddenly as the sinister meaning of the assurance dawned upon her and she saw the awful confirmation of her fears in the other's averted face. She caught her breath, and turning to her slower-witted husband, laid her trembling old hand upon his. There was a long silence.

"He was caught in the machinery," said the visitor at length, in a low voice.

"Caught in the machinery," repeated Mr. White, in a dazed fashion, "yes."

He sat staring blankly out at the window, and taking his wife's hand between his own, pressed it as he had been wont to do in their old courting days nearly forty years before.

"He was the only one left to us," he said, turning gently to the visitor. "It is hard."

The other coughed, and rising, walked slowly to the window. "The firm wished me to convey their sincere sympathy with you in your great loss," he said, without looking round. "I beg that you will understand I am only their servant and merely obeying orders."

There was no reply; the old woman's face was white, her eyes staring, and her breath inaudible; on the husband's face was a look such as his friend the sergeant might have carried into his first action.

"I was to say that Maw and Meggins disclaim all responsibility," continued the other. "They admit no liability at all, but in consideration of your son's services they wish to present you with a certain sum as compensation."

Mr. White dropped his wife's hand, and rising to his feet, gazed with a look of horror at his visitor. His dry lips shaped the words, "How much?"

"Two hundred pounds," was the answer.

Unconscious of his wife's shriek, the old man smiled faintly, put out his hands like a sightless man, and dropped, a senseless heap, to the floor.

III

In the huge new cemetery, some two miles distant, the old people buried their dead, and came back to a house steeped in shadow and silence. It was all over so quickly that at first they could hardly realize it, and remained in a state of expectation as though of something else to happen—something else which was to lighten this load, too heavy for old hearts to bear. But the days passed, and expectation gave place to resignation—the hopeless resignation of the old, sometimes miscalled apathy. Sometimes they hardly exchanged a word, for now they had nothing to talk about, and their days were long to weariness.

It was about a week after that that the old man, waking suddenly in the night, stretched out his hand and found himself alone. The room was in darkness, and the sound of subdued weeping came from the window. He raised himself in bed and listened.

"Come back," he said tenderly. "You will be cold."

"It is colder for my son," said the old woman, and wept afresh.

The sound of her sobs died away on his ears. The bed was warm, and his eyes heavy with sleep. He dozed fitfully, and then slept until a sudden wild cry from his wife awoke him with a start.

"The monkey's paw!" she cried wildly. "The monkey's paw!"

He started up in alarm. "Where? Where is it? What's the matter?"

She came stumbling across the room toward him. "I want it," she said quietly. "You've not destroyed it?"

"It's in the parlor, on the bracket," he replied, marveling. "Why?"

She cried and laughed together, and bending over, kissed his cheek.

"I only just thought of it," she said hysterically. "Why didn't I think of it before? Why didn't you think of it?"

"Think of what?" he questioned.

"The other two wishes," she replied rapidly. "We've only had one."

"Was that not enough?" he demanded fiercely.

"No," she cried triumphantly; "we'll have one more. Go down and get it quickly, and wish our boy alive again."

The man sat up in bed and flung the bedclothes from his quaking limbs. "Good God, you are mad!" he cried, aghast.

"Get it," she panted; "get it quickly, and wish—Oh, my boy, my boy!"

Her husband struck a match and lit the candle. "Get back to bed," he said unsteadily. "You don't know what you are saying."

"We had the first wish granted," said the old woman feverishly; "why not the second?"

"A coincidence," stammered the old man.

"Go and get it and wish," cried the old woman, and dragged him toward the door.

He went down in the darkness, and felt his way to the parlor and then to the mantelpiece. The talisman was in its place, and a horrible fear that the unspoken wish might bring his mutilated son before him ere he could escape from the room seized upon him, and he caught his breath as he found that he had lost the direction of the door. His brow cold with sweat, he felt his way round the table, and groped along the wall until he found himself in the small passage with the unwholesome thing in his hand.

Even his wife's face seemed changed as he entered the room. It was white and expectant, and to his fears seemed to have an unnatural look upon it. He was afraid of her.

"Wish!" she cried in a strong voice.

"It is foolish and wicked," he faltered.

"Wish!" repeated his wife.

He raised his hand. "I wish my son alive again."

The talisman fell to the floor, and he regarded it shudderingly. Then he sank trembling into a chair as the old woman, with burning eyes, walked to the window and raised the blind.

He sat until he was chilled with the cold, glancing occasionally at the figure of the old woman peering through the window. The candle end, which had burnt below the rim of the china candlestick, was throwing pulsating shadows on the ceiling and walls, until, with a flicker larger than the rest it expired. The old man, with an unspeakable sense of relief at the failure of the talisman, crept back to his bed, and a minute or two afterward the old woman came silently and apathetically beside him.

Neither spoke, but both lay silently listening to the ticking of the clock. A stair creaked, and a squeaky mouse scurried noisily through the wall. The darkness was oppressive, and after lying for some time screwing up his courage, the husband took the box of matches, and striking one, went downstairs for a candle.

At the foot of the stairs the match went out, and he paused to strike another, and at the same moment a knock, so quiet and stealthy as to be scarcely audible, sounded on the front door.

The matches fell from his hand. He stood motionless, his breath suspended until the knock was repeated. Then he turned and fled swiftly back to his room, and closed the door behind him. A third knock sounded through the house.

"*What's that?*" cried the old woman, starting up.

"A rat," said the old man, in shaking tones—"a rat. It passed me on the stairs."

His wife sat up in bed listening. A loud knock resounded through the house.

"It's Herbert!" she screamed. "It's Herbert!"

She ran to the door, but her husband was before her, and catching her by the arm, held her tightly.

"What are you going to do?" he whispered hoarsely.

"It's my boy; it's Herbert!" she cried, struggling mechanically. "I forgot it was two miles away. What are you holding me for? Let go. I must open the door."

"For God's sake don't let it in," cried the old man, trembling.

"You're afraid of your own son," she cried, struggling. "Let me go. I'm coming, Herbert; I'm coming."

There was another knock, and another. The old woman with a sudden wrench broke free and ran from the room. Her husband followed to the landing, and called after her appealingly as she hurried downstairs. He heard the chain rattle back and the bottom bolt drawn slowly and stiffly from the socket. Then the old woman's voice, strained and panting.

"The bolt," she cried loudly. "Come down. I can't reach it."

But her husband was on his hands and knees groping wildly on the floor in search of the paw. If he could only find it before the thing outside got in. A perfect fusillade of knocks reverberated through the house, and he heard the scraping of a chair as his wife put it down in the passage against the door. He heard the creaking of the bolt as it came slowly back, and at the same moment he found the monkey's paw, and frantically breathed his third and last wish.

The knocking ceased suddenly, although the echoes of it were still in the house. He heard the chair drawn back and the door opened. A cold wind rushed up the staircase, and a long loud wail of disappointment and misery from his wife gave him courage to run down to her side and then to the gate beyond. The street lamp flickering opposite shone on a quiet and deserted road.

Check Your Reading

1. Why does Mr. White complain about the location of his house?

2. What aspects of Indian life would Mr. White like to see?

3. What story does the paw bring to Mrs. White's mind?

4. What piece of information causes Mr. White to faint?

5. What keeps Mrs. White from opening the door?

Further Exploration

1. How does the sergeant-major's description of the final wish of the first man who owned the paw add to the suspense of the story?

2. How does Jacobs illustrate the dangers of greed?

3. What elements in Part 1 of the story foreshadow the tragedy of the remainder of the story? Does Mr. White receive enough warning of the consequences of his wishes?

4. What would you do with the paw if Mr. White gave it to you? Do you think he passed it on to someone else? What advice would you give someone who just received the paw?

5. Do you agree with the old fakir that fate rules human life and "those who interfere with it do so to their sorrow"? Can you name other characters from literature, television, or movies who have known the future and tried to change it?

Encountering the Unexpected

Thinking It Over

These activities offer opportunities for you to consider how the stories in Part Three relate to one another and to the theme of *Encountering the Unexpected.*

1. In each of these four stories, at least one character displays a serious flaw. Select one of these characters and explain how that flaw influences the story.

2. Often humor and terror exist side by side in fiction. Explain how Vonnegut pairs comic elements with horror in "Harrison Bergeron."

3. Compare the role of the Handicapper General in "Harrison Bergeron" with that of the Investigator of Moral Climates in "Usher II." Which character makes the greater change in the society?

4. Describe the role of music, dancing, art, literature, and story-telling in these four stories. How do the four authors utilize the arts to emphasize terror?

5. Discuss the appeal to the five senses—seeing, hearing, touching, smelling, and tasting—in "The Fall of the House of Usher." Which sense seems to dominate the details? Which sense is used least often? How does the narrator's use of sensual imagery increase the level of terror?

6. Writers of horror stories play upon people's natural fears, by carrying them to extremes. Give examples from these four stories.

7. Have any of the prophecies contained in these stories already come true? Why do warnings of future catastrophe fail to change society's ways?

PART FOUR

Confronting Prejudice

In an ideal society there would be no need to study prejudice. However, we do not live in a utopia where prejudice does not exist. In our world, prejudice based on race, sex, religion, physical characteristics, age, intelligence, and political ideas is something we all must cope with. It is important to understand the difference between prejudice and discrimination. Prejudice is an attitude whereas discrimination is an act. We might never know one is prejudiced unless that person discriminates. It is these acts of discrimination that reveal prejudice.

Where does one develop a prejudice? By analyzing the word *prejudice*, we can gain some insight into the source of biased thinking. The word means pre-judging or forming an opinion before you know all of the facts. Intellectually we know that prejudice is wrong. The basis for every sound decision is a complete knowledge of all the facts. Then why do people pre-judge?

Unfortunately, fear plays an important part in pre-judging. Sometimes we fear that someone will take our jobs, disturb the harmony of our neighborhoods, do better on a test or be a better athlete, beat us in an election, or make fun of our appearance. To prevent these seemingly unfair occurrences, we discriminate against other persons whom we suspect may harm us.

When we observed discrimination in the form of exclusion or humiliation of an innocent person, we have many choices of response. We may react with anger, we may intervene on behalf of the injured party, or we may choose to say nothing. Unfortunately, in many instances it is to our advantage not to fight back, for the forces of prejudice can be much larger than one person can combat, for example our society's neglect and mistreatment of elderly people. Whatever the situation, our awareness of other people's feelings is the key issue, for concern for individual human needs is a quality that sets us apart from animals.

As you study these stories that deal with prejudice and discrimination, determine the reasons for the characters' actions. When you isolate their motivation, consider your own actions and decide whether you are guilty of similar faulty reasoning. At the same time concentrate on the uniqueness of people and the rich heritage they bring to our heterogeneous society. Consider what you might be missing if you allow prejudice to rob you of a wide range of interesting, talented people.

Borden Deal (1922–1985)

Born on a farm in Pontotoc, Mississippi, during the Depression, Borden Deal understood the meaning of hard times. Following his years in the Navy during World War II, he earned a B.A. degree from the University of Alabama in 1949 and worked in various jobs, including a circus, the Civilian Conservation Corps, and the Labor Department, before becoming a freelance writer. Deal wrote regional novels, such as *Walk Through My Valley* (1956) *and Dunbar's Cove* (1957), describing people closely associated with agriculture; adaptations for stage, film, radio, and television; and more than one hundred short stories, which have appeared in *Saturday Review* and *Best American Short Stories 1949.*

A critic praised Deal's characters because they "live and work in real time in real places." This description fits T.J., a character in "Antaeus," who must learn to cope with new pals and an urban environment. The story was selected for inclusion in *The Best American Short Stories 1962.*

*Antaeus**
Borden Deal

This was during the wartime, when lots of people were coming North for jobs in factories and war industries, when people moved around a lot more than they do now, and sometimes kids were thrown into new groups and new lives that were completely different from anything they had ever known before. I remember this one kid, T. J. his name was, from somewhere down South, whose family moved into our building during that time. They'd come North with everything they owned piled into the back seat of an old-model sedan that you wouldn't expect could make the trip, with T. J. and his three younger sisters riding shakily on top of the load of junk.

Our building was just like all the others there, with families crowded into a few rooms, and I guess there were twenty-five or thirty kids about my age in that one building. Of course, there were a few of us who formed a gang and ran together all the time after school, and I was the one who brought T. J. in and started the whole thing.

The building right next door to us was a factory where they made walking dolls. It was a low building with a flat, tarred roof that had a parapet all around it about head-high, and we'd found out a long time before that no one, not even the watchman, paid any attention to the roof because it was higher than any of the other buildings around. So my gang used the roof as a headquarters. We could get up there by crossing over to the fire escape from our own roof on a plank and then going on up. It was a secret place for us, where nobody else could go without our permission.

I remember the day I first took T. J. up there to meet the gang. He was a stocky, robust kid with a shock of white hair, nothing sissy about

---

*Antaeus in Greek mythology is a giant who invariably won wrestling matches with his enemies because his mother, the Earth goddess, renewed his strength each time he was thrown. Hercules killed Antaeus by holding him in the air and crushing him.

him except his voice; he talked in this slow, gentle voice like you never heard before. He talked different from any of us and you noticed it right away. But I liked him anyway, so I told him to come on up.

We climbed up over the parapet and dropped down on the roof. The rest of the gang were already there.

"Hi," I said. I jerked my thumb at T. J. "He just moved into the building yesterday."

He just stood there, not scared or anything, just looking, like the first time you see somebody you're not sure you're going to like.

"Hi," Blackie said. "Where are you from?"

"Marion County," T. J. said.

We laughed. "Marion County?" I said. "Where's that?"

He looked at me for a moment like I was a stranger, too. "It's in Alabama," he said, like I ought to know where it was.

"What's your name?" Charley said.

"T. J.," he said, looking back at him. He had pale blue eyes that looked washed-out, but he looked directly at Charley, waiting for his reaction. He'll be all right, I thought. No sissy in him, except that voice. Who ever talked like that?

"T. J.," Blackie said. "That's just initials. What's your real name? Nobody in the world has just initials."

"I do," he said. "And they're T. J. That's all the name I got."

His voice was resolute with the knowledge of his rightness, and for a moment no one had anything to say. T. J. looked around at the rooftop and down at the black tar under his feet. "Down yonder where I come from," he said, "we played out in the woods. Don't you-all have no woods around here?"

"Naw," Blackie said. "There's the park a few blocks over, but it s full of kids and cops and old women. You can't do a thing."

T. J. kept looking at the tar under his feet. "You mean you ain't got no fields to raise nothing in?—no watermelons or nothing?"

"Naw," I said scornfully. "What do you want to grow something for? The folks can buy everything they need at the store."

He looked at me again with that strange, unknowing look. "In Marion County," he said, "I had my own acre of cotton and my own acre of corn. It was mine to plant and make ever' year."

He sounded like it was something to be proud of, and in some obscure way it made the rest of us angry. Blackie said, "Who'd want to have their own acre of cotton and corn? That's just work. What can you do with an acre of cotton and corn?"

T. J. looked at him. "Well, you get part of the bale offen your acre," he said seriously. "And I fed my acre of corn to my calf."

We didn't really know what he was talking about, so we were more puzzled than angry; otherwise, I guess, we'd have chased him off the roof and wouldn't let him be part of our gang. But he was strange and different, and we were all attracted by his stolid sense of rightness and belonging, maybe by the strange softness of his voice contrasting our own tones of speech into harshness.

He moved his foot against the black tar. "We could make our own field right here," he said softly, thoughtfully. "Come spring we could raise us what we want to—watermelons and garden truck and no telling what all."

"You'd have to be a good farmer to make these tar roofs grow any watermelons," I said. We all laughed.

But T. J. looked serious. "We could haul us some dirt up here," he said. "And spread it out even and water it, and before you know it, we'd have us a crop in here." He looked at us intently. "Wouldn't that be fun?"

"They wouldn't let us," Blackie said quickly.

"I thought you said this was you-all's roof," T. J. said to me. "That you-all could do anything you wanted to up here."

"They've never bothered us," I said. I felt the idea beginning to catch fire in me. It was a big idea, and it took a while for it to sink in; but the more I thought about it, the better I liked it. "Say," I said to the gang. "He might have something there, just make us a regular roof garden, with flowers and grass and trees and everything. And all ours, too," I said. "We wouldn't let anybody up here except the ones we wanted to."

"It'd take a while to grow trees," T. J. said quickly, but we weren't paying any attention to him. They were all talking about it suddenly, all excited with the idea after I'd put it in a way they could catch hold of it. Only rich people had roof gardens, we knew, and the idea of our own private domain excited them.

"We could bring it up in sacks and boxes," Blackie said. "We'd have to do it while the folks weren't paying any attention to us, for we'd have to come up to the roof of our building and then cross over with it."

"Where could we get the dirt?" somebody said worriedly.

"Out of those vacant lots over close to school," Blackie said. "Nobody'd notice if we scraped it up."

I slapped T. J. on the shoulder. "Man, you had a wonderful idea," I said, and everybody grinned at him, remembering that he had started it. "Our own private roof garden."

He grinned back. "It'll be ourn," he said. "All ourn." Then he looked thoughtful again. "Maybe I can lay my hands on some cotton seed, too. You think we could raise us some cotton?"

We'd started big projects before at one time or another, like any gang of kids, but they'd always petered out for lack of organization and direction. But this one didn't; somehow or other T. J. kept it going through the winter months, He kept talking about the watermelons and the cotton we'd raise, come spring, and when even that wouldn't work, he'd switch around to my idea of flowers and grass and trees, though he was always honest enough to add that it'd take a while to get any trees started. He always had it on his mind and he'd mention it in school, getting them lined up to carry dirt that afternoon, saying in a casual way that he reckoned a few more weeks ought to see the job through.

Our little area of private earth grew slowly. T. J. was smart enough to start in one corner of the building, heaping up the carried earth two or three feet thick so that we had an immediate result to look at, to contemplate with awe. Some of the evenings T. J. alone was carrying earth up to the building, the rest of the gang distracted by other enterprises or interests, but T. J. kept plugging along his own, and eventually we'd all come back to him again and then our own little acre would grow more rapidly.

He was careful about the kind of dirt he'd let us carry up there, and more than once he dumped a sandy load over the parapet into the areaway below because it wasn't good enough. He found out the kinds of earth in all the vacant lots for blocks around. He'd pick it up and feel it and smell it, frozen though it was sometimes, and then he'd say it was good growing soil or it wasn't worth anything, and we'd have to go on somewhere else.

Thinking about it now, I don't see how he kept us at it. It was hard work lugging around sacks and boxes of dirt all the way up the stairs of our own building, keeping out of the way of the grownups so they wouldn't catch on to what we were doing. They probably wouldn't have cared, for they didn't pay much attention to us, but we wanted to keep it secret anyway. Then we had to go through the trap door to our roof, teeter over a plank to the fire escape, then climb two or three stories to the parapet and drop down onto the roof. All that for a small pile of earth that sometimes didn't seem worth the effort. But T. J. kept the vision bright within us, his words shrewd and calculated toward the fulfillment of his dream; and he worked harder than any of us. He seemed driven toward a goal that we couldn't see, a particular point in time that would be definitely marked by signs and wonders that only he could see.

The laborious earth just lay there during the cold months, inert and lifeless, the clods lumpy and cold under our feet when we walked over it. But one day it rained, and afterward there was a softness in the air, and the earth was live and giving again with moisture and warmth.

That evening T. J. smelled the air, his nostrils dilating with the odor of the earth under his feet. "It's spring," he said, and there was a gladness rising in his voice that filled us all with the same feeling "It's mighty late for it, but it's spring. I'd just about decided it wasn't never gonna get here at all."

We were all sniffing at the air, too, trying to smell it the way that T. J. did, and I can still remember the sweet odor of the earth under our feet. It was the first time in my life that spring and spring earth had meant anything to me. I looked at T. J. then, knowing in a faint way the hunger within him through the toilsome winter months, knowing the dream that lay behind his plan. He was a new Antaeus, preparing his own bed of strength.

"Planting time," he said, "We'll have to find us some seed."

"What do we do?" Blackie said "How do we do it?"

"First we'll have to break up the clods," T. J. said. "That won't be hard to do. Then we plant the seeds, and after a while they come up. Then you got you a crop." He frowned. "But you ain't got it raised yet. You got to tend it and hoe it and take care of it, and all the time it's growing and growing, while you're awake and while you're asleep. Then you lay it by when it's growed and let it ripen, and then you got you a crop."

"There's those wholesale seed houses over on Sixth," I said. "We could probably swipe some grass seed over there."

T. J. looked at the earth. "You-all seem mighty set on raising some grass," he said. "I ain't never put no effort into that. I spent all my life trying not to raise grass."

"But it's pretty," Blackie said. "We could play on it and take sunbaths on it. Like having our own lawn. Lots of people got lawns."

"Well," T. J. said. He looked at the rest of us, hesitant for the first time. He kept on looking at us for a moment. "I did have it in mind to raise some corn and vegetables. But we'll plant grass."

He was smart. He knew where to give in. And I don't suppose it made any difference to him, really. He just wanted to grow something, even if it was grass.

"Of course," he said, "I do think we ought to plant a row of watermelons. They'd be mighty nice to eat while we was a-laying on that grass."

We all laughed. "All right," I said. "We'll plant us a row of watermelons."

Things went very quickly then. Perhaps half the roof was covered with the earth, the half that wasn't broken by ventilators, and we swiped pocketfuls of grass seed from the open bins in the wholesale seed house, mingling among the buyers on Saturdays and during the school lunch hour. T. J. showed us how to prepare the earth, breaking up the clods and smoothing it and sowing the grass seed. It looked rich and black now with moisture, receiving of the seed, and it seemed that the grass sprang up overnight, pale green in the early spring.

We couldn't keep from looking at it, unable to believe that we had created this delicate growth. We looked at T. J. with understanding now, knowing the fulfillment of the plan he had carried along within his mind. We had worked without full understanding of the task, but he had known all the time.

We found that we couldn't walk or play on the delicate blades, as we had expected to, but we didn't mind. It was enough just to look at it, to realize that it was the work of our own hands, and each evening the whole gang was there, trying to measure the growth that had been achieved that day.

One time a foot was placed on the plot of ground, one time only, Blackie stepping onto it with sudden bravado. Then he looked at the crushed blades and there was shame in his face. He did not do it again. This was his grass, too, and not to be desecrated. No one said anything, for it was not necessary.

T. J. had reserved a small section for watermelons, and he was still trying to find some seed for it. The wholesale house didn't have any watermelon seeds, and we didn't know where we could lay our hands on them. T. J. shaped the earth into mounds, ready to receive them, three mounds lying in a straight line along the edge of the grass plot.

We had just about decided that we'd have to buy the seeds if we were to get them. It was a violation of our principles, but we were anxious to get the watermelons started. Somewhere or other, T. J. got his hands on a seed catalog and brought it one evening to our roof garden.

"We can order them now," he said, showing us the catalog. "Look!"

We all crowded around, looking at the fat, green watermelons pictured in full color on the pages. Some of them were split open, showing the red, tempting meat, making our mouths water.

"Now we got to scrape up some seed money," T. J. said, looking at us. "I got a quarter. How much you-all got?"

We made up a couple of dollars among us and T. J. nodded his head. "That'll be more than enough. Now we got to decide what kind to get. I think them Kleckley Sweets. What do you-all think?"

He was going into esoteric matters beyond our reach. We hadn't even known there were different kinds of melons. So we just nodded our heads and agreed that yes, we thought the Kleckley Sweets too. "I'll order them tonight," T. J. said. "We ought to have them in a few days."

"What are you boys doing up here?" an adult voice said behind us. It startled us, for no one had ever come up here before in all the time we had been using the roof of the factory. We jerked around and saw three men standing near the trap door at the other end of the roof. They weren't policemen or night watchmen, but three men in plump business suits looking at us. They walked toward us.

"What are you boys doing up here?" the one in the middle said again.

We stood still, guilt heavy among us, levied by the tone of voice, and looked at the three strangers.

The men stared at the grass flourishing behind us. "What's this?" the man said. "How did this get up here?"

"Sure is growing good, ain't it?" T. J. said conversationally, "We planted it."

The men kept looking at the grass as if they didn't believe it. It was a thick carpet over the earth now, a patch of deep greenness startling in the sterile industrial surroundings.

"Yes, sir," T. J. said proudly. "We toted that earth up here and planted that grass." He fluttered the seed catalog. "And we're just fixing to plant us some watermelon,"

The man looked at him then, is eyes strange and faraway. "What do you mean, putting this on the roof of my building?" he said. "Do you want to go to jail?"

T. J. looked shaken. The rest of us were silent, frightened by the authority of his voice. We had grown up aware of adult authority, of policemen and night watchmen and teachers, and this man sounded like all the others. But it was a new thing to T. J.

"Well, you wasn't using the roof," T. J. said. He paused a moment and added shrewdly, "So we just thought to pretty it up a little bit."

"And sag it so I'd have to rebuild it" the man said sharply. He started turning away, saying to another man beside him, "See that all that junk is shoveled off by tomorrow."

"Yes, sir," the man said.

T. J. started forward. "You can't do that," he said. "We toted it up here, and it's our earth. We planted it and raised it and toted it up here."

The man stared at him coldly. "But it's my building," he said. "It's to be shoveled off tomorrow."

"It's our earth," T. J. said desperately. "You ain't got no right!"

The men walked on without listening and descended clumsily through the trapdoor. T. J. stood looking after them, his body tense with anger, until they had disappeared. They wouldn't even argue with him, wouldn't let him defend his earth-rights.

He turned to us. "We won't let 'em do it," he said fiercely. "We'll stay up here all day tomorrow and the day after that, and we won't let 'em do it."

We just looked at him. We knew there was no stopping it.

He saw it in our faces, and his face wavered for a moment before he gripped it into determination. "They ain't got no right," he said. "It's our earth. It's our land. Can't nobody touch a man's own land."

We kept looking at him, listening to the words but knowing that it was no use. The adult world had descended on us even in our richest dream, and we knew there was no calculating the adult world, no fighting it, no winning against it.

We started moving slowly toward the parapet and the fire escape, avoiding a last look at the green beauty of the earth that T. J. had planted for us, had planted deeply in our minds as well as in our experience. We filed slowly over the edge and down the steps to the plank, T. J. coming last, and all of us could feel the weight of his grief behind us.

"Wait a minute," he said suddenly, his voice harsh with the effort of calling.

We stopped and turned, held by the tone of his voice, and looked up at him standing above us on the fire escape.

"We can't stop them?" he said, looking down at us, his face strange in the dusky light. "There ain't no way to stop'em?"

"No," Blackie said with finality. "They own the building."

We stood still for a moment, looking up at T. J., caught into inaction by the decision working in his face. He stared back at us, and his face was pale and mean in the poor light, with a bald nakedness in his skin like cripples have sometimes.

"They ain't gonna touch my earth," he said fiercely. "They ain't gonna lay a hand on it! Come on."

He turned around and started up the fire escape agin, almost running against the effort of climbing. We followed more slowly, not knowing what he intended. By the time we reached him, he had seized a board and and thrust it into the soil, scooping it up and flinging it over the parapet into the areaway below. He straightened and looked at us.

"They can't touch it," he said. "I won't let 'em lay a dirty hand on it!"

We saw it then. He stooped to his labor again and we followed, the gusts of his anger moving in frenzied labor among us as we scattered along the edge of earth, scooping it and throwing it over the parapet, destroying with anger the growth we had nurtured with such tender care. The soil carried so laboriously upward to the light and the sun cascaded swiftly into the dark areaway, the green blades of grass crumpled and twisted in the falling.

It took less time than you would think; the task of destruction is infinitely easier than that of creation. We stopped at the end, leaving only a scattering of loose soil, and when it was finally over, a stillness stood among the group and over the factory building. We looked down at the bare sterility of black tar, felt the harsh texture of it under the soles of our shoes, and the anger had gone out of us, leaving only a sore aching in our minds like overstretched muscles.

T. J. stood for a moment his breathing slowing from anger and effort, caught into the same contemplation of destruction as all of us. He stooped slowly, finally, and picked up a lonely blade of grass left trampled under our feet and put it between his teeth, tasting it sucking the greenness out of it into his mouth. Then he started walking toward the fire escape, moving before any of us were ready to move, and disappeared over the edge.

We followed him, but he was already halfway down to the ground, going on past the board where we crossed over, climbing down into the areaway. We saw the last section swing down with his weight, and then he stood on the concrete below us, looking at the small pile of anonymous earth scattered by our throwing. Then he walked across the place where we could see him and disappeared toward the street without glancing back, without looking up to see us watching him.

They did not find him for two weeks.

Then the Nashville police caught him just outside the Nashville freight yards. He was walking along the railroad track, still heading south, still heading home.

As for us, who had no remembered home to call us, none of us ever again climbed the escapeway to the roof.

Check Your Reading

1. Where do the boys plan to get watermelon seeds?

2. How do the boys get to the roof without going through the building?

3. What had T. J. grown on his two acres in the South?

4. What sense tells T. J. that spring has come?

5. Where do the police find T. J. after he disappears?

Further Exploration

1. Contrast T. J.'s idea of a garden with the ideas of the other boys. Why would he choose to plant food? Do the other boys understand his need to grow things?

2. How do the boys react to the landlord? How might the landlord have confronted the boys without defeating their sense of accomplishment?

3. What pleasure would a boy like T. J. enjoy in open fields? Why does the park not fill those needs? What do urban residents miss by not having open land they can enjoy?

4. Why does T. J. depart from the roof and his friends without looking back? How did T. J. change the boys' lives?

5. To create a garden on a tar roof seems an almost impossible task, but the boys show confidence in T. J.'s leadership. What qualities of a leader does T. J. possess? Explain why you would or would not have joined in the project.

Paul Laurence Dunbar (1872–1906)

Acutely aware of the disadvantages faced by black Americans, Paul Laurence Dunbar wrote:

I know why the caged bird sings, ah me,
When his wing is bruised and his bosom sore, —
When he beats his bars and he would be free;
It is not a carol of joy or glee,
But a prayer that he sends from his heart's deep core. . . .

The son of slaves who ran away from unjust servitude by way of the Underground Railroad, Dunbar made an attempt to educate himself but could not afford college.

While working in Dayton, Ohio, as an elevator operator, he produced his first book of verse, *Oak and Ivy* (1893), followed by *Majors and Minors* (1895). The sponsorship of William Dean Howells, a powerful voice in American literature, resulted in a third books, *Lyrics of Lowly Life* (1896), and national recognition as a leading black writer. His unfortunate battle with tuberculosis ended his life at the age of thirty-four.

Dunbar's four novels, including *The Sport of the Gods* (1902), and three short story collections, *Folks from Dixie* (1898), *The Strength of Gideon* (1900), and *The Heart of Happy Hollow* (1904), contain some of the America's first encounters with the black's point of view. In "The Finish of Patsy Barnes," Dunbar focuses on the struggles of a poor young man who must find a way to distinguish himself and earn enough money to assist his ailing mother.

The Finish of Patsy Barnes

Paul Laurence Dunbar

His name was Patsy Barnes, and he was a denizen of Little Africa. In fact, he lived on Douglass Street. By all the laws governing the relations between people and their names, he should have been Irish—but he was not. He was colored, and very much so. That was the reason he lived on Douglass Street. The Negro has very strong within him the instinct of colonization and it was in accordance with this that Patsy's mother had found her way to Little Africa when she had come North from Kentucky.

Patsy was incorrigible. Even into the confines of Little Africa had penetrated the truant officer and the terrible penalty of the compulsory education law. Time and time again had poor Eliza Barnes been brought up on account of the shortcomings of that son of hers. She was a hardworking, honest woman, and day by day bent over her tub, scrubbing away to keep Patsy in shoes and jackets that would wear out so much faster than they could be bought. But she never murmured, for she loved the boy with a deep affection, though his misdeeds were a sore thorn in her side.

She wanted him to go to school. She wanted him to learn. She had the notion that he might become something better, something higher than she had been. But for him school had no charms; his school was the cool stalls in the big livery stable near at hand; the arena of his pursuits its sawdust floor; the height of his ambition, to be a horseman. Either here or in the racing stables at the Fair-grounds he spent his truant hours. It was a school that taught much, and Patsy was as apt a pupil as he was a constant attendant. He learned strange things about horses, and fine, sonorous oaths that sounded eerie on his young lips, for he had only turned into his fourteenth year.

A man goes where he is appreciated; then could this slim black boy be blamed for doing the same thing? He was a great favorite with the horsemen, and picked up many a dime or nickel for dancing or singing, or even a quarter for warming up a horse for its owner. He was not to be blamed for this, for, first of all, he was born in Kentucky, and had spent the very days of his infancy about the paddocks near Lexington, where his father had sacrificed his life on account of his love for horses. The little fellow had shed no tears when he looked at his father's bleeding body, bruised and broken by the fiery young two-year-old he was trying to subdue. Patsy did not sob or whimper, though his heart ached, for over all the feeling of his grief was a mad, burning desire to ride that horse.

His tears were shed, however, when, actuated by the idea that times would be easier up North, they moved to Dalesford. Then, when he learned that he must leave his old friends, the horses and their masters, whom he had known, he wept. The comparatively meagre appointments of the Fair-grounds at Dalesford proved a poor compensation for all these. For the first few weeks Patsy had dreams of running away—back to Kentucky and the horses and stables. Then after a while he settled himself with heroic resolution to make the best of what he had, and with a mighty effort took up the burden of life away from his beloved home.

Eliza Barnes, older and more experienced though she was, took up her burden with a less cheerful philosophy than her son. She worked hard, and made a scanty livelihood it is true, but she did not make the best of what she had. Her complainings were loud in the land, and her wailings for her old home smote the ears of any who would listen to her.

They had been living in Dalesford for a year nearly, when hard work and exposure brought the woman down to bed with pneumonia. They were very poor—too poor even to call in a doctor, so there was nothing to do but to call in the city physician. Now this medical man had too frequent calls into Little Africa, and he did not like to go there. So he was very gruff when any of its denizens called him, and it was even said that he was careless of his patients.

Patsy's heart bled as he heard the doctor talking to his mother:

"Now, there can't be any foolishness about this," he said "You've got to stay in bed and not get yourself damp."

"How long you thing I got to lay hyeah, doctah?" she asked.

"I'm a doctor, not a fortune-teller," was the reply. "You'll lie there as long as the disease holds you."

"But I can't lay hyeah long, doctah, case I ain't got nuffin' to go on."

"Well, take your choice: the bed or the boneyard."

Eliza began to cry.

"You needn't sniffle," said the doctor; "I don't see what you people want to come up here for anyhow. Why don't you stay down South where you belong? You come up here and you're just a burden and a trouble to the city. The South deals with all of you better, both in poverty and crime." He knew that these people did not understand him, but he wanted an outlet for the heat within him.

There was another angry being in the room, and that was Patsy. His eyes were full of tears that scorched him and would not fall. The memory of many beautiful and appropriate oaths came to him; but he dared not let his mother hear him swear. Oh! to have a stone—to be across the street from that man!

When the physician walked out, Patsy went to the bed, took his mother's hand, and bent over shamefacedly to kiss her. He did not know that with that act the Recording Angel blotted out many a curious damn of his.

The little mark of affection comforted Eliza unspeakably. The mother-feeling overwhelmed her in one burst of tears. Then she dried her eyes and smiled at him

"Honey," she said; "mammy ain' gwine lay hyeah long. She be all right putty soon."

"Nevah you min'," said Patsy with a choke in his voice. "I can do somep'n', an' we'll have anothah doctah."

"La, listen at de chile; what kin you do?"

"I'm goin' down to McCarthy's stable and see if I kin git some horses to exercise."

A sad look came into Eliza's eyes as she said: "You'd bettah not go, Patsy; dem hosses'll kill you yit, des lak dey did yo' pappy."

But the boy, used to doing pretty much as be pleased, was obdurate, and even while she was talking, put on his ragged jacket and left the room.

Patsy was not wise enough to be diplomatic. He went right to the point with McCarthy, the liveryman.

The big red-faced fellow slapped him until he spun round and round. Then he said, "Ye little devil, ye, I've a mind to knock the whole head off o' ye. Ye want harses to exercise, do ye? Well git on that 'un, an' see what ye kin do with him."

The boy's honest desire to be helpful had tickled the big generous Irishman's peculiar sense of humor, and from now on, instead of giving

Patsy a horse to ride now and then as he had formerly done, he put into his charge all the animals that needed exercise.

It was with a king's pride that Patsy marched home with his first considerable earnings.

They were small yet, and would go for food rather than a doctor, but Eliza was inordinately proud, and it was this pride that gave her strength and the desire of life to carry her through the days approaching the crisis of her disease.

As Patsy saw his mother growing worse, saw her gasping for breath, heard the rattling as she drew in the little air that kept going her clogged lungs, felt the heat of her burning hands, and saw the pitiful appeal in her poor eyes, he became convinced that the city doctor was not helping her. She must have another. But the money?

That afternoon, after his work with McCarthy, found him at the Fair-grounds. The spring races were on, and he thought he might get a job warming up the horse of some independent jockey. He hung around the stables, listening to the talk of men he knew and some he had never seen before. Among the latter was a tall, lanky man, holding forth to a group of men.

"No, suh," he was saying to them generally, "I'm goin' to withdraw my hoss, because thaih ain't nobody to ride him as he ought to be rode. I haven't brought a jockey along with me, so I've got to depend on pick-ups. Now, the talent's set again my hoss, Black Boy, because he's been losin' regular, but that hoss had lost for the want of ridin', that's all."

The crowd looked in at the slim-legged, raw-boned horse, and walked away laughing.

"The fools!" muttered the stranger. "If I could ride myself I'd show 'em!"

Patsy was gazing into the stall at the horse.

"What are you doing thaih?" called the owner to him.

"Look hyeah, mistah," said Patsy, "ain't that a bluegrass hoss?"

"Of co'se it is, an' one o' the fastest that evah grazed."

"I'll ride that hoss, mistah."

"What do you know 'bout ridin'?"

"I used to gin'ally be' roun' Mistah Boone's Paddock in Lexington, an'—"

"Aroun' Boone's paddock—what! Look here, little nigger, if you can ride that hoss to a winnin' I'll give you more money than you ever seen before."

"I'll ride him."

Patsy's heart was beating very wildly beneath his jacket. That horse. He knew that glossy coat. He knew that rawboned frame and those flashing nostrils. That black horse there owed something to the orphan he had made.

The horse was to ride in the race before the last. Somehow out of odds and ends, his owner scraped together a suit and colors for Patsy. The colors were maroon and green, a curious combination. But then it was a curious horse, a curious rider, and a more curious combination that brought the two together.

Long before the time for the race Patsy went into the stall to become better acquainted with his horse. The animal turned its wild eyes upon him and neighed. He patted the long, slender head, and grinned as the horse stepped aside as gently as a lady.

"He sholy is full o' ginger," he said to the owner, whose name he had found to be Brackett.

"He'll show 'em a thing or two," laughed Brackett.

"His dam was a fast one," said Patsy, unconsciously.

Brackett whirled on him in a flash. "What do you know about his dam?" he asked.

The boy would have retracted, but it was too late. Stammeringly he told the story of his father's death and the horse's connection therewith.

"Well," said Brackett, "if you don't turn out a hoodoo, you're a winner, sure. But I'll be blessed if this don't sound like a story! But I've heard that story before. The man I got Black Boy from, no matter how I got him, you're too young to understand the ins and outs of poker, told it to me."

When the bell sounded and Patsy went out to warm up, he felt as if he were riding on air. Some of the jockeys laughed at his get-up, but there was something in him—or under him, maybe—that made him scorn their derision. He saw a sea of faces about him, then saw no more. Only a shining white track loomed ahead of him, and a restless steed was cantering with him around the curve. Then the bell called him back to the stand.

They did not get away at first, and back they trooped. A second trial was a failure. But at the third they were off in a line as straight as a chalk-mark. There were Essex and Firefly, Queen Bess and Mosquito, galloping away side by side, and Black Boy a neck ahead. Patsy knew the family reputation of his horse for endurance as well as fire and began riding the race from the first. Black Boy came of blood that would not be passed, and to this his rider trusted. At the eighth the line was hardly broken, but as the quarter was reached Black Boy had forged a length ahead and Mosquito was at his flank. Then, like a flash, Essex shot out ahead under whip and spur, his jockey standing straight in the stirrups.

The crowd in the stand screamed; but Patsy smiled as he lay low over his horse's neck. He saw that Essex had made her best spurt. His only fear was for Mosquito, who hugged and hugged his flank. They were nearing the three-quarter post, and he was tightening his grip on the black. Essex fell back; his spurt was over. The whip fell unheeded on his sides. The spurs dug him in vain.

Black Boy's breath touches the leader's ear. They are neck and neck—nose to nose. The black stallion passes him.

Another cheer from the stand, and again Patsy smiles as they turn into the stretch. Mosquito has gained a head. The colored boy flashes one glance at the horse and rider who are so surely gaining upon him, and his lips close in a grim line. They are half-way down the stretch, and Mosquito's head is at the stallion's neck.

For a single moment Patsy thinks of the sick woman at home and what that race will mean to her, and then his knees close against the horse's sides with a firmer dig. The spurs shoot deeper into the steaming flanks. Black Boy shall win; he must win. The horse that has taken away his father shall give him back his mother. The stallion leaps away like a flash, and goes under the wire—a length ahead.

Then the band thundered, and Patsy was off his horse, very warm and very happy, following his mount to the stable. There, a little later, Brackett found him. He rushed to him, and flung his arms around him.

"You little devil," he cried, "You rode like you were kin to that hoss! We've won! We've won!" And he began sticking banknotes at the boy. At first Patsy's eyes bulged, and then he seized the money and got into his clothes.

"Goin' out to spend it?" asked Brackett.

"I'm goin' for a doctah fu' my mother," said Patsy, "she's sick."

"Don't let me lose sight of you."

"Oh, I'll see you again. So long," said the boy.

An hour later he walked into his mother's room with a very big doctor, the greatest the druggist could direct him to. The doctor left his medicines and his orders, but, when Patsy told his story, it was Eliza's pride that started her on the road to recovery. Patsy did not tell his horse's name.

Check Your Reading

1. How does McCarthy reward Patsy's hard work?

2. Where did Brackett get Black Boy?

3. What name does Patsy mention that gains him influence with Brackett?

4. What curious combination of colors does Patsy wear?

5. What fact about his winnings does Patsy keep from Eliza?

Further Exploration

1. Comment on the tone of the doctor's advice when he says, "the bed or the boneyard." Why does he object to house calls in Little Africa?

2. Dunbar states, "A man goes where he is appreciated." Where is Patsy appreciated? How does he earn a reputation for understanding horses? Why does he prefer stables to schools?

3. Why is life in Dalesford difficult for Patsy? Why are most people upset by a move away from the area they know best? What would you miss most if you had to move to another place?

4. What is the significance of the title of the story?

5. Why does a feeling of pride assist Eliza in regaining her health? Is it truly possible for a young person to save a parent? Explain why feelings of worth and dignity are important to the general well-being of all people.

Kurt Vonnegut (1922–)

According to Kurt Vonnegut, humanity's insistence on inflicting catastrophes upon itself can be countered by only one human trait—the ability to laugh at its own folly. The humor found in Vonnegut's major works, *Cat's Cradle* (1962), *Welcome to the Monkey House* (1968) and *Breakfast of Champions* (1973), is often unsettling to readers who are lured by his playful tone only to find a gloomy view of mankind. Vonnegut seems to have devoted his work to revealing the potential harm of man-made systems.

"D.P." is an example of how Vonnegut uses humor to make social comment. He expresses his disillusionment with war, which resulted in displaced persons, children who "might have wandered off the edges of the earth, searching for parents who had long ago stopped searching for them."

D.P.
Kurt Vonnegut

Eighty-one small sparks of human life were kept in an orphanage set up by Catholic nuns in what had been the gamekeeper's house on a large estate overlooking the Rhine. This was in the German village of Karlswald, in the American Zone of Occupation. Had the children not been kept there, not been given the warmth and food and clothes that could be begged for them, they might have wandered off the edges of the earth, searching for parents who had long ago stopped searching for them.

Every mild afternoon the nuns marched the children, two by two, through the woods, into the village and back, for their ration of fresh air. The village carpenter, an old man who was given to thoughtful rests between strokes of his tools, always came out of his shop to watch the bobbing, chattering, cheerful, ragged parade, and to speculate, with idlers his shop attracted, as to the nationalities of the passing children's parents.

"See the little French girl," he said one afternoon. "Look at the flash of those eyes!"

"And look at that little Pole swing his arms. They love to march, the Poles," said a young mechanic.

"Pole? Where do you see any Pole?" said the carpenter.

"There—the thin, sober-looking one in front," the other replied.

"Aaaaah. He's too tall for a Pole," said the carpenter. "And what Pole has flaxen hair like that? He's a German."

The mechanic shrugged. "They're all German now, so what difference does it make?" he said. "Who can prove what their parents were? If you had fought in Poland, you would know he was a very common type."

"Look—look who's coming now," said the carpenter, grinning. "Full of arguments as you are, you won't argue with me about *him*. There we

have an American!" He called out to the child. "Joe—when you going
to win the championship back?"

"Joe!" called the mechanic. "How is the Brown Bomber today?"

At the very end of the parade, a lone, blue-eyed colored boy, six
years old, turned and smiled with sweet uneasiness at those who called
out to him every day. He nodded politely, murmuring a greeting in
German, the only language he knew.

His name, chosen arbitrarily by the nuns, was Karl Heinz. But the
carpenter had given him a name that stuck, the name of the only
colored man who had ever made an impression on the villagers' minds,
the former heavyweight champion of the world, Joe Louis.

"Joe!" called the carpenter. "Cheer up! Let's see those white teeth
sparkle, Joe."

Joe obliged shyly.

The carpenter clapped the mechanic on the back. "And if *he* isn't a
German too! Maybe it's the only way we can get another heavyweight
champion."

Joe turned a corner, shooed out of the carpenter's sight by a nun bringing
up the rear. She and Joe spent a great deal of time together, since Joe,
no matter where he was placed in the parade, always drifted to the end.

"Joe," she said, "you are such a dreamer. Are all your people such dreamers?"

"I'm sorry, sister," said Joe. "I was thinking."

"Dreaming."

"Sister, am I the son of an American soldier?"

"Who told you that?"

"Peter. Peter said my mother was a German, and my father was an
American soldier who went away. He said she left me with you, and then
went away too." There was no sadness in his voice—only puzzlement.

Peter was the oldest boy in the orphanage, an embittered old man
of fourteen, a German boy who could remember his parents and brothers
and sisters and home, and the war, and all sorts of food that Joe found
impossible to imagine. Peter seemed superhuman to Joe, like a man
who had been to heaven and hell and back many times, and knew
exactly why they were where they were, how they had come there, and
where they might have been.

"You mustn't worry about it, Joe," said the nun. "No one knows who
your mother and father were. But they must have been very good people
because you are so good."

"What is an American?" said Joe.

"It's a person from another country."

"Near here?"

"There are some near here, but their homes are far, far away—across a great deal of water."

"Like the river."

"More water than that, Joe. More water than you have ever seen. You can't even see the other side. You could get on a boat and go for days and days and still not get to the other side. I'll show you a map sometime. But don't pay any attention to Peter, Joe. He makes things up. He doesn't really know anything about you. Now, catch up."

Joe hurried, and overtook the end of the line, where he marched purposefully and alertly for a few minutes. But then he began to dawdle again, chasing ghostlike words in his small mind: . . . soldier . . . German . . . American . . . your people . . . champion . . . Brown Bomber . . . more water than you've ever seen.

"Sister," said Joe, "are Americans like me? Are they brown?"

"Some are, some aren't, Joe."

"Are there many people like me?"

"Yes. Many, many people."

"Why haven't I seen them?"

"None of them have come to the village. They have places of their own."

"I want to go there."

"Aren't you happy here, Joe?"

"Yes. But Peter says I don't belong here, I'm not a German and never can be."

"Peter! Pay no attention to him."

"Why do people smile when they see me, and try to make me sing and talk, and then laugh when I do?"

"Joe, Joe! Look quickly," said the nun. "See—up there, in the tree. See the little sparrow with the broken leg. Oh poor, brave little thing—he still gets around quite well. See him, Joe? Hop, hop, hippity-hop."

One hot summer day, as the parade passed the carpenter's shop, the carpenter came out to call something new to Joe, something that thrilled and terrified him.

"Joe! Hey, Joe! Your father is in town. Have you seen him yet?"

"No, sir—no, I haven't," said Joe. "Where is he?"

"He's teasing," said the nun sharply.

"You see if I'm teasing, Joe," said the carpenter. "Just keep your eyes open when you go past the school. You have to look sharp, up the slope and into the woods. You'll see, Joe."

"I wonder where our little friend the sparrow is today," said the nun brightly. "Goodness, I hope his leg is getting better, don't you, Joe?"

"Yes, yes I do, sister."

She chattered on about the sparrow and the clouds and the flowers as they approached the school, and Joe gave up answering her.

The woods above the school seemed still and empty.

But then Joe saw a massive brown man, naked to the waist and wearing a pistol, step from the trees. The man drank from a canteen, wiped his lips with the back of his hand, grinned down on the world with handsome disdain, and disappeared again into the twilight of the woods.

"Sister!" gasped Joe. "My father—I just saw my father!"

"No, Joe—no you didn't."

"He's up there in the woods. I saw him. I want to go up there, sister."

"He isn't your father, Joe. He doesn't know you. He doesn't want to see you."

"He's one of my people, sister!"

"You can't go up there, Joe, and you can't stay here." She took him by the arm to make him move. "Joe—you're being a bad boy, Joe."

Joe obeyed numbly. He didn't speak again for the remainder of the walk, which brought them home by another route, far from the school. No one else had seen his wonderful father, or believed that Joe had. Not until prayers that night did he burst into tears.

At ten o'clock, the young nun found his cot empty.

Under a great spread net that was laced with rags, an artillery piece squatted in the woods, black and oily, its muzzle thrust at the night sky. Trucks and the rest of the battery were hidden higher on the slope.

Joe watched and listened tremblingly through a thin screen of shrubs as the soldiers, indistinct in the darkness, dug in around their gun. The words he overheard made no sense to him.

"Sergeant, why we gotta dig in, when we're movin' out in the mornin', and it's just maneuvers anyhow? Seems like we could kind of conserve our strength, and just scratch around a little to show where we'd of dug if there was any sense to it."

"For all you know, boy, there may *be* sense to it before mornin'," said the sergeant. "You got ten minutes to get to China and bring me back a pigtail. Hear?"

The sergeant stepped into a patch of moonlight, his hands on his hips, his big shoulders back, the image of an emperor. Joe saw that it was the same man he'd marveled at in the afternoon. The sergeant listened with satisfaction to the sounds of digging, and then, to Joe's alarm, strode toward Joe's hiding place.

Joe didn't move a muscle until the big boot struck his side. "*Ach!*"

"Who's that?" The sergeant snatched Joe from the ground, and set him on his feet hard. "My golly, boy, what you doin' here? Scoot! Go on home! This ain't no place for kids to be playin'." He shined a flashlight in Joe's face. "Doggone," he muttered. "Where you come from?" He held Joe at arm's length, and shook him gently, like a rag doll. "Boy, how you get here—swim?"

Joe stammered in German that he was looking for his father.

"Come on—how you get here? What you doin'? Where's your mammy?"

"What you got there, sergeant?" said a voice in the dark.

"Don't rightly know what to call it," said the sergeant. "Talks like a Kraut and dresses like a Kraut, but just look at it a minute."

Soon a dozen men stood in a circle around Joe, talking loudly, then softly, to him, as though they thought getting through to him were a question of tone.

Every time Joe tried to explain his mission, they laughed in amazement.

"How he learn German? Tell me that."

"Where your daddy, boy?"

"Where your mammy, boy?"

"Sprecken zee Dutch, boy? Looky there. See him nod. He talks it, all right."

"Oh, you're fluent, man, mighty fluent. Ask him some more."

"Go get the lieutenant," said the sergeant. "He can talk to this boy, and understand what he's tryin' to say. Look at him shake. Scared to death. Come here, boy; don't be afraid, now." He enclosed Joe in his great arms. "Just take it easy, now—everything's gonna be all-l-l-l right. See what I got? By golly, I don't believe the boy's ever seen chocolate before. Go on—taste it. Won't hurt you."

Joe, safe in a fort of bone and sinew, ringed by luminous eyes, bit into the chocolate bar. The pink lining of his mouth, and then his whole soul, was flooded with warm, rich pleasure, and he beamed.

"He smiled!"

"Look at him light up!"

"Doggone if he didn't stumble right into heaven! I mean!"

"Talk about displaced persons," said the sergeant, hugging Joe, "this here's the most displaced little old person I *ever* saw. Upside down and inside out and ever' which way."

"Here, boy—here's some more chocolate."

"Don't give him no more," said the sergeant reproachfully. "You want to make him sick?"

"Naw, sarge, naw—don't wanna make him sick. No, sir."

"What's going on here?" The lieutenant, a small, elegant Negro, the beam of his flashlight dancing before him, approached the group.

"Got a little boy here, lieutenant," said the sergeant. "Just wandered into the battery. Must of crawled past the guards."

"Well, send him on home, sergeant."

"Yessir. I planned to." He cleared his throat. "But this ain't no ordinary little boy, lieutenant." He opened his arms so that the light fell on Joe's face.

The lieutenant laughed incredulously, and knelt before Joe. "How'd you get here?"

"All he talks is German, lieutenant," said the sergeant.

"Where's your home?" said the lieutenant in German.

"Over more water than you've ever seen," said Joe.

"Where do you come from?"

"God made me," said Joe.

"This boy is going to be a lawyer when he grows up," said the lieutenant in English. "Now, listen to me," he said to Joe, "what's your name, and where are your people?"

"Joe Louis," said Joe, "and you are my people. I ran away from the orphanage, because I belong with you."

The lieutenant stood, shaking his head, and translated what Joe had said.

The woods echoed with glee.

"Joe Louis *thought* he was awful big and powerful-lookin'!"

"Jus' keep away from that left—*tha's* all!"

"If he's Joe, he's sure found his people. He's got us there!"

"Shut up!" commanded the sergeant suddenly. "All of you just shut up. This ain't no joke! Ain't nothing funny in it! Boy's all alone in the world. Ain't no joke."

A small voice finally broke the solemn silence that followed. "Naw—ain't no joke at all."

"We better take the jeep and run him back into town, sergeant," said the lieutenant. "Corporal Jackson, you're in charge."

"You tell 'em Joe was a *good* boy," said Jackson.

"Now, Joe," said the lieutenant in German, softly, "you come with the sergeant and me. We'll take you home."

Joe dug his fingers into the sergeant's forearms. "Papa! No—papa! I want to stay with you."

"Look, sonny, I ain't your papa," said the sergeant helplessly. "I *ain't* your papa."

"Papa!"

"Man, he's glued to you, ain't he, sergeant?" said a soldier. "Looks like you ain't never goin' to pry him loose. You got yourself a boy there, sarge, and he's got hisself a papa."

The sergeant walked over to the jeep with Joe in his arms. "Come on, now," he said, "you leggo, little Joe, so's I can drive. I can't drive with you hangin' on, Joe. You sit in the lieutenant's lap right next to me."

The group formed again around the jeep, gravely now, watching the sergeant try to coax Joe into letting go.

"I don't want to get tough, Joe. Come on—take it easy, Joe. Let go, now, Joe, so's I can drive. See, I can't steer or nothin' with you hanging on right there."

"Papa!"

"Come on, over to my lap, Joe," said the lieutenant in German.

"Papa!"

"Joe, Joe, looky," said a soldier. "Chocolate! Want some more chocolate, Joe? See? Whole bar, Joe, all yours. Jus' leggo the sergeant and move over into the lieutenant's lap."

Joe tightened his grip on the sergeant.

"Don't put the chocolate back in your pocket, man! Give it to Joe anyways," said a soldier angrily. "Somebody get a case of D bars off the truck, and throw'em in the back for Joe. Give that boy chocolate enough for the nex' twenny years."

"Look, Joe," said another soldier, "ever see a wristwatch? Look at the wristwatch, Joe. See it glow, boy? Move over in the lieutenant's lap, and I'll let you listen to it tick. Tick, tick, tick, Joe. Come on, want to listen?"

Joe didn't move.

The soldier handed the watch to him. "Here, Joe, you take it anyway. It's yours." He walked away quickly.

"Man," somebody called after him, "you crazy? You paid fifty dollars for that watch. What business a little boy got with any fifty-dollar watch?"

"No—I ain't crazy. Are you?"

"Naw, I ain't crazy. Neither one of us crazy, I guess. Joe—want a knife? You got to promise to be careful with it now. Always cut *away* from yourself. Hear? Lieutenant, when you get back, you tell him always cut *away* from hisself."

"I don't want to go back. I want to stay with *papa*," said Joe tearfully.

"Soldiers can't take little boys with them, Joe," said the lieutenant in German. "And we're leaving early in the morning." "Will you come back for me?" said Joe.

"We'll come back if we can, Joe. Soldiers never know where they'll be from one day to the next. We'll come back for a visit, if we can."

"Can we give old Joe this case of D bars, lieutenant?" said a soldier carrying a cardboard carton of chocolate bars.

"Don't ask me," said the lieutenant. "I don't know anything about it. I never saw anything of any case of D bars, never heard anything about it."

"Yessir." The soldier laid his burden down on the jeep's back seat.

"He ain't gonna let go," said the sergeant miserably. "You drive, lieutenant, and me and Joe'll sit over there."

The lieutenant and the sergeant changed places, and the jeep began to move.

"By, Joe!"

"You be a good boy, Joe!"

"Don't you eat all that chocolate at once, you hear?"

"Don't cry, Joe. Give us a smile."

"Wider, boy—that's the stuff!"

"Joe, Joe, wake up, Joe." The voice was that of Peter, the oldest boy in the orphanage, and it echoed damply from the stone walls.

Joe sat up, startled. All around his cot were the other orphans, jostling one another for a glimpse of Joe and the treasures by his pillow.

"Where did you get the hat, Joe—and the watch, and knife?" said Peter. "And what's in the box under your bed?"

Joe felt his head, and found a soldier's wool knit cap there. "Papa," he mumbled sleepily.

"Papa!" mocked Peter, laughing.

"Yes," said Joe. "Last night I went to see my papa, Peter."

"Could he speak German, Joe?" said a little girl wonderingly.

"No, but his friend could," said Joe.

"He didn't see his father," said Peter. "Your father is far, far away, and will never come back. He probably doesn't even know you're alive."

"What did he look like?" said the girl.

Joe glanced thoughtfully around the room. "Papa is as high as this ceiling," he said at last. "He is wider than that door." Triumphantly, he took a bar of chocolate from under his pillow. "And as brown as that!" He held out the bar to the others. "Go on, have some. There is plenty more."

"He doesn't look anything like that," said Peter. "You aren't telling the truth, Joe."

"My papa has a pistol as big as this bed, almost, Peter," said Joe happily, "and a cannon as big as this house. And there were hundreds and hundreds like him."

"Somebody played a joke on you, Joe," said Peter. "He wasn't your father. How do you know he wasn't fooling you?"

"Because he cried when he left me," said Joe simply. "And he promised to take me back home across the water as fast as he could." He smiled airily. "Not like the river, Peter—across more water than you've *ever* seen. He promised, and then I let him go."

Check Your Reading

1. Why is Peter "an embittered old man of fourteen"?

2. Why do the villagers associate Karl with Joe Louis?

3. Why does the boy prefer the sergeant over the lieutenant?

4. What promise does the sergeant make?

5. What do you think "D.P." stands for?

Further Exploration

1. How does the nun try to distract Karl from his worry about his father? Why is she unsuccessful?

2. Why do the children in the story have difficulty understanding where America is? How would you explain the ocean to children who had never seen it? How would you describe the skin color of Americans?

3. How does the lieutenant explain a soldier's unpredictable life?

4. Do you think the sergeant will return to get Karl? If not, describe Karl's reaction.

5. How would a "D.P." adjust in America? What new problems would Karl face in an American home?

Murray Heyert (1913–)

A civil technician for the Air Force during World War II, Murray Heyert has worked in the legal department of a film company and lectured at New York University. His stories and articles capture the flavor of ethnic mixtures characteristic of New York City, his hometown.

"The New Kid" depicts some of the uncertainty of childhood that accompanies growing up, especially when most of the neighborhood is older and streetwise. Marty learns the lesson only too well—that strength over others is an advantage worth having, and that the pain of being the outsider quickly disperses in the sweet joy of power over the next victim.

The New Kid
Murray Heyert

By the time Marty ran up the stairs, past the dentist's office, where it smelled like the time his father was in the hospital, past the fresh paint smell, where the new kid lived, past the garlic smell from the Italians in 2D; and waited for Mommer to open the door; and threw his schoolbooks on top of the old newspapers that were piled on the sewing machine in the hall; and drank his glass of milk ("How many times must I tell you not to gulp! Are you going to stop gulping like that or must I smack your face!"); and set the empty glass in the sink under the faucet; and changed into his brown keds; and put trees into his school shoes ("How many times must I talk to you! God in heaven— when will you learn to take care of your clothes and not make me follow you around like this!"); and ran downstairs again, past the garlic and the paint and the hospital smells; by the time he got into the street and looked breathlessly around him, it was too late. The fellows were all out there, all ready for a game, and just waiting for Eddie Deakes to finish chalking a base against the curb.

Running up the street with all his might, Marty could see that the game would start any minute now. Out in the gutter Paulie Dahler was tossing high ones to Ray-Ray Stickerling, whose father was a bus driver and sometimes gave the fellows transfers so they could ride free. The rest were sitting on the curb, waiting for Eddie to finish making the base and listening to Gelberg, who was a Jew, explain what it meant to be bar-mizvah'd, like he was going to be next month.

They did not look up as Marty galloped up to them all out of breath. Eddie finished making his base and after looking at it critically a moment, with his head on one side, moved down toward the sewer that was home plate and began drawing a scoreboard alongside of it. With his nose running from excitement Marty trotted over to him.

"Just going to play with two bases?" he said, wiping his nose on the sleeve of his lumber jacket, and hoping with all his might that Eddie would think he had been there all the while and was waiting for a game like all the other fellows.

Eddie raised his head and saw that it was Marty. He gave Marty a shove. "Why don't you watch where you're walking?" he said. "Can't you see I'm making a scoreboard!"

He bent over again and with his chalk repaired the lines that Marty had smudged with his sneakers. Marty hopped around alongside him, taking care to keep his feet off the chalked box. "Gimme a game, Eddie?" he said.

"What are you asking me for?" Eddie said without looking up. "It ain't my game."

"Aw, come on, Eddie. I'll get even on you!" Marty said.

"Ask Gelberg. It's his game," Eddie said, straightening himself and shoving his chalk into his pants pocket. He trotted suddenly into the middle of the street and ran sideways a few feet. "Here go!" he hollered. "All the way!"

From his place up near the corner Paulie Dahler heaved the ball high into the air, higher than the telephone wires. Eddie took a step back, then a step forward, then back again, and got under it.

Marty bent his knees like a catcher, pounded his fist into his palm as though he were wearing a mitt, and held out his hands. "Here go, Eddie!" he hollered. "Here go!"

Holding the ball in his hand, and without answering him, Eddie walked toward the curb, where the rest of the fellows were gathered around Gelberg. Marty straightened his knees, put down his hands, and, sniffling his nose, trotted after Eddie.

"All right, I'll choose Gelberg for sides," Eddie said.

Gelberg heaved himself off the curb and put on his punchball glove, which was one of his mother's old kid gloves, with the fingers and thumb cut off short. "Odds, once takes it," he said.

After a couple of preparatory swings of their arms they matched fingers. Gelberg won. He chose Albie Newbauer. Eddie looked around him and look Wally Reinhard. Gelberg took Ray-Ray Stickerling. Eddie took Wally Reinhard's brother Howey.

Marty hopped around on the edge of the group. "Hey, Gelberg," he hollered in a high voice. "Gimme a game, will you?"

"I got Arnie," Gelberg said.

Eddie looked around him again. "All right, I got Paulie Dahler."

They counted their men. "Choose you for up first," Gelberg said. Feeling as though he were going to cry, Marty watched them as they swung their arms, stuck out their fingers. This time Eddie won. Gelberg gathered his men around him and they trotted into the street to take up positions on the field. They hollered, "Here go!" threw the ball from first to second, then out into the field, and back again to Gelberg in the pitcher's box.

Marty ran over to him. "Gimme a game, will you, Gelberg?"

"We're all choosed up," Gelberg said, heaving a high one to Arnie out in center field.

Marty wiped his nose on his sleeve. "Come on, gimme a game. Didn't I let you lose my Spaulding Hi-Bouncer down the sewer once?"

"Want to give the kid a game?" Gelberg called to Eddie, who was seated on the curb, figuring out his batting order with his men.

"Aw, we got the sides all choosed up!" Eddie said.

Marty stuck out his lower lip and wished that he would not have to cry. "You give Howey Reinhard a game!" he said, pointing at Howey sitting on the curb next to Eddie. "He can't play any better than me!"

"Yeah," Howey yelled, swinging back his arm as though he were going to punch Marty in the jaw. "You couldn't hit the side of the house!"

"Yeah, I can play better than you any day!" Marty hollered.

"You can play left outside!" Howey said, looking around to see how the joke went over.

"Yeah, I'll get even on you!" Marty hollered, hoping that maybe they would get worried and give him a game after all.

With a fierce expression on his face, as if to indicate that he was through joking and now meant serious business, Howey sprang up from the curb and sent him staggering with a shove. Marty tried to duck, but Howey smacked him across the side of the head. Flinging his arms up about his ears, Marty scrambled down the street; for no reason at all Paulie Dahler booted him in the pants as he went by.

"I'll get even on you!" Marty yelled when he was out of reach. With a sudden movement of his legs Howey pretended to rush at him. Almost falling over himself in panic, Marty dashed toward the house, but stopped, feeling ashamed, when he saw that Howey had only wanted to make him run.

For a while he stood there on the curb, wary and ready to dive into the house the instant any of the fellows made a move toward him. But presently he saw that the game was beginning, and that none of them was paying any more attention to him. He crept toward them again and, seating himself on the curb a little distance away, watched the game start. For a moment he thought of breaking it up, rushing up to the scoreboard and smudging it with his sneakers before anyone could stop him, and then dashing into the house before they caught him. Or grabbing the ball when it came near him and flinging it down the sewer. But he decided not to; the fellows would catch him in the end, smack him, and make another scoreboard or get another ball, and then he would never get a game.

Every minute feeling more and more like crying, he sat there on the curb, his elbow on his knee, his chin in his palm, and tried to think where he could get another fellow, so that they could give him a game and still have even sides. Then he lifted his chin from his palm and saw that the new kid was sitting out on the stoop in front of the house, chewing something and gazing toward the game; and all at once the feeling that he was going to cry disappeared. He sprang up from the curb.

"Hey, Gelberg!" he hollered. "If I get the new kid for even sides can I get a game?"

Without waiting for an answer he dashed down the street toward the stoop where the new kid was sitting.

"Hey, fellow!" he shouted. "Want a game? Want a game of punchball?"

He could see now that what the new kid was eating was a slice of rye bread covered with applesauce. He could see too that the new kid was smaller than he was, and had a narrow face and a large nose with a few little freckles across the bridge. He was wearing Boy Scout pants and a brown woolen pullover, and on the back of his head was a skullcap made from the crown of a man's felt hat, the edge turned up and cut into sharp points that were ornamented with brass paper clips.

All out of breath, he stopped in front of the new kid. "What do you say?" he hollered. "Want a game?"

The new kid looked at him and took another bite of rye bread. "I don't know," he said, with his mouth full of bread, turning to take another look at the fellows in the street. "I guess I got to go to the store soon."

"You don't have to go to the store right away, do you?" Marty said in a high voice.

The new kid swallowed his bread and continued looking up toward the game. "I got to stay in front of the house in case my mother calls me."

"Maybe she won't call you for a while," Marty said. He could see that the inning was ending, that they would be starting a new inning in a minute, and his legs twitched with impatience.

"I don't know," the new kid said, still looking up at the game. "Anyway, I got my good shoes on."

"Aw, I bet you can't even play punchball!" cried Marty.

The new kid looked at him with his lower lip stuck out. "Yeah, I can so play! Only I got to go to the store!"

Once more he looked undecidedly up toward the game. Marty could see that the inning was over now. He turned pleadingly to the new kid.

"You can hear her if she calls you, can't you? Can't you play just till she calls you? Come on, can't you?"

Putting the last of his rye bread into his mouth, the new kid got up from the stoop. "Well, when she calls me," he said, brushing off the seat of his pants with his hand, "when she calls me I got to quit and go to the store."

As fast as he could run Marty dashed up the street with the new kid trailing after him. "Hey, I got another man for even sides!" he yelled. "Gimme a game now? I got another man!"

The fellows looked at the new kid coming up the street behind Marty.

"You new on the block?" Howey Reinhard asked, eying the Boy Scout pants, as Marty and the new kid came up to them.

"You any good?" Gelberg demanded, bouncing the ball at his feet and looking at the skull cap ornamented with brass paper clips. "Can you hit?"

"Come on!" Marty said. He wished that they would just give him a game and not start asking a lot of questions. "I got another man for even sides, didn't I?"

"Aw, we got the game started already!" Ray-Ray Stickerling hollered.

Marty sniffled his nose, which was beginning to run again, and looked at him as fiercely as he was able. "It ain't your game!" he yelled. "It's Gelberg's game! Ain't it your game, Gelberg?"

Gelberg gave him a shove. "No one said you weren't going to get a game!" With a last bounce of his ball he turned to Eddie, who was looking the new kid over carefully.

"All right, Eddie. I'll take the new kid and you can have Marty." Eddie drew his arm back as though he were going to hit him. "Like fun! Why don't you take Marty, if you're so wise?"

"I won the choose-up!" Gelberg hollered.

"Yeah, that was before! I'm not taking Marty!"

"I won the choose-up, didn't I?"

"Well, you got to choose up again for the new kid!"

Marty watched them as they stood up to each other, each eying the other suspiciously, and swung their arms to choose. Eddie won. "Cheating shows!" he yelled, seizing the new kid by the arm and pulling him into the group on his side.

Trying to look like the ballplayers he had seen the time his father had taken him to the Polo Grounds, Marty ran into the outfield and took the position near the curb that Gelberg had selected for him. He tried not to feel bad because Eddie had taken the new kid, that no one knew anything about, how he could hit, or anything; and that he had had to go to the loser of the choose-up. As soon as he was out in the field he leaned forward, with his hands propped on his knees, and hollered: "All right, all right, these guys can't hit!" Then he straightened up and pounded his fist into his palm as though he were wearing a fielder's glove and shouted: "Serve it to them on a silver platter, Gelberg! These guys are just bunch of fan artists!" He propped his hands on his knees again, like a bigleaguer, but all the while he felt unhappy, not nearly the way he should have felt, now that they had finally given him a game. He hoped that they would hit to him, and he would make one-handed catches over his head, run way out with his back to the ball and spear them blind, or run in with all his might and pick them right off the tops of his shoes.

A little nervous chill ran through his back as he saw Paulie Dahler get up to hit. On Gelberg's second toss Paulie stepped in and sent the ball sailing into the air. A panic seized Marty as he saw it coming at him. He took a step nervously forward, then backward, then forward again, trying as hard as he could to judge the ball. It smacked into his cupped palms, bounced out and dribbled toward the curb. He scrambled after it, hearing them shouting at him, and feeling himself getting more scared every instant. He kicked the ball with his sneaker, got his hand on it, and, straightening himself in a fever of fright, heaved it with all his strength at Ray-Ray on first. The moment the ball left his hand he knew he had done the wrong, thing. Paulie was already on his way to second; and besides, the throw was wild. Ray-Ray leaped into the air, his arms flung up, but it was way over his head, bouncing beyond him on the sidewalk and almost hitting a woman who was jouncing a baby carriage at the door of the apartment house opposite.

With his heart beating the same way it did whenever anyone chased him, Marty watched Paulie gallop across the plate. He sniffled his nose, which was beginning to run again, and felt like crying.

"Holy Moses!" he heard Gelberg yell. "What do you want, a basket?

Can't you hold on to them once in a while?"

"Aw, the sun was in my eyes!" Marty said.

"You wait until you want another game!" Gelberg shouted.

Breathing hard, Ray-Ray got back on first and tossed the ball to Gelberg. "Whose side are you on anyway?" he hollered.

Eddie Deakes put his hands to his mouth like a megaphone. "Attaboy, Marty!" he yelled. "Having you out there is like having another man on our side!"

The other fellows on the curb laughed, and Howey Reinhard made them laugh harder by pretending to catch a fly ball with the sun in his eyes, staggering around the street with his eyes screwed up and his hands cupped like a sissy, so that the wrists touched and the palms were widely separated.

No longer shouting or punching his fist into his palm, Marty took his place out in the field again. He stood there, feeling like crying, and wished that he hadn't dropped that ball, or thrown it over Ray-Ray's head. Then, without knowing why, he looked up to see whether the new kid was laughing at him like all the rest. But the new kid was sitting a little off by himself at one end of the row of fellows on the curb, and with a serious expression on his face gnawed at the skin at the side of his thumbnail. Marty began to wonder if the new kid was any good or not. He saw him sitting there, with the serious look on his face, his ears sticking out, not joking like the other fellows, and from nowhere the thought leaped into Marty's head that maybe the new kid was no good. He looked at the skinny legs, the Boy Scout pants, and the mama's-boy shoes, and all at once he began to hope that Eddie would send the new kid in to hit, so that he could know right away whether he was any good or not.

But Wally Reinhard was up next. He fouled out on one of Gelberg's twirls, and after him Howey popped up to Albie Newbauer and Eddie was out on first. The fellows ran in to watch Eddie chalk up Paulie's run on the scoreboard alongside the sewer. They were still beefing and hollering at Marty for dropping that ball, but he pretended he did not hear them and sat down on the curb to watch the new kid out in the field.

He was over near the curb, playing in closer than Paulie Dahler. Marty could see that he was not hollering "Here go!" or "All the way!" like the others, but merely stood there with that serious expression on his face and watched them throw the ball around. He held one leg bent at the ankle, so that the side of his shoe rested on the pavement, his belly was stuck out, and he chewed the skin at the side of his thumbnail.

Gelberg got up to bat. Standing in the pitcher's box, Eddie turned around and motioned his men to lay out. The new kid looked around him to see what the other fellows did, took a few steps backward, and then, with his belly stuck out again, went on chewing his thumb.

Marty felt his heart begin to beat hard. He watched Gelberg stand up to the plate and contemptuously fling back the first few pitches.

"Come on, gimme one like I like!" Gelberg hollered.

"What's the matter! You afraid to reach for them?" Eddie yelled.

"Just pitch them to me, that's all!" Gelberg said.

Eddie lobbed one in that bounced shoulder high. With a little sideways skip Gelberg lammed into it.

The ball sailed down toward the new kid. Feeling his heart begin to beat harder, Marty saw him take a hurried step backward and at the same moment fling his hands before his face and duck his head. The ball landed beyond him and bounded up on the sidewalk. For an instant the new kid hesitated, then he was galloping after it, clattering across the pavement in his polished shoes.

Swinging his arms in mock haste, Gelberg breezed across the plate. "Get a basket!" he hollered over his shoulder. "Get a basket!"

Marty let his nose run without bothering to sniffle. He jumped up from the curb and curved his hands around his mouth like a megaphone. "He's scared of the ball!" he yelled at the top of his lungs. "He's scared of the ball! That's what he is, scared of the ball!"

The new kid tossed the ball back to Eddie. "I wasn't scared!" he said, moistening his lips with his tongue. "I wasn't scared! I just couldn't see it coming!"

With an expression of despair on his face Eddie shook his head. "Holy Moses! If you can't see the ball why do you try to play punchball?" He bounced the ball hard at his feet and motioned Gelberg to send in his next batter. Arnie got up from the curb and, wiping his hands on his pants, walked toward the plate.

Marty felt his heart pounding in his chest. He hopped up and down with excitement and, seizing Gelberg by the arm, pointed at the new kid.

"You see him duck?" he yelled. "He's scared of the ball, that's what he is!" He hardly knew where to turn first. He rushed up to Ray-Ray, who was sitting on the curb making marks on the asphalt with the heel of his sneaker. "The new kid's scared to stop a ball! You see him duck!"

The new kid looked toward Marty and wet his lips with his tongue. "Yeah," he yelled, "didn't you muff one that was right in your hands?"

He was looking at Marty with a sore expression on his face, and his

lower lip stuck out; and a sinking feeling went through Marty, a sudden
sick feeling that maybe he had started something he would be sorry for.
Behind him on the curb he could hear the fellows sniggering in that
way they did when they picked on him. In the pitcher's box Eddie let
out a loud cackling laugh.

"Yeah, the new kid's got your number!"

"The sun was in my eyes!" Marty said. He could feel his face getting
red, and in the field the fellows were laughing. A wave of self-pity
flowed through him.

"What are you picking on me for!" he yelled in a high voice. "The
sun was so in my eyes. Anyway, I ain't no yellowbelly! I wasn't scared
of the ball!"

The instant he said it he was sorry. He sniffled his nose uneasily as
he saw Gelberg look at Ray-Ray. For an instant he thought of running
into the house before anything happened. But instead he just stood
there, sniffling his nose and feeling his heart beating, fast and heavy.

"You hear what he called you?" Paulie Dahler yelled at the new kid.

"You're not going to let him get away with calling you a yellowbelly,
are you?" Eddie said, looking at the new kid.

The new kid wet his lips with his tongue and looked at Marty. "I
wasn't scared!" he said. He shifted the soles of his new-looking shoes on
the pavement. "I wasn't scared! I just couldn't see it coming, that's all!"

Eddie was walking toward the new kid now, bouncing the ball slowly
in front of him as he walked. In a sudden panic Marty looked back toward
the house where Old Lady Kipnis lived. She always broke up fights; maybe
she would break up this one; maybe she wouldn't even let it get started.
But she wasn't out on her porch. He sniffled his nose, and with all his
might hoped that the kid's mother would call him to go to the store.

"Any kid that lets himself be called a yellowbelly must be a yellowbelly!" Albie Newbauer said, looking around him for approval.

"Yeah," Gelberg said. "I wouldn't let anyone call me a yellowbelly."

With a sudden shove Eddie sent the new kid scrambling forward
toward Marty. He tried to check himself by stiffening his body and
twisting to one side, but it was no use. Before he could recover his
balance another shove made him stagger forward.

Marty sniffled his nose and looked at the kid's face close in front of
him. It seemed as big as the faces he saw in the movies; and he could
see that the kid's nose was beginning to run just like his own; and he
could see in the corner of his mouth a crumb of the rye bread he had
eaten on the stoop. For a moment the kid's eyes looked squarely into

Marty's, so that he could see the little dark specks in the colored part around the pupil. Then the glance slipped away to one side; and all at once Marty had a feeling that the new kid was afraid of him.

"You gonna let him get away with calling you a yellowbelly?" he heard Eddie say. From the way it sounded he knew that the fellows were on his side now. He stuck out his jaw and waited for the new kid to answer.

"I got to go to the store!" the new kid said. There was a scared look on his face and he took a step back from Marty.

Paulie Dahler got behind him and shoved him against Marty. Although he tried not to, Marty couldn't help flinging his arms up before his face. But the new kid only backed away and kept his arms at his sides. A fierce excitement went through Marty as he saw how scared the look on the kid's face was. He thrust his chest up against the new kid.

"Yellowbelly!" he hollered, making his voice sound tough. "Scared of the ball!"

The new kid backed nervously away, and there was a look on his face as though he wanted to cry.

"Yeah, he's scared!" Eddie yelled.

"Slam him, Marty!" Wally Reinhard hollered. "The kid's scared of you!"

"Aw, sock the yellowbelly!" Marty heard Gelberg say, and he smacked the kid as hard as he could on the shoulder. The kid screwed up his face to keep from crying and tried to back through the fellows ringed around him.

"Lemme alone!" he yelled.

Marty looked at him fiercely, with his jaw thrust forward, and felt his heart beating. He smacked the kid again, making him stagger against Arnie in back of him.

"Yeah, yellowbelly!" Marty hollered, feeling how the fellows were on his side, and how scared the new kid was. He began smacking him again and again on the shoulder.

"Three, six, nine, a bottle of wine, I can fight you any old time!" he yelled. With each word he smacked the kid on the shoulder or arm. At the last word he swung with all his strength. He meant to hit the kid on the shoulder, but at the last instant, even while his arm was swinging, something compelled him to change his aim; his fist caught the kid on the mouth with a hard, wet, socking sound. The shock of his knuckles against the kid's mouth, and that sound of it, made Marty want to hit him again and again. He put his head down and began swinging wildly, hitting the new kid without any aim on the head and shoulders and arms.

The new kid buried his head in his arms and began to cry. "Lemme alone!" he yelled. He tried to rush through the fellows crowded around him.

With all his might Marty smacked him on the side of the head. Rushing up behind him, Arnie smacked him too. Paulie Dahler shoved the skullcap, with its paper-clip ornaments, over the kid's eyes; and as he went by Gelberg booted him in the pants.

Crying and clutching his cap, the new kid scampered over to the curb out of reach.

"I'll get even on you!" he cried.

With a fierce expression on his face Marty made a sudden movement of his legs and pretended to rush at him. The kid threw his arms about his head and darted down the street toward the house. When he saw that Marty was not coming after him he sat down on the stoop; and Marty could see him rubbing his knuckles against his mouth.

Howey Reinhard was making fun of the new kid, scampering up and down the pavement with his arms wrapped around his head and hollering, "Lemme alone! Lemme alone!" The fellows laughed, and although he was breathing hard, and his hand hurt from hitting the kid, Marty had to laugh too.

"You see him duck when that ball came at him?" he panted at Paulie Dahler.

Paulie shook his head. "Boy, just wait until we get the yellowbelly in the schoolyard!"

"And on Halloween," Gelberg said. "Wait until we get him on Halloween with our flour stockings!" He gave Marty a little shove and made as though he were whirling an imaginary flour stocking round his head.

Standing there in the middle of the street, Marty suddenly thought of Halloween, of the winter and snowballs, of the schoolyard. He saw himself whirling a flour stocking around his head and rushing at the new kid, who scampered in terror before him, hollering, "Lemme alone! Lemme alone!" As clearly as if it were in the movies, he saw himself flinging snowballs and the new kid backed into a corner of the schoolyard, with his hands over his face. Before he knew what he was doing, Marty turned fiercely toward the stoop where the new kid was still sitting, rubbing his mouth and crying.

"Hey, yellowbelly!" Marty hollered; and he pretended he was going to rush at the kid.

Almost falling over himself in fright, the new kid scrambled inside the house. Marty stood in the middle of the street and sniffled his nose. He shook his fist at the empty doorway.

"You see him run?" he yelled, so loud that it made his throat hurt. "Boy, you see him run?" He stood there shaking his fist, although the new kid was no longer there to see him. He could hardly wait for the winter, for Halloween, or the very next day in the schoolyard.

Check Your Reading

1. What must Marty do to get into the game?

2. What two essentials does Eddie draw with the chalk?

3. What excuse does Marty give for dropping the ball?

4. What name does Marty inadvertently call the new kid?

5. When do the boys plan to make use of "flour stockings" on the new kid?

Further Exploration

1. What effect does Heyert create by the long opening sentence, which ends with ". . . it was too late"? How does he emphasize Marty's youth? Why does Mommer seem impatient with Marty?

2. Why does there have to be a victim in order for Marty to assert himself? What do you think will happen the next day in the schoolyard?

3. When the boys choose sides for the game, why is Marty excluded? Is Marty ever accepted by the boys?

4. Why do you think the shock and sound of Marty's knuckles against the new kid's mouth make Marty want to go on fighting? Why does he continue swinging without taking aim? What is Heyert suggesting about violence?

5. How would you counsel a person like Marty or a new kid who feels left out? What experiences from your own childhood could you use as examples?

Langston Hughes (1902–1967)

A multi-talented artist, a recipient of a Guggenheim Fellowship, and the first black American to earn a living solely from writing, Langston Hughes excelled in the art of poetry, novels, plays, short stories, songs, and radio scripts. In addition he was known for translation, lectures, and his travels to Europe, Africa, Mexico, and the Soviet Union. A native of Joplin, Missouri, Hughes became a literary leader and unofficial "poet laureate of the Negro people."

Hughes got his start in 1925 while working as a busboy at a Washington hotel. After depositing a sheaf of poems by the plate of Vachel Lindsay, a popular poet of the 1920s, Hughes was startled to hear his own works included in Linday's public reading and his name introduced to the press as an exciting new talent. The following year DuBose Heyward wrote: "Langston Hughes, although only twenty-four years old, is already conspicuous in the group of Negro intellectuals who are dignifying Harlem with a genuine art life."

"One Friday Morning" captures the feelings of a young artist who, like the author, looks forward to recognition and a chance to contribute to America. The cold slap of rejection that Nancy Lee receives symbolizes the pain inflicted on anyone who suffers the ugliness of discrimination.

One Friday Morning
Langston Hughes

The news did not come directly to Nancy Lee, but it came in little indirections that finally added themselves up to one tremendous fact: she had won the prize! But being a calm and quiet young lady, she did not say anything although the whole high school buzzed with rumors, guesses, reportedly authentic announcements on the part of students who had no right to be making announcements at all—since no student really knew yet who had won this year's art scholarship.

But Nancy Lee's drawing was so good, her lines so sure, her colors so bright and harmonious that certainly no other student in the senior art class at George Washington High was thought to have very much of a chance. Yet you never could tell. Last year nobody had expected Joe Williams to win the Artist Club scholarship with that funny modernistic water color he had done of the high-level bridge. In fact, it was hard to make out there was a bridge until you had looked at the picture a long time. Still, Joe Williams got the prize, was feted by the community's leading painters, club women, and society folks at a big banquet at the Park-Rose Hotel, and was now an award student at the Art School—the city's only art school.

Nancy Lee Johnson was a black girl, a few years out of the South. But seldom did her high-school classmates think of her as black. She was smart, pretty and brown, and fitted in well with the life of the school. She stood high in scholarship, played a swell game of basketball, had taken part in the senior musical in a soft velvety voice, and had never seemed to intrude or stand out except in pleasant ways, so it was seldom even mentioned—her color.

Nancy Lee sometimes forgot she was black herself. She liked her

classmates and her school. Particularly she liked her art teacher, Miss
Dietrich, the tall red-haired woman who taught her to keep her brush
strokes firm and her colors clean, who taught her law and order in doing
things; and the beauty of working step by step until a job is done; a
picture finished; a design created; or a block print carved out of nothing
but an idea and a smooth square of linoleum, inked, proofs made, and
finally put down on paper—clean, sharp, beautiful, individual, unlike
any other in the world, thus making the paper have a meaning nobody
else could give it except Nancy Lee. That was the wonderful thing
about true creation. You made something nobody else on earth could
make—but you.

Miss Dietrich was the kind of teacher who brought out the best in
her students—but their own best, not anybody else's copied best. For
anybody else's best, great though it might be, even Michelangelo's,
wasn't enough to please Miss Dietrich dealing with the creative impulses
of young men and women living in an American city in the Middle
West, and being American.

Nancy Lee was proud of being American, a Black American with
blood out of Africa a long time ago, too many generations back to
count. But her parents had taught her the beauties of Africa, its strength,
its song, its mighty rivers, its early smelting of iron, its building of the
pyramids, and its ancient and important civilizations. And Miss Dietrich
had discovered for her the sharp and humorous lines of African sculpture,
Benin, Congo, Makonde. Nancy Lee's father was a mail carrier, her
mother a social worker in a city settlement house. Both parents had
been to black colleges in the South. And her mother had gotten a
further degree in social work from a Northern university. Her parents
were, like most Americans, simple ordinary people who had worked
hard and steadily for their education. Now they were trying to make it
easier for Nancy Lee to achieve learning than it had been for them.
They would be very happy when they learned of the award to their
daughter—yet Nancy did not tell them. To surprise them would be
better. Besides, there had been a promise.

Casually, one day, Miss Dietrich asked Nancy Lee what color frame
she thought would be best on her picture. That had been the first inkling.

"Blue," Nancy Lee said. Although the picture had been entered in
the Artist Club contest a month ago, Nancy Lee did not hesitate in
her choice of a color for the possible frame since she could still see her
picture clearly in her mind's eye—for that picture waiting for the blue
frame had come out of her soul, her own life, and had bloomed into

miraculous being with Miss Dietrich's help. It was, she knew, the best water color she had painted in her four years as a high-school art student, and she was glad she had made something Miss Dietrich liked well enough to permit her to enter in the contest before she graduated.

It was not a modernistic picture in the sense that you had to look at it a long time to understand what it meant. It was just a simple scene in the city park on a spring day with the trees still leaflessly lacy against the sky, the new grass fresh and green, a flag on a tall pole in the center, children playing, and an old black woman sitting on a bench with her head turned. A lot for one picture, to be sure, but it was not there in heavy and final detail like a calendar. Its charm was that everything was light and airy, happy like spring, with a lot of blue sky, paper-white clouds, and air showing through. You could tell that the old black woman was looking at the flag; and that the flag was proud in the spring breeze; and that the breeze helped to make the children's dresses billow as they played.

Miss Dietrich had taught Nancy Lee how to paint spring, people and a breeze on what was only a plain white piece of paper from the supply closet. But Miss Dietrich had not said make it like any other spring-people-breeze ever seen before. She let it remain Nancy Lee's own. That is how the old black woman happened to be there looking at the flag—for in her mind the flag, the spring and the woman formed a kind of triangle holding a dream Nancy Lee wanted to express. White stars on a blue field, spring, children, ever-growing life, and an old woman. Would the judges at the Artist Club like it?

One wet rainy April afternoon Miss O'Shay, the girl's vice-principal, sent for Nancy Lee to stop by her office as school closed. Pupils without umbrellas or raincoats were clustered in doorways hoping to make it home between showers. Outside the skies were gray. Nancy Lee's thoughts were suddenly gray, too.

She did not think she had done anything wrong, yet that tight little knot came in her throat just the same as she approached Miss O'Shay's door. Perhaps she had banged her locker too often and too hard. Perhaps the note in French she had written to Sallie halfway across the study hall just for fun had never gotten to Sallie but into Miss O'Shay's hands instead. Or maybe she was failing in some subject and wouldn't be allowed to graduate. Chemistry! A pang went through the pit of her stomach.

She knocked on Miss O'Shay's door. That familiarly solid and competent voice said, "Come in."

Miss O'Shay had a way of making you feel welcome even if you came to be expelled.

"Sit down, Nancy Lee Johnson," said Miss O'Shay. "I have something to tell you." Nancy Lee sat down. "But I must ask you to promise not to tell anyone yet."

"I won't, Miss O'Shay," Nancy Lee said, wondering what on earth the principal had to say to her.

"You are about to graduate," Miss O'Shay said. "And we shall miss you. You have been an excellent student, Nancy, and you will not be without honors on the senior list, as I am sure you know."

At that point there was a light knock on the door. Miss O'Shay called out, "Come in" and Miss Dietrich entered. "May I be a part of this, too?" she asked, tall and smiling.

"Of course," Miss O'Shay said. "I was just telling Nancy Lee what we thought of her. But I hadn't gotten around to giving her the news. Perhaps, Miss Dietrich, you'd like to tell her yourself."

Miss Dietrich was always direct. "Nancy Lee," she said, "your picture has won the Artist Club scholarship."

The slender brown girl's eyes widened, her heart jumped, then her throat tightened again. She tried to smile, but instead tears came to her eyes.

"Dear Nancy Lee," Miss O'Shay said, "we are so happy for you." The elderly white woman took her hand and shook it warmly while Miss Dietrich beamed with pride.

Nancy Lee must have danced all the way home. She never remembered quite how she got there through the rain. She hoped she had been dignified. But certainly she hadn't stopped to tell anybody her secret on the way. Raindrops, smiles, and tears mingled on her brown cheeks. She hoped her mother hadn't yet gotten home and that the house was empty. She wanted to have time to calm down and look natural before she had to see anyone. She didn't want to be bursting with excitement— having a secret to contain.

Miss O'Shay's calling her to the office had been in the nature of a preparation and a warning. The kind, elderly vice-principal said she did not believe in catching young ladies unawares, even with honors, so she wished her to know about the coming award. In making acceptance speeches she wanted her to be calm, prepared, not nervous, overcome, and frightened, so Nancy Lee was asked to think what she would say when the Scholarship award was conferred upon her a few days hence, both at the Friday morning high-school assembly hour when the announcement would be made, and at the evening banquet of the Artist Club. Nancy Lee promised the vice-principal to think calmly about what she would say.

Miss Dietrich had then asked for some facts about her parents, her background and her life, since it would probably all be desired for the papers. Nancy Lee had told her how, six years before, they had come up from the Deep South, her father having been successful in achieving a transfer from one post office to another, a thing he had long sought in order to give Nancy Lee a chance to go to school in the North. Now, they lived in a modest black neighborhood, went to see the best plays when they came to town, and had been saving to send Nancy Lee to art school, in case she were permitted to enter. But the scholarship would help a great deal, for they were not rich people.

"Now Mother can have a new coat next winter," Nancy Lee thought, "because my tuition will all be covered for the first year. And once in art school, there are other scholarships I can win."

Dreams began to dance through her head, plans and ambitions, beauties she would create for herself, her parents and the black people—for Nancy Lee possessed a deep and reverent race pride. She could see the old woman in her picture (really her grandmother in the South) lifting her head to the bright stars on the flag in the distance. A black in America! Often hurt, discriminated against, sometimes lynched—but always there were the stars—the blue body of the flag. Was there any other flag in the world that had so many stars? Nancy Lee thought deeply but she could remember none in all the encyclopedias or geographies she had ever looked into.

"Hitch your wagon to a star," Nancy Lee thought, dancing home in the rain. "Who were our flag makers?"

Friday morning came, the morning when the world would know—her high-school world, the newspaper world, her mother and dad. Dad could not be there at the assembly to hear the announcement, nor see her prize picture displayed on the stage, nor listen to Nancy Lee's little speech of acceptance, but Mother would be able to come, although Mother was much puzzled as to why Nancy Lee was so insistent she be at school on that particular Friday morning.

When something is happening, something new and fine, something that will change your very life, it is hard to go to sleep at night for thinking about it, and hard to keep your heart from pounding, or a strange little knot of joy gathering in your throat. Nancy Lee had taken her bath, brushed her hair until it glowed, and had gone to bed thinking about the next day, the big day when, before three thousand students, she would be the one student honored, her painting the one painting to be acclaimed as the best of the year from all the art classes of the city. Her short speech of gratitude was ready. She went over it in her mind, not word for word (because she didn't want it to sound as if she had learned it by heart) but she let the thoughts flow simply and sincerely through her consciousness many times.

When the president of the Artist Club presented her with the medal and scroll of the scholarship award, she would say:

"Judges, and members of the Artist Club. I want to thank you for this award that means so much to me personally and through me to my people, the black people of this city who, sometimes, are discouraged and bewildered, thinking that color and poverty are against them. I accept this award with gratitude and pride, not for myself alone but for my race that believes in American opportunity and American fairness — and the bright stars in our flag. I thank Miss Dietrich and the teachers of this school who made it possible for me to have the knowledge and training that lie behind this honor you have conferred upon my painting. When I came here from the South a few years ago, I was not sure how you would receive me. You received me well. You have given me a chance, and helped me along the road I wanted to follow. I suppose the judges know that every week here at assembly the students of this school pledge allegiance to the flag. I shall try to be worthy of that pledge, and of the help and friendship and understanding of my fellow citizens of whatever race or creed, and of our American dream of 'Liberty and justice for all!'"

That would be her response before the students in the morning. How proud and happy the black pupils would be, perhaps as proud as they were of the one black star on the football team. Her mother would probably cry with happiness. Thus Nancy Lee went to sleep dreaming of a wonderful tomorrow. The bright sunlight of an April morning woke her. There was breakfast with her parents — their half-amused and puzzled faces across the table, wondering what could be this secret that made her eyes so bright. The swift walk to school; the clock in the tower almost nine; hundreds of pupils streaming into the long rambling old building that was the city's largest high school; the sudden quiet of the home room after the bell rang; then the teacher opening her record book to call the roll. But just before she began, she looked across the room until her eyes located Nancy Lee.

"Nancy," she said, "Miss O'Shay would like to see you in her office, please."

Nancy Lee rose and went out while the names were being called and the word "present" added its period to each name. Perhaps, Nancy Lee thought, the reporters from the papers had already come. Maybe they wanted to take her picture before assembly, which wasn't until ten o'clock. (Last year they had had the photograph of the winner of the award in the morning papers as soon as the announcement had been made.)

Nancy Lee knocked at Miss O'Shay's door.

"Come in."

The vice-principal stood at her desk. There was no one else in the room. It was very quiet.

"Sit down, Nancy Lee," she said. Miss O'Shay did not smile. There was a long pause. The seconds went by slowly. "I do not know how to tell you what I have to say," the elderly woman began, her eyes on the papers on her desk. "I am indignant and ashamed for myself and for this city." Then she lifted her eyes and looked at Nancy Lee in the neat blue dress sitting there before her. "You are not to receive the scholarship this morning."

Outside in the hall the electric bells announcing the first period rang, loud and interminably long. Miss O'Shay remained silent. To the brown girl there in the chair, the room grew suddenly smaller, smaller, smaller, and there was no air. She could not speak.

Miss O'Shay said, "When the committee learned that you were black they changed their plans."

Still Nancy Lee said nothing, for there was no air to give breath to her lungs.

"Here is the letter from the committee, Nancy Lee." Miss O'Shay picked it up and read the final paragraph to her.

"It seems to us wiser to arbitrarily rotate the award among the various high schools of the city from now on. And especially in this case since the student chosen happens to be black, a circumstance which unfortunately, had we known, might have prevented this embarrassment. But there have never been any black students in the local art school and the presence of one there might create difficulties for all concerned. We have high regard for the quality of Nancy Lee Johnson's talent, but we do not feel it would be fair to honor it with the Art Club award." Miss O'Shay paused. She put the letter down.

"Nancy Lee, I am very sorry to have to give you this message."

"But my speech," Nancy Lee said, "was about . . ." The words stuck in her throat.". . . about America . . . ."

Miss O'Shay had risen, she turned her back and stood looking out the window at the spring tulips in the school yard.

"I thought, since the award would be made at assembly right after our oath of allegiance," the words tumbled almost hysterically from Nancy Lee's throat now, "I would put part of the flag salute in my speech. You know, Miss O'Shay, that part about "liberty and justice for all.'"

"I know," said Miss O'Shay slowly facing the room again. "But America is only what we who believe in it, make it. I am Irish. You may not know, Nancy Lee, but years ago, we were called the dirty Irish, and mobs rioted against us in the big cities, and we were invited to go back where we came from. But we didn't go. And we didn't give up, because we believed in the American dream, and in our power to make that dream come true. Difficulties, yes. Mountains to climb, yes. Discouragements to face, yes. Democracy *to make*, yes. That is it, Nancy Lee! We still have in this world of ours, democracy to make. You and I, Nancy Lee. But the premise and the base is here, the lines of the Declaration of Independence and the words of Lincoln are here, and the stars in our flag. Those who deny you this scholarship do not know the meaning of these stars, but it's up to us to make them know. As a teacher in the public schools of this city, I myself will go before the school board and ask them to remove from our system the offer of any prizes or awards denied to any student because of race or color." Suddenly Miss O'Shay stopped speaking. Her clear, clear blue eyes looked into those of the girl before her. The woman's eyes were full of strength and courage. "Lift up your head, Nancy Lee, and smile at me."

Miss O'Shay stood against the open window with the green lawn and the tulips beyond, the sunlight tangled in her gray hair, her voice an electric flow of strength to the hurt spirit of Nancy Lee. The Abolitionists who believed in freedom when there was slavery must have been like that. The first white teachers who went into the Deep South to teach the freed slaves must have been like that. All those who stand against ignorance, narrowness, hate and mud on stars must be like that.

Nancy Lee lifted her head and smiled. The tears were only drops of April rain.

The bell for assembly rang. Nancy Lee went through the long hall filled with students toward the auditorium.

"There will be other awards," Nancy Lee thought. "There're schools in other cities. This won't keep me down. But when I'm a woman, I'll fight to see that these things don't happen to other girls as this has happened to me. And men and women like Miss O'Shay will help me."

She took her seat among the seniors. The doors of the auditorium closed. As the principal came onto the platform the students rose and turned their eyes to the flag on the stage with its red and white stripes and the stars on its field of blue.

One hand went to the heart, the other outstretched toward the flag. Three thousand voices spoke. Among them was the voice of a dark girl whose cheeks were suddenly wet with tears.

"I pledge allegiance to the flag of the United States of America and to the Republic for which it stands." The words grew stronger, the dark girl's voice stronger, too. "One nation indivisible, with liberty and justice for all."

"That is the land we must make," she thought.

Check Your Reading

1. Why is Nancy Lee summoned to Miss O'Shay's office a second time?

2. What medium does Nancy Lee use to express herself?

3. What relative is represented in Nancy Lee's picture?

4. What event was to take place just before Nancy Lee's speech?

5. What ethnic group does Miss O'Shay describe to Nancy Lee?

Further Exploration

1. Describe the speech Nancy Lee has planned to deliver. Why do you think the audience would be moved by such a speech? How might her speech have aided other students?

2. What is the focal point of Nancy Lee's picture? What season does it depict? What kinds of people does she feature? How are these aspects symbolic of Nancy Lee's own beliefs?

3. How does the vice-principal plan to help "make" America a democracy? Do you think her actions will cause embarrassment to the committee? How could she help change their discriminatory actions against school children?

4. Why have Nancy Lee's parents moved to the North? Has her father achieved what he hoped for his daughter? Would Nancy Lee have profited by staying the South?

5. How has the committee cheated the art school? How does discrimination cheat the nation as a whole of talent?

Confronting Prejudice

Thinking It Over

These activities offer opportunities for you to consider how the stories in Part Four relate to one another and to the theme of *Confronting Prejudice*.

1. Write an essay in which you describe in detail a place that strongly connotes home for you. Tell why this is a home and why it gives you a sense of belonging.

2. Borden Deal writes that "the task of destruction is infinitely easier than that of creation." Support his opinion with evidence from at least two stories from this selection and with evidence from your own experience.

3. Write a letter to one of the characters from this section in which you help build a person's self-esteem. Mention the character's actions that you found most praiseworthy.

4. Pretend you are having a birthday party and can invite four guests. Select four characters from these short stories to invite to your party and explain why you made each choice.

5. The stories you have read in this section deal with young people. Explain how prejudice might take a different form when applied to adults. Do people ever learn to cope with discrimination?

6. Compare Nancy Lee Johnson's relationship with her parents to the parent/son relationships of Patsy Barnes and Marty. Did each characters' parent(s) help him or her deal with discrimination? If so, explain how.

PART FIVE

Getting Along

John Donne, an English poet of the seventeenth century, summarizes the theme of this section in few words: "No man is an island." As the poet implies, people cannot live apart from each other like separate stretches of earth in a great body of water. It is impossible for our lives not to touch those of the people around us, sometimes casually, but often significantly. For all of us, learning to get along with others can be the major ingredient in establishing a satisfying life.

As we grow, develop, and move through life, we build and clarify relationships with parents, brothers and sisters, classmates, spouses, and neighbors. When reconciling your hopes and desires with those close to you, problems can and often do develop, especially when you can't have the thing you most want. Learning to fill those holes in your life can take a tremendous amount of understanding—of others and of yourself.

All four stories in this section provide examples of adjustment to loss, such as Minta's loss of her mother, Al's injured self-esteem, Sucker's attempts to find a place in a family, and Holly's search for security after the divorce of her parents. In each case the characters must make difficult choices in order to put their lives back into balance.

Although home should be the most peaceful place we can go, relationships with parents and siblings (brothers and sisters) can become very tense and difficult at times. The stories by Sherburne, Saroyan, Cormier, and McCullers illustrate the tensions of strife and unhappiness at home. When we encounter problems in our lives with those closest to us, we suffer a most painful feeling—isolation.

Isolation is an unsettling experience—of not belonging, of having no place to call your own, of being unwelcome. The character in these stories must recognize something about loss and isolation before finding new ways to cope with rejection, humiliation, divorce, and death. In all of the stories there is a feeling that returning to a former sense of security is impossible—in that respect, the examples are realistic.

Learning to get along implies an ability to accept loss and to search for new expressions of belonging, new sources of warmth and security. We never stop losing the things we count on, the aspects of our lives that we love most. Sometimes change occurs as a natural part of growing, such as our enjoyment of school friends. At some point we must bid farewell to them with nostalgia, a bittersweet emotion.

Unfortunately, other aspects of our lives are wrenched from our grasp by violence, ill fortune, and death. The first time we lose a pet, we begin to see that life is not always fair—that adjustments must be made, even when they hurt. After we have lived through a number of these losses, we have learned ways to cope with sorrow. By surrounding ourselves with loving relationships, we learn to substitute one form of love for another.

Zoa Sherburne (1912–)

It is not surprising that Zoa Sherburne was chosen Woman of the Year by Phi Delta Nu. A native of Seattle, Washington, she spent many years as a housewife before launching a writing career that focuses on the conflicts and concerns of young people. Best known for her novels, Sherburne's *Almost April* has sustained its popularity for more than fifty years. *The High White Wall* and *Ballerina on Skates* have also found favor with young readers. A novel of the mid-60s, *Too Bad About the Haines Girl* displays the author's concern for unwed pregnant teenagers, a subject that had received little attention in young adult fiction before Sherburne's book.

"From Mother. . . With Love" describes the emotional turmoil of a young girl who must face the approaching loss of her mother in silence. Sherburne's sensitive treatment of Minta's problem reveals how Minta is able to recover and at the same time bring comfort to her father.

From Mother. . . With Love

Zoa Sherburne

The day that Minta Hawley grew up was a crisp golden day in early September.

Afterwards she was to remember everything about that day with poignant clarity. She remembered the slapping sound the waves made, the pungent smell of the logs burning, even the gulls that soared and swooped overhead; but most of all she remembered her father's face when he told her.

It began like any other Saturday, with Minta lying in bed an extra hour. Breakfast was always lazy and unhurried on Saturday mornings. The three of them in the breakfast room—Minta's father engrossed in his paper; her mother flying around in a gayly colored housecoat mixing waffles and frying bacon; Minta setting the table.

They talked, the casual happy talk of people who love each other and don't have to make conversation. About neighborhood doings . . . about items in the paper . . . about the clothes Minta would need when she went away to school in a couple of weeks.

It was after the dishes were finished that Minta's father asked her if she would like to go down to the beach for a little while.

"Low tide," he said. "Might get a few clams."

Minta nodded agreement, but her mother made a little face.

"Horrors, clam chowder for another week!"

"Sure you wouldn't like to go, Mary?" Minta's father asked. "The salt air might help your headache."

"No. You two run along. I'll curl up with an apple and a television program." She yawned and stretched, looking almost as young as Minta.

Minta ran upstairs and got into her heavy shoes and jeans. "Shall I call Sally and ask her if she wants to go?" she yelled, leaning far over the bannister.

"Let's just go by ourselves this time," her father answered rather shortly.

He was silent as they drove toward the beach, but it wasn't the companionable silence that Minta had come to expect from him. There was something grim about it.

"He's going to talk to me about school," Minta told herself, "He's going to try to talk me out of it again."

It was funny the way her father had acted when she announced her intention of going to MaryHill this term. It had always been such an accepted thing; her mother had graduated from MaryHill and it followed that Minta should be enrolled there as a matter of course.

Last year was different. With Mother just recovering from that operation it was natural that he should expect Minta to stay home; she had even *wanted* to stay. But now going to MaryHill was something special. She would live in a dormitory and be part of all the campus fun. It wasn't as if MaryHill were clear across the country, either, she'd probably be getting home every month or so . . . and there were the Christmas holidays . . . and then spring vacation.

Minta's chin was lifted in a stubborn line as her father parked the car and went around to get the shovels and pail from the trunk.

It wasn't like him to be so stubborn, usually he was jolly and easygoing and inclined to leave such matters entirely up to Minta's mother.

She followed him down to the beach, her boots squishing in the wet sand. The tide was far out and farther up the beach she could see bent figures busily digging along the water's edge.

A scattered beach fire smoldered near the bank and Minta poked it into place and revived it with splinters of driftwood until she had coaxed back a steady warming blaze. When she sat back on her heels to smile up at her father she felt her throat constrict with a smothering fear. His eyes looked the way they had when . . .

When?

Suddenly she remembered. He was looking at her and trying to smile, just the way he had looked at her the time her appendix burst and they were taking her to the hospital. She could almost hear the wail of the ambulance siren and feel the way he had held her hands tightly, trying to make it easier. His eyes had told her then, as they told her now, that he would a thousand times rather bear the pain than watch her suffer.

It seemed like a long time that she knelt there by the beach fire, afraid to move, childishly willing herself to wake from the nightmarish feeling that gripped her.

He took her hand and pulled her to her feet and they started walking up the beach slowly, not toward the group of people digging clams, but in the other direction, toward the jagged pile of rocks that jutted out into the bay.

She heard a strange voice, her own voice.

"I thought . . . I thought you wanted to talk to me about school, but it isn't that, is it, Father?"

Father.

She never called him Father. It was always "Dad" or "Pops" or, when she was feeling especially gay, "John Henry."

His fingers tightened around hers. "In a way it is . . . about school."

And then, before the feeling of relief could erase the fear he went on. "I went to see Dr. Morton last week, Minta. I've been seeing him pretty regularly these last few months."

She flashed a quick frightened look up at him. "You aren't ill?"

"No." He sighed and it was a heartbreaking sound. "No. It isn't me. It's your mother. That's why I don't want you to go to MaryHill this year."

"But . . . but she's feeling so much better, Dad. Except for these headaches once in a while. She's even taking on a little weight—" She broke off and stopped walking and her hand was steady on his arm. "Tell me," she said quietly.

The look was back in his eyes again but this time Minta scarcely noticed it, she was aware only of his words, the dreadful echoing finality of his words.

Her mother was going to die.

To die.

Her mother.

To die, the doctor said. Three months, perhaps less . . . .

Her mother who was gay and scatterbrained and more fun than anyone else in the world. Her mother who could be counted on to announce in the spring that she was going to do her Christmas shopping early *this* year, and then left everything until the week before Christmas.

No one was worse about forgetting anniversaries and birthdays and things like that; but the easy-to-remember dates, like Valentine's Day and St. Patrick's Day and Halloween were always gala affairs complete with table favors and three-decker cakes.

Minta's mother wore the highest heels and the maddest hats of any mother on the block. She was so pretty. And she always had time for things like listening to new records and helping paste pictures in Minta's scrapbook.

She wasn't ever sick—except for the headaches and the operation last year which she had laughingly dismissed as a rest cure.

"I shouldn't have told you." Her father was speaking in a voice that Minta had never heard from him before. A voice that held loneliness and fear and a sort of angry pain. "I was afraid I couldn't make you understand, why you had to stay home . . . why you'd have to forget about MaryHill for this year." His eyes begged her to forgive him and for some reason she wanted to put her arms around him, as if she were much older and stronger.

"Of course you had to tell me," she said steadily. "Of course I had to know." And then—"Three months, but Dad, that's *Christmas.*"

He took her hand and tucked it under his arm and they started walking again.

It was like walking through a nightmare. The steady squish-squish of the wet sand and the little hollows their feet made filling up almost as soon as they passed.

He talked quietly, explaining, telling her everything the doctor had said, and Minta listened without tears, without comment.

She watched his face as though it were the face of a stranger.
She thought about a thousand unrelated things.

Last winter when he had chased her and her mother around the back yard to wash their faces in the new snow. She could still see the bright red jacket her mother had worn . . . the kerchief that came off in the struggle . . . the way the neighbors had watched from their windows, laughing and shaking their heads.

She remembered all the times they had gone swimming this past summer. Minta and her father loved to swim but her mother had preferred to curl up on a beach blanket and watch them.

"You have the disposition of a Siamese cat," Minta had accused her mother laughingly. "A cushion by the fire in the winter and a cushion in the sun in the summer . . . ."

"And a bowl of cream nearby," her mother had agreed instantly.

She was always good-natured about their teasing.

But in spite of her apparent frailty and her admitted laziness she managed to accomplish an astounding amount of work. Girl Scouts, PTA, Church bazaars, Red Cross. People were always calling her to head a committee or organize a drive. Young people congregated in her home. Not just Minta's gang, but the neighborhood youngsters. She had Easter egg hunts for them; she bought their raffle tickets and bandaged their skinned knees.

It was like coming back from a long journey when her father stopped talking and they turned back toward the car.

"So that's why I can't let you go away, Midge." Her father's voice was very low and he didn't seem to realize that he had called her by the babyish name she had discarded when she started to first grade. "It isn't just your mother I'm thinking about . . . it's me. I need you."

She looked at him quickly and her heart twisted with pity. He did need her. He would need her more than ever.

In the car she sat very close to him.

"We didn't get the clams," she reminded him once, but he only nodded.

Just before they reached home he reached over and took her hand in a tight hurting grip.

"We can't tell her, Minta. The doctor left it up to me and I said not to tell her. We have to let her have this last time . . . this last little time . . . without that hanging over her. We have to go on as if everything were exactly the same."

She nodded to show that she understood. After a moment she spoke past the ache in her throat. "About school. I'll . . . I'll tell her that I decided to wait until next year. Or that I'm afraid I'd be lonesome without the gang. I've been sort of . . . sort of seesawing back and forth, anyway."

It seemed impossible that life could go on exactly as before.

The small private world peopled by the three of them was as snug and warm and happy as though no shadow had touched them.

They watched television and argued good-naturedly about the programs. Minta's friends came and went and there was the usual round of parties and dances and games. Her father continued to bowl two evenings a week and her mother became involved in various pre-holiday pursuits.

"I really must get at my Christmas shopping," she mentioned the day she was wrapping trick-or-treat candy for Halloween.

Minta shook her head and sighed gustily.

Her mother started this "I-must-get-at-my-Christmas-shopping" routine every spring and followed it up until after Thanksgiving but she never actually got around to it until two or three days before Christmas.

It was amazing that Minta could laugh and say, "Oh, *you* . . ." the way she did year after year.

It was a knife turning in her heart when her mother straightened up from the gay cellophane-wrapped candies and brushed a stray wisp of taffy-colored hair back from one flushed cheek.

"Don't laugh," she said, pretending to be stern. "You know you're just exactly like me."

It was a warming thought. She was like her mother. Inside, where it really mattered she was like her mother, even though she had her father's dark eyes and straight black hair, even though she had his build and the firm chin of all the Hawleys.

She wanted to put her arm around her mother and hug her, hard. She wanted to say, "I hope I am like you. I want to be."

But instead she got up and stretched and wrinkled her nose.

"Perish forbid" she said, "that I should be such a scatterbrain."

She was rewarded by the flash of a dimple in her mother's cheek.

It seemed to Minta as week followed week, that the day at the beach had been something out of a nightmare: something that she could push away from her and forget about. Sometimes she looked at her father, laughing, teasing them, or howlimg about the month-end bills and she thought, "It didn't happen . . . it isn't true."

And then at night she would lie sleepless in her room, the pretty room that had been reconverted from her nursery. She watched the moonlight drift patterns across the yellow bedspread and the breeze billow the curtains that her mother had made by hand, because that was the only way she could be sure of an absolute match.

"Yellow is such a difficult color to match," she had explained around a mouthful of pins.

And in the dark hours of the night Minta had known it wasn't a nightmare. It was true. It was true.

One windy November day she hurried home from school and found her mother in the yard raking leaves. She wore a bright kerchief over her head and she had Minta's old polo coat belted around her. She looked young and gay and carefree and her eyes were shining.

"Hi!" She waved the rake invitingly. "Change your clothes and come help. We'll have a smudge party in the alley."

Minta stopped and leaned on the gate. She saw with a new awareness that there were dark circles under her mother's eyes and that the flags of color in her cheeks were too bright. But she managed a chuckle.

"I wish you could see yourself, Mom. For two cents I'd get my camera and take a picture of you."

She ran into the house and got her camera and they took a whole roll of pictures.

"Good," her mother said complacently. "Now we can show them to your father the next time he accuses me of being a Sally-Sit-by-the-Fire."

They piled the leaves into a huge damp stack, with the help of half a dozen neighborhood children. It wouldn't burn properly but gave out with clouds of thick, black, wonderfully pungent smoke.

Her mother was tired that night. She lay on the davenport and made out her Christmas card list while Minta and her father watched the wrestling matches. It was like a thousand other such evenings but in some unaccountable way it was different.

"Because it's the last time," Minta told herself. "The last time we'll ever rake the leaves and make a bonfire in the alley. The last time I'll snap a picture of her with her arms around the Kelly kids, The last time . . . the last time. . . ."

She got up quickly and went out into the kitchen and made popcorn in the electric popper, bringing a bowl to her mother first, remembering just the way she liked it, salt and not too much butter.

But that night she wakened in the chilly darkness of her room and began to cry, softly, her head buried in the curve of her arm. At first it helped, loosening the tight bands about her heart, washing away the fear and the loneliness, but when she tried to stop she found that she couldn't. Great wracking sobs shook her until she could no longer smother them against her pillow. And then the light was on and her mother was there bending over her, her face concerned, her voice soothing.

"Darling, what is it? Wake up, baby, you're having a bad dream."

"No . . . no, it isn't a dream," Minta choked, "It's true . . . it's true."

The thin hand kept smoothing back her tumbled hair and her mother went on talking in the tone she had always used to comfort a much smaller Minta.

She was aware that her father had come to the doorway. He said nothing, just stood there watching them while Minta's sobs diminished into hiccupy sighs.

Her mother pulled the blanket up over Minta's shoulder and gave her a little spank. "The idea! Gollywogs, at your age," she said reprovingly. "Want me to leave the light on in case your spook comes back?"

Minta shook her head, blinking against the tears that crowded against her eyelids, even managing a wobbly smile.

She never cried again.

Not even when the ambulance came a week later to take her mother to the hospital. Not even when she was standing beside her mother's high white hospital bed, holding her hand tightly, forcing herself to chatter of inconsequential things.

"Be sure that your father takes his vitamin pills, won't you, Minta? He's so careless unless I'm there to keep eye on him."

"I'll watch him like a beagle," Minta promised lightly. "Now you behave yourself and get out of here in a hurry, you hear?"

Not even at the funeral. . . .

The friends and relatives came and went and it was as if she stood on the sidelines watching the Minta who talked with them and answered their questions. As if her heart were encased in a shell that kept it from breaking.

She went to school and came home afterwards to the empty house. She tried to do the things her mother had done but even with the help of well-meaning friends and neighbors it was hard. She tried not to hate the people who urged her to cry.

"You'll feel better, dear," her Aunt Grace had insisted and then had lifted her handkerchief to her eyes and walked away when Minta had only stared at her with chilling indifference.

She overheard people talking about her mother.

"She never knew, did she?" they asked.

And always Minta's father answered, "No, she never knew. Even at the very last, when she was waiting for the ambulance to come she looked around the bedroom and said, "I must get these curtains done up before Christmas."

Minta knew that her father was worried about her and she was sorry, but it was as if there were a wall between them, a wall that she was too tired to surmount.

One night he came to the door of her room where she was studying.

"I wonder if you'd like to go through those clothes before your Aunt Grace takes them to the church bazaar," he began haltingly. And then when she looked up at him, not understanding, he went on gently, "Your mother's clothes. We thought someone might as well get some good out of them."

She stood up and closed the book and went past him without another word, but she closed the door behind her when she went into her mother's room.

There were some suit boxes by the closet door and Minta vaguely remembered that the women from the bazaar committee had called several times.

Her hands felt slightly unsteady as she pulled open the top dresser drawer and looked down at the stacks of clean handkerchiefs, the stockings in their quilted satin case, the gloves folded into tissue wrappings.

"I can't do it," she told herself, but she got a box and started putting the things into it, trying not to look at them, trying to forget how delighted her mother had been with the pale green slip, trying not to remember.

Once she hesitated and almost lifted a soft wool sweater from the pile that was growing in the suit box. She had borrowed it so often that her mother used to complain that she felt like a criminal every time she borrowed it back again. She didn't mean it though . . . she loved having Minta borrow her things.

Minta put the sweater with the other things and closed the box firmly.

Now, the things in the closet—

Opening the door was almost like feeling her mother in the room beside her. A faint perfume clung to most of her garments. The housecoat . . . the woolly robe . . . the tan polo coat . . . the scarlet jacket . . . her new blue wool with the pegtop skirt.

Minta started folding the things with almost frantic haste, stuffing them into boxes, cramming the lids on and then starting on another box.

At the very back of the closet were the two pieces of matched luggage that had been her mother's last birthday gift from her father. They were heavy when she tried to move them—too heavy.

She brought them out into the room and put them side by side on her mother's bed. Her breath caught in her throat when she opened them.

Dozens and dozens of boxes, all tied with bright red ribbon, the gift tags written out in her mother's careful script. Gayly colored Christmas stickers, sprigs of holly. To Minta from Mother and Dad . . . to Grace from Mary . . . to John from Mary . . . to the Kelly Gremlims from Aunt Mary . . . to Uncle Art from the Hawley family . . .

"So you knew," Minta whispered the words. "You knew all the time."

She looked down in surprise as a hot tear dropped on her hand and she dashed it away almost impatiently.

She picked up another package and read the tag. To Minta from Mother . . . with love.

Without opening it she knew that it was a picture frame and she remembered the way she had teased her mother to have a good photograph taken.

"The only one I have of you looks like a fugitive from a chain gang," she had pointed out. "I can't very well go away to school next year with *that.*"

She put the package back in the suitcase with all the others and carried the cases back into the closet.

Poor Dad, she thought.

"She never knew," she could hear him saying. "Not even at the last."

Minta opened the box beside the bed and took out the sweater and the pale green slip.

"You know perfectly well that you're just exactly like me," she remembered her mother saying.

She brushed the tears away and went down the stairs and out into the cheerless living room.

"I'd like to keep these things, Dad," she said in her most matter-of-fact voice, and she showed him the sweater and slip. "The slip is a little big but I'll grow into it. It . . . it looks like her, I think."

She went around the room, snapping on the lamps, turning on the television that had been silent for so long. She was aware that his eyes followed her, that he could hardly avoid noticing the tear stains on her cheeks.

"I think I'll have an apple," she said. "Want one?"

He nodded. "Sure. Bring me one as long as you're making the trip."

It was natural. It was almost like old times, except that the blue chair by the fireplace was vacant.

She went out into the kitchen hurriedly.

"I'll tell him that I pestered mother to do her shopping early this year," she told herself as she got the apples from the refrigerator. "I'll tell him that it was my idea about the photographs. She wanted him to believe that she didn't know."

The vitamin pills were pushed back on a shelf. She took them out of the refrigerator and put them on the window sill where she would be sure to see them in the morning.

When she came back into the living room she noticed that a light in a Christmas wreath was winking on and off in the Kelly's window across the street.

"I guess we should start thinking about Christmas, Dad." She tossed him an apple as she spoke and he caught it deftly.

She hesitated for just a moment and then walked over and sat down in the blue chair by the fire, as if she belonged there, and looked across at her father, and smiled.

Check Your Reading

1. Where does Minta's father take her to discuss her mother's illness?

2. To what animal does Minta compare her mother?

3. At what time of the year does Minta's mother die?

4. What does Minta discover in her mother's luggage?

5. Which of her mother's possessions does Minta keep for herself?

Further Exploration

1. How might the last three months of Minta's mother's life have changed if she had spoken openly with her family about death? Explain which approach you would prefer—deception or honesty.

2. How do the vitamin pills become a symbol of responsibility? What is Minta's mother indicating about her hopes for the family? Why is the blue chair significant?

3. Describe the relationship Minta has had with her father. How would Minta have adjusted if her father had died?

4. What happy memories does Minta have of her mother? Why will holidays be especially significant after her mother's death?

5. Explain how Minta knows that her mother accepted death. Why is that knowledge comforting to Minta?

William Saroyan (1908–1981)

Blessed with a joy in the diversity of life, William Saroyan produced more than five hundred stories during the period between 1934 and 1940. Saroyan, born in Fresno, California, to a family of Armenian-American workers, was a close observer of people and situations. After leaving school at thirteen and working in various jobs, he found his place in writing and entertained an appreciative audience for his stories, plays, and novels during the '30s and '40s. His first collection of stories, *The Daring Young Man on the Flying Trapeze* (1934), was followed two years later by a larger collection, *Inhale and Exhale*. Two of his most famous plays are *My Heart's in the Highlands* (1939) and *The Time of Your Life* (1939).

Of his emphasis on the family, Saroyan explains, ". . .if a writer misunderstands the members of his own family, there is little chance he will understand the whole human race." He summarizes his generous view of mankind, "They can drive a man crazy with their awful limitations, their stupidities, or meannesses, and then all of a sudden they can make him rejoice, literally jump for joy, because they are so really handsome and brave and proud and true and real, after all—just a little misunderstood, along the way." The character Al Condraj in "The Parsley Garden" exemplifies Saroyan's faith in people who need that bit of understanding.

The Parsley Garden
William Saroyan

One day in August Al Condraj was wandering through Woolworth's without a penny to spend when he saw a small hammer that was not a toy but a real hammer, and he was possessed with a longing to have it. He believed it was just what he needed by which to break the monotony and with which to make something. He had gathered some first-class nails from Foley's Packing House where the boxmakers worked and where they had carelessly dropped at least fifteen cents' worth. He had gladly gone to the trouble of gathering them together, because it had seemed to him that a nail, as such, was not something to be wasted. He had the nails, perhaps a half pound of them, at least two hundred of them, in a paper bag in the apple box in which he kept his junk at home.

Now, with the ten-cent hammer he believed he could make something out of box wood and the nails, although he had no idea what. Some sort of a table perhaps, or a small bench.

At any rate, he took the hammer and slipped it into the pocket of his overalls, but just as he did so, a man took him firmly by the arm without a word and pushed him to the back of the store into a small office. Another man, an older one, was seated behind a desk in the office, working with papers. The younger man, the one who had captured him, was excited, and his forehead was covered with sweat.

"Well," he said, "here's one more of them."

The man behind the desk got to his feet and looked Al Condraj up and down.

"What's *he* swiped?"

"A hammer." The young man looked at Al with hatred. "Hand it over," he said.

The boy brought the hammer out of his pocket and handed it to the young man, who said, "I ought to hit you over the head with it, that's what I ought to do."

He turned to the older man, the boss, the manager of the store, and he said, "What do you want me to do with him?"

"Leave him with me," the older man said.

The younger man stepped out of the office, and the older man sat down and went back to work. Al Condraj stood in the office fifteen minutes before the older man looked at him again.

"Well," he said.

Al didn't know what to say. The man wasn't looking at him; he was looking at the door.

Finally Al said, "I didn't mean to steal it. I just need it, and I haven't got any money."

"Just because you haven't got any money doesn't mean you've got a right to steal things," the man said. "Now, does it?"

"No, sir."

"Well, what am I going to do with you? Turn you over to the police?"

Al didn't say anything, but he certainly didn't want to be turned over to the police. He hated the man, but at the same time he realized somebody else could be a lot tougher than he was being.

"If I let you go, will you promise never to steal from this store again?"

"Yes, sir."

"All right," the man said. "Go out this way, and don't come back to this store until you've got some money to spend."

He opened a door to the hall that led to the alley, and Al Condraj hurried down the hall and out into the alley.

The first thing he did when he was free was laugh, but he knew he had been humiliated, and he was deeply ashamed. It was not in his nature to take things that did not belong to him. He hated the young man who had caught him, and he hated the manager of the store who had made him stand in silence in the office so long. He hadn't liked it at all when the young man had said he ought to hit him over the head with the hammer.

He should have had the courage to look him straight in the eye and say, "You and who else?"

Of course he *had* stolen the hammer, and he had been caught, but it seemed to him he oughtn't to have been so humiliated.

After he had walked three blocks, he decided he didn't want to go home just yet, so he turned around and started walking back to town.

He almost believed he meant to go back and say something to the young man who had caught him. And then he wasn't sure he didn't mean to go back and steal the hammer again, and this time *not* get caught. As long as he had been made to feel like a thief anyway, the least he ought to get out of it was the hammer.

Outside the store he lost his nerve, though. He stood in the street, looking in, for at least ten minutes.

Then, crushed and confused and now bitterly ashamed of himself, first for having stolen something, then for having been caught, then for having been humiliated, then for not having guts enough to go back and do the job right, he began walking home again, his mind so troubled that he didn't greet his pal Pete Wawchek when they came face to face outside Graf's Hardware.

When he got home, he was too ashamed to go inside and examine his junk, so he had a long drink of water from the faucet in the back yard. The faucet was used by his mother to water the stuff she planted every year: okra, bell peppers, tomatoes, cucumbers, onions, garlic, mint, eggplants, and parsley.

His mother called the whole business the parsley garden, and every night in the summer she would bring chairs out of the house and put them around the table she had had Ondro, the neighborhood handyman, make for her for fifteen cents, and she would sit at the table and enjoy the cool of the garden and the smell of the things she had planted and tended.

Sometimes she would even make a salad and moisten the flat old-country bread and slice some white cheese, and she and he would have supper in the parsley garden. After supper she would attach the water hose to the faucet and water her plants, and the place would be cooler than ever, and it would smell real good, real fresh and cool and green, all the different growing things making a green-garden smell out of themselves and the air and the water.

After the long drink of water he sat down where the parsley itself was growing, and he pulled a handful of it out and slowly ate it. Then he went inside and told his mother what had happened. He even told her what he had *thought* of doing after he had been turned loose: to go back and steal the hammer again.

"I don't want you to steal," his mother said in broken English. "Here is ten cents. You go back to that man and you give him this money and you bring it home, that hammer."

"No," Al Condraj said. "I won't take your money for something I don't really need. I just thought I ought to have a hammer, so I could make something if I felt like it. I've got a lot of nails and some box wood, but I haven't got a hammer."

"Go buy it, that hammer," his mother said.

"No," Al said.

"All right," his mother said. "Shut up."

That's what she always said when she didn't know what else to say.

Al went out and sat on the steps. His humiliation was beginning to really hurt now. He decided to wander off along the railroad tracks to Foley's because he needed to think about it some more. At Foley's he watched Johnny Gale nailing boxes for ten minutes, but Johnny was too busy to notice him or talk to him, although one day at Sunday school, two or three years ago, Johnny had greeted him and said, "How's the boy?" Johnny worked with a boxmaker's hatchet, and everybody in Fresno said he was the fastest boxmaker in town. He was the closest thing to a machine any packing house ever saw. Foley himself was proud of Johnny Gale.

Al Condraj finally set out for home because he didn't want to get in the way. He didn't want somebody working hard to notice that he was being watched and maybe say to him, "Go on, beat it." He didn't want Johnny Gale to do something like that. He didn't want to invite another humiliation.

On the way home he looked for money, but all he found was the usual pieces of broken glass and rusty nails, the things that were always cutting his bare feet every summer.

When he got home, his mother had made a salad and set the table, so he sat down to eat, but when he put the food in his mouth, he just didn't care for it. He got up and went into the three-room house and got his apple box out of the corner of his room and went through his junk. It was all there, the same as yesterday.

He wandered off back to town and stood in front of the closed store, hating the young man who had caught him, and then he went along to the Hippodrome and looked at the display photographs from the two movies that were being shown that day.

Then he went along to the public library to have a look at all the books again, but he didn't like any of them, so he wandered around town some more, and then around half-past eight he went home and went to bed.

His mother had already gone to bed because she had to be up at five to go to work at Inderrieden's, packing figs. Some days there would be work all day, some days there would be only a half a day of it, but whatever his mother earned during the summer had to keep them the whole year.

He didn't sleep much that night, because he couldn't get over what had happened, and he went over six or seven ways by which to adjust the matter. He went so far as to believe it would be necessary to kill the young man who had caught him. He also believed it would be necessary for him to steal systematically and successfully the rest of his life. It was a hot night and he couldn't sleep.

Finally, his mother got up and walked barefooted to the kitchen for a drink of water, and on the way back she said to him softly, "Shut up."

When she got up at five in the morning, he was out of the house, but that had happened many times before. He was a restless boy, and he kept moving all the time every summer. He was making mistakes and paying for them, and he had just tried stealing and had been caught at it, and he was troubled. She fixed her breakfast, packed her lunch, and hurried off to work, hoping it would be a full day.

It was a full day, and then there was overtime, and although she had no more lunch, she decided to work for the extra money, anyway. Almost all the other packers were staying on too, and her neighbor across the alley, Leeza Ahboot, who worked beside her, said, "Let us work until the work stops; then we'll go home and fix supper between us and eat it in your parsley garden where it's so cool. It's a hot day, and there's no sense not making an extra fifty or sixty cents."

When the two women reached the garden, it was almost nine o'clock, but still daylight, and she saw her son nailing pieces of box wood together, making something with a hammer. It looked like a bench. He had already watered the garden and tidied up the rest of the yard, and the place seemed very nice, and her son seemed very serious and busy. She and Leeza went straight to work for their supper, picking bell peppers and tomatoes and cucumbers and a great deal of parsley for the salad.

Then Leeza went to her house for some bread which she had baked the night before, and some white cheese, and in a few minutes they were having supper together and talking pleasantly about the successful day they had had. After supper they made Turkish coffee over an open fire in the yard. They drank the coffee and smoked a cigarette apiece and told one another stories about their experiences in the old country and here in Fresno, and then they looked into their cups at the grounds to see if any good fortune was indicated, and there was: health and work and supper out of doors in the summer and enough money for the rest of the year.

Al Condraj worked and overheard some of the things they said, and then Leeza went home to go to bed, and his mother said, "Where you get it, that hammer, Al?"

"I got it at the store."

"How you get it? You steal it?"

Al Condraj finished the bench and sat on it. "No," he said "I didn't steal it."

"How you get it?"

"I worked at the store for it," Al said.

"The store where you steal it yesterday?"

"Yes."

"Who give you job?"

"The boss."

"What you do?"

"I carried different stuff to the different counters."

"Well, that's good," the woman said. "How long you work for that little hammer?"

"I worked all day," Al said. "Mr. Clemmer gave me the hammer after I'd worked one hour, but I went right on working. The fellow who caught me yesterday showed me what to do, and we worked together. We didn't talk, but at the end of the day he took me to Mr. Clemmer's office, and he told Mr. Clemmer that I'd worked hard all day and ought to be paid at least a dollar."

"That's good," the woman said.

"So Mr. Clemmer put a silver dollar on his desk for me, and then the fellow who caught me yesterday told him the store needed a boy like me every day, for a dollar a day, and Mr. Clemmer said I could have the job."

"That's good," the woman said."You can make it a little money for yourself."

"I left the dollar on Mr. Clemmer's desk," Al Condraj said, "and I told them both I didn't want the job."

"Why you say that?" the woman said. "Dollar a day for eleven-year-old boy good money. Why you not take job?"

"Because I hate the both of them," the boy said. "I would never work for people like that. I just looked at them and picked up my hammer and walked out. I came home and I made this bench."

"All right," His mother said. "Shut up."

His mother went inside and went to bed, but Al Condraj sat on the bench he had made and smelled the parsley garden and didn't feel humiliated any more.

But nothing could stop him from hating the two men, even though he knew they hadn't done anything they shouldn't have done.

Check Your Reading

1. How much money does Mrs. Condraj offer her son?

2. What kind of work does Al's mother do?

3. What words does Al's mother use when she does not know what else to say?

4. What does Al build with his hammer?

5. What does Al do with the silver dollar?

Further Exploration

1. What fuels Al's hatred for the two men who humiliated him? Does he have good reason to continue hating them? How can he rid himself of bad feelings?

2. Describe Al's treatment after he is caught. How might Mr. Clemmer have punished Al without shaming him? Does a youthful offender deserve mercy and understanding?

3. What good feelings do Al and his mother get from the parsely garden? Why is the garden essential to their lives? How does Al demonstrate his respect for his mother and her garden?

4. How does poverty affect Al and his mother? Is poverty the reason for Al's dishonesty?

5. Will Al eventually find happiness in his life or will he only find sadness and frustration? Explain the reasons for your prediction.

Robert Cormier (1925–)

Robert Cormier does not believe in writing endings where the characters live happily ever after. A journalist and author of novels and short stories, he says that "As long as what I write is true and believable, why should I have to create happy endings?" Cormier's personal philosophy appears in many of his works. His short stories have appeared in current periodicals, including *McCall's*, *Redbook*, *Woman's Day*, and *The Saturday Evening Post*. Three of his novels have won the *New York Times*'s Outstanding Book of the Year Award: *The Chocolate War (1974)*, *I Am the Cheese* (1977), and *After the First Death* (1979).

Mine on Thursdays

Robert Cormier

To begin with, it took more than two hours to drive from Boston to Monument, twice the usual time, because of an accident near Concord that caused a traffic backup that turned a three-mile line of cars into a giant metal caterpillar, inching ponderously forward. Meanwhile, I had a splitting headache, my eyes were like raw onions and my stomach lurched on the edge of nausea, for which I fully accepted the blame. Ordinarily, the night before my Thursdays with Holly, I took it easy, avoided involvements and went to bed early. But yesterday afternoon, I'd had a futile clash with McClafflin—all arguments with employers are futile—and had threatened to quit, an empty gesture that caused him to smile because he knew about all my traps. This led to a few solitary and self-pitying drinks at the bar across the street, leaving me vulnerable to an invitation to a party in Cambridge, a party that turned out to be nothing more than pseudo-intellectual talk, plus liquor, the effect of which was pseudo: promising so much and delivering little except a clanging hangover and the familiar and desperate taste of old regrets. Somehow, I managed to survive the morning and left at my usual hour, aware that McClaffin was watching my painful progress through the office. And I thought: "The hell with you, Mac. You think I'm going to leave her waiting uselessly, while I take a cold shower and sleep it off. But Holly expects me and I'll be there."

I *was* there, late maybe but present and accounted for, and Holly leaped with delight when she saw me drive into her street. I made a reckless U-turn, knowing that Alison would be watching from the window, frowning her disapproval. The scarlet convertible in itself was sufficient to insult her cool gray New England eyes and my lateness was an affront to her penchant for punctuality (she'd been a teacher before our marriage and still loved schedules and timetables). Anyway, the brakes squealed as I pulled up in front of the house on the sedate street. On impulse, I blew the horn, long and loud. I always did things like that, to provoke her, killing myself with her, or killing whatever was left of what we'd had together, like a dying man hiding the medicine in the palm of his hand instead of swallowing the pill that might cure him.

Holly came streaking off the porch, dazzling in something pink and lacy and gay. Holly, my true love, the one person who could assuage my hangovers, comfort my aching limbs and give absolution to my sins.

"Oh, Daddy, I knew you'd come. I just knew it," she said, flinging herself at me.

I dug my face into her shampoo-scented hair and clutched the familiar geography of her bones and flesh. "Did I ever stand you up?" Then, laughing: "Don't answer that." Because there had been times, of course, when it had been impossible for me to come.

"Wonder World today, Dad?" she asked.

The sun hurled its rays against my eyeballs, penetrating the dark glasses, and the prospect of those whirling rides at the amusement park spread sickness through my veins. But aware that Alison was there behind the white curtains, I assured Holly: "Whatever you say, baby, whatever you say." Wanting Alison to know that somebody loved me. "The sky's the limit."

Holly was mine on Thursdays, and during the two years of our Thursdays together, we had made the circuit many times—shopping trips to fancy stores, movie matinees, picnics on Moosock Ridge, bowling, Wonder World in season—all the things an adult can do with a child. I'd always been careful to indulge her, basking in her delight. We shared the unspoken knowledge that we were playing a special kind of hooky, each of us a truant, she from that well-regulated and orderly world of her mother's and I from the world of too many martinis, too many girls, too many long shots that had never come in.

For some reason, I thought of my father. Occasionally, Holly and I journeyed out to the cemetery where I stood at his grave and tried to recall him. I most often remembered the time, a few weeks before he died, when we sat together at the nursing home. After long minutes of silence, he'd said: "The important thing, Howie, is to be a man."

He began to cry, tears overflowing his red-rimmed eyes, and I pitied him, pitied all the old people who could only look back, look back. After a while, I asked: "What's a man, Dad?" Not really curious but wanting to say something.

My poor father. Who'd had too much booze and too little love and no luck at all, at cards or dice or all those jobs. And all the deals that had collapsed.

"To be a man," my father said, wiping his cheeks, "is to look at the wreckage of your life and to confront it all without pity for yourself. Without alibis. And to go on. To endure—"

It had been a long day and I had been impatient to get away from the ancient abandoned man who called himself my father. I left shortly afterward, thinking: he'd always had a way with words, hadn't he? And what had it gotten him in the end? A wife whose early death had given him an excuse to drown himself in bottle after bottle, while his son, whose birth was the cause of that death, was shunted from uncle to aunt to cousin. Yet, he had tried hard to be a father, in his way, always showing up on holidays, bundled with gifts and stories of great adventures in the cities he visited on his sales routes.

Now, Holly and I drove along soft-shaded Spruce Street and I was relieved that a trip to the cemetery was not on the agenda that day. Holly chatted gaily. She told me about the neighborhood carnival she and her friends had staged and how their names had appeared in the newspaper because they'd donated the proceeds to charity. She described the shopping trips for school clothes, because September loomed ahead. She brought me up to date on all the things that make up the life and times of a ten-year-old girl, and I barely listened, taking pleasure in her presence alone. She wore pigtails, and she was dark, unlike Alison, who was blond, and this secretly delighted me. Holly prattled on: there was a fabulous new ride at Wonder World, "The Rocket Trip to the Moon," that all the kids were crazy about, and could we go on it, could we, huh, please?

"Why not?" I asked. All the "why nots" I had tossed her on Thursdays, like bouquets of love. I agreed so quickly because I knew she would change her mind at the last moment. Holly was shy, timid, and she usually avoided the more adventurous and perilous rides. Ordinarily, she was content to stroll through the park at my side while we made up stories about people passing by. She liked the merry-go-round and the distorted mirrors in the fun house and she was reluctant to attempt such daring exploits as the roller coaster or the loop-the-loop. For which I was grateful. Particularly on days such as this when my head pounded and my stomach revolted at the slightest movement.

"How's your mother?" I asked, the question ritual.

Usually, the answer was ritual, too. "Fine" or "swell." As if Holly'd received instructions. But today, she hesitated, sighed, and said: "Tired."

"Tired?" I was searching for a parking place in the busy Wonder World lot.

"Oh, she's been on a committee to get blood donors—"

That was Alison. Conscientious and community-minded and always willing to help. She had a desire for service to others and she dearly loved Monument and had no wish to venture to other places. Which was part of our trouble, or at least the beginning of it all. I had always regarded Monument as a starting point, not a destination. Alison and I had met the summer I'd been planning to leave, ready to knock on a thousand doors in New York City, seeking a job, something, anything— just to get away. But Alison had been so beautiful and I had loved her so incredibly that I'd remained in Monument, writing obituaries and other equally dismal stories for the town newspaper. However, I was always aware of the world outside of Monument and I had wanted to see it, to know a million people, visit a million places, all of which was ridiculous, of course, and eminently impractical. Sometimes, my frustration would burst out. "Alison," I'd plead, "let's try, let's pack up and take our chances. I don't mean go to the other side of the world. But somewhere. The world's so big and Monument's so small, our lives are so small—"

Alison had held up little Holly, who smiled at me in her infant innocence. "Is she so small, too, that you can't be a father to her?"

Defeated, I remained in Monument but spent more and more time away from that confining claustrophobic apartment. In a bar or cocktail lounge, there were kind shadows and when you'd consumed just the right amount of beer or rye or whatever, all the sharp edges blurred and Monument itself receded. Inevitably, if you go often enough to a bar, a girl walks in. And, finally, Sally arrived. She was a member of a television unit dispatched to Monument by a Boston station to capture, on tape, the one-hundred-fifth birthday of Harrison Shanks, the oldest man in the county. Sally and I had a drink or two; she confessed that she was only a secretary for the film crew, an errand girl, really. Laughing, she reversed the cliché and wondered what a fellow like me was doing in a place like that. Meaning Monument, of course. She leaned against me warmly, a frankness about her body. Alison hid herself in tailored suits or loose, comfortable sweaters while Sally wore clothes that made me constantly aware that she was a woman. Sitting beside her on that first night, before I had said two dozen words to her, I felt as though I had known her body before, probably in a thousand adolescent dreams.

The television people were in Monument only two days. I served as their unofficial guide, arranging the interview with Harrison Shanks, who sat bewildered in a wicker chair on the porch of his ancient house, croaking monosyllabic answers to the inane questions placed by the interviewer. "How does it feel to be one hundred five years old?" The old man, confused by time and place, kept muttering about the banks closing and Herbert Hoover, which caused a few laughs and quips off camera, and I felt myself tightening inside. Someone pressed my arm.

"You're a sensitive one, aren't you?" Sally asked.

"He's an old man. I've known him all my life."

"Poor boy," she said, touching the tip of my nose with a delicate finger. "You need a little tender loving care."

The interview with Harrison Shanks used up only ninety-three seconds of a special show dealing with the problems of the aged but my alliance with Sally lasted much longer than that. But not long enough. That was the terrible part: leaving Alison and Holly for Sally and all the bright promises of Boston, to dislocate our lives and make Holly that pitiable object—the child of a broken home—to do all that and then to end up alone, after all. Sally found other sensitive men upon whom to bestow her tender loving care. Her care wasn't really loving, I had learned, and I drifted from one job to another, sideways, not upward. To go upward demanded more than talent. It demanded ruthlessness and cunning, the necessity for sitting up nights plotting the next day's maneuver, the next day's presentation. But I found more allure in a drink or two, which became three or four, and then, what the hell, let's have a party, let's have some fun. And then it wasn't fun anymore.

"Daddy, you look kooky," Holly said now, giggling uncontrollably.

"You're not exactly Cinderella at the ball" I retorted.

We were regarding ourselves in the fun-house mirrors: Holly suddenly short and fat as if invisible hands had clapped her head down into her body, and I ludicrously tall and thin, pencil-like, my head a soiled eraser. Then we moved and exchanged grotesqueries, laughing some more at our reversed roles. At one point, I picked her up and whirled her around, basking in the gaiety of her laughter, despite the pain that stabbed my head. Dizziness overtook me and I set her down. "Let's rest awhile, baby." But she was carried on the momentum of her excitement and pulled me on. "The Rocket Ride, Dad, the Rocket Ride."

I let myself be led through the sun-dazzled park, telling myself to hold out for a little while. There was a small bar across the street and maybe I could duck in there for a cool one while Holly went on the rocket. On those Thursdays with Holly, I had seldom cheated that way, had devoted all my time to her, perhaps to show Alison that I wasn't completely without a conscience. When I had first called her after finding my loneliness intolerable, she'd been skeptical.

"We've been doing nicely, thanks," she said, cool and crisp. "Don't upset things, Howie. We haven't seen you for—how long? Three years?— and we've arranged our lives. It doesn't hurt anymore."

"You mean, you don't need me," I said.

When she didn't answer, I took the plunge. "But I need you."

Her laughter infuriated me. I wanted to hurt her. "All right, maybe not you. But Holly. I need her. She's mine, too. My blood runs—"

"I know. Your blood runs in her veins. But nothing else, I hope."

I was startled by her bitterness but, upon reflection, I saw that she was justified. When the divorce had become final, I hadn't made any particular demands about Holly. Alison had been generous enough to leave the terms open: I could see the child whenever and however I wished. Terms that I did not take her up on, because I was too intoxicated with my freedom and Sally and later the others. Until that day I called, alone and desperate in that hotel room, abandoned by everyone, needing somebody. And so we decided, over the telephone, that Holly would be mine on Thursdays. Thursday afternoon to be precise. Those first few weeks, I clutched at those hours with Holly as if they were gulps of oxygen in an airless world. We made the rounds, stiff and awkward at first, but finally Holly began to laugh at my jokes and eventually she accepted me. Alison remained distant, however, and never ventured out of the house. I was not invited inside, of course.

One day she addressed me through the screen door as I met Holly at the porch. She told Holly to go to the car.

"You know what you're doing?" she asked. But it wasn't a question: more an accusation.

"What?"

"Disrupting her life, her routine. Cruising in here every week like a year-round Santa Claus."

"Are you jealous? Or don't you think a kid needs a little fun now and then?"

She recoiled as if I'd slapped her or had stumbled upon the truth, and I felt a twist of triumph.

"Here we are, Dad," Holly said.

"My God," I cried, confronted by the huge and elaborate piece of machinery rising from the ground in front of us. Ordinarily, the rides in amusement parks all resemble one another, but the Rocket Ride seemed to be an exception, a roaring and revolving device that emitted billows of smoke and showers of sparks. Circular in design, the machinery contained small, simulated rockets with room for two or three people in each rocket. As the entire device moved in circular motion, the individual rockets swung up and down and occasionally poised daringly fifty feet above the ground before descending in a roar of smoke and flame. As we watched, the ride was apparently completing its circuit. I realized, finally, that the smoke was simulated and that the flames were actually paper streamers cunningly devised to resemble the real thing.

"Isn't it cool, Dad?" Holly asked.

I chuckled at my shy little girl, who had yet to find the courage for a trip on the roller coaster.

"You're not going on *this*, are you?" Although the ride was not as awesome as it had seemed at first glance, there was still that fifty-foot swoop.

"All the kids have," Holly said, eyes blazing with challenge. "If I don't, they'll think I'm—" she groped for the alien word—"chicken."

My poor sweet. So small and worried, risking an encounter with the monster to prove to her friends that she was not afraid. The ride came to a stop with screams and shouts and bellows and a muffled explosion. The pain between my eyes increased, my stomach rose.

"Please, Daddy?"

"Tickets," called the attendant.

"Boy, oh, boy," exulted a fellow coming off the ramp, his arm around a small blond girl who was flushed and excited, her body ripe and full. Somehow, our eyes met. She was young, but her eyes held the old message, the ancient code I had deciphered a thousand times.

"Can I, Daddy?" Holly's voice was poised on the edge of victory, interpreting my sudden preoccupation as acquiescence.

I watched the blond and her boyfriend as they made their way to a nearby refreshment stand. As a test. Sure enough, her eyes found their way to mine.

Holly had been leading me to the ticket booth, and I found myself with wallet in hand.

"You really want to go on this thing?" I asked, thinking that perhaps she had started to grow up, beginning to leave childhood behind. And yet I doubted her endurance. She was still only a baby.

"Oh, Daddy," she said impatiently, the woman emerging from the girl, a hint of the future.

I thought of a tall cool one in the bar across the street. Or maybe an approach to the blond. Handing a dollar to the cashier, I said: "One."

"Child or adult?"

"Child," I answered. Adult? What sane adult would risk a ride on that terrible parody of a rocket shot?

"Aren't you coming with me?" Holly asked.

"Look, Holly, your daddy's getting old for these kinds of capers. Rocket ships are for the young." Leading her toward the entrance, I urged: "Better hurry. You won't get a seat."

"Do you think I should go on the ride alone?" she asked, doubts gathering, almost visible in her eyes.

I squinted at the mechanism, conjuring up the vision of myself, complete with pounding head and queasy stomach, being tossed and turned and lifted and dashed down. Ridiculous. It was impossible for me to accompany her. I was not equipped for Rocket Rides, with or without a hangover. Blond or no blond.

The crowd jostled us, pushing forward, carrying us to the entrance. Placing the ticket in Holly's hand, I waved her on. She was swept along in the crowd and then emerged on the ramp leading to the platform where customers entered the individual capsules. The attendant on the platform took her ticket. I hoped he would realize how young she was and guide her to a rocket where other people would be near her. He led her to a small rocket, a capsule with enough room for only one person, installed no doubt for those who preferred to ride alone. She hesitated for a moment and then entered the compartment She seemed small and wan and abandoned. She snapped a thin bar in place—her only protection from falling out. But, of course, nobody ever fell out of those things. Did they? I told myself to stop being melodramatic; it was only a lousy ride in an amusement park and she wasn't a child any longer.

Damn it. I walked over to the cashier's booth, drawing my wallet. But I was halted in my tracks by the attendant's cry: "All aboard. We're off to the moon."

"You can just make it, mister," the cashier offered. But I'd look foolish scurrying up the ramp. And, besides, all the rockets were probably filled.

A belch of smoke escaped the rocket, the roar of an engine filled the air and the entire mechanism seemed to come alive. I ran back near the entrance, eager to see Holly before the ride began. She was sitting erect in her seat, as if she were a dutiful fifth-grader being obedient for her teacher. Her hands were folded in her lap. Our eyes met and I garlanded my face with a smile, assuring her that she was gong to have fun. She nodded back, sighed a little, and with a roar and swish and boom, the trip started.

It all resembled a merry-go-round gone mad, the rockets whirling madly and individually, rising and falling and twisting, often at crazy impossible angles. I was grateful for my restraint, for having refused to go with Holly; I'd have been sick as a dog already. I glanced toward the refreshment stand; the blond was gone. Like so many others.

When I turned back to the ride again, it was in full swing. People screamed, those peculiar screams of terror and delight. The machinery *whooshed* and I sought Holly. At first, I couldn't find her in the nightmare of motion and color and sound. And then the small rocket swung into view and I spotted her. Her eyes were wide with surprise, her body tense, her hands clinging to the bar. Then she was gone, whisked away out of sight. The other people passed like blurs before my eyes. On the next turn Holly's eyes were closed and her face resembled melted wax, as if a mad sculptor had molded her flesh into a mask of fright. As she began to rise, far up, I wondered whether there was an element of danger, after all. Suppose she lost her grip on the bar. I walked toward the attendant who stood at bored attention near the entrance, but I finally decided not to bother him. Stop dramatizing, I told myself. Then Holly swept by, her eyes wild with horror, terrible eyes, agonized. I hurried to the attendant and asked him how long the ride went on.

"What?" he shouted above the din.

"How long's the ride?"

"Five minutes. They get their money's worth," he yelled.

Stalking to my vantage point, I cursed myself. A moment later, she came into view, her eyes closed once more, her body crouched and tense, pitifully small and vulnerable. I remembered that as a child of three or so she'd been subject to nightmares. And she'd been afraid of thunder and lightning. I thought of all the thunderstorms she had endured and how I hadn't been there to comfort her.

Now, the rocket swept around again and began the long ascent. Her eyes were open, in a gaze of desperation. She looked downward and saw me. Her lips were pressed tight, her cheeks taut. In that precious moment, I tried to hold her in my view. I smiled, more than smiled: I attempted to inject courage and love and protection into my smile. And our eyes met for a long moment—and then she was gone. Up and away. Around and around. And I closed my own eyes.

The ride finally ended and I rushed to the exit to greet her, arms ready to welcome her, happy to have her safe at last. I watched as she carefully let herself out of the rocket. She walked, one foot after the other, across the ramp, a little unsteady, perhaps, but determined. I held out my arms as she approached.

"Holly!" I cried.

She looked up thoughtfully, startled, as if she were surprised to find me there.

"Say, that was quite a trip, wasn't it?" I inquired. "Holy mackerel, I was ready to rip off my clothes, show my Superman outfit and leap to the rescue."

She smiled distantly. But not at my words. She was smiling at something else. It was a terrible smile. Private. The kind of smile that didn't belong on the face of a child.

"Are you all right?" I asked.

"I'm fine," she said.

"I'm sorry you were alone. Too bad you couldn't have gotten into a rocket with somebody else. I was afraid you might fall out."

"I'm safe and sound," she said.

But she wasn't looking at me.

"Well," I said, "what's next on the schedule?" Trying to induce enthusiasm into my voice.

"I think I'd like to go home, please," she replied, in her best polite-little-girl manner.

"It's early," I pointed out. "How about something to eat?" Ordinarily, she was ravenous for the things I bought her: popcorn and cotton candy and triple-header ice-cream cones.

"I'm not hungry," she said.

We were passing the fun house. I thought of those crazy mirrors inside and grimaced at the thought of myself bloated and distorted. With Holly walking beside me—beside me and yet getting farther and farther away with every step we took—I wondered if the mirrors weren't true reflections, after all. Forget it, I ridiculed myself, stop thinking of yourself as a poor man's Dorian Gray.

"Look, Holly, it's early. You said school's starting. How about a trip downtown? To Norton's? For some new clothes?" Everybody went to Norton's and I was sure that I would be able to charge purchases there without any fuss.

She blew air out of the side of her mouth. "I think I'd rather just go home," she said. "Besides, Mom isn't feeling too well. I might be able to help her."

"Your wish is my command," I said, keeping it light, keeping it gay.

And Alison. How tired did she get? And why wasn't she feeling well? Should I have inquired once in a while? But who inquired about me?

We made our way to the car under a sky suddenly subdued with clouds. The brilliance of the sun was muted, for which my eyes were thankful.

Once in the car, I asked: "Sure you want to go right home?" Clinging to her presence.

She looked straight ahead. I realized she hadn't looked at me directly since she'd emerged from the Rocket Ride.

"Oh, Daddy," she said.

Oh, Daddy. Without anguish, without any reprimand. Oh, Daddy. With a tired, weary acceptance that echoed a thousand other acceptances that had marked my life. A comment on all my defections.

"Next Thursday," I said, "we should do something different, something crazy." Thinking wildly. "Maybe your mother would let you come in to Boston. We could really do the town."

"I don't know," she said. "I think there's something special going on next Thursday. At school. Orientation Day—getting ready for September."

"But—" I began. And then stopped. I'd been about to say: you are mine on Thursdays. But I saw, of course, that she was not actually mine, not on Thursdays or any other day of the week, or the year. We'd been playing truant, sure enough, but not as father and daughter, merely as adult and child. All those why nots I had tossed her—not bouquets of love, but bribes. I glanced at her as we drove along. She sat erect, composed, that elegance of Alison's so much in evidence, and I ached with love and longing and tenderness, knowing that she was more Alison than me, despite the dark hair. Where was I in her? Was I there at all?

I turned the car away from Spruce Street. "I'd like to drive by the cemetery," I told her.

"All right," she said, eyes still on the road ahead. I stopped the car at the comfortless place of gray and green, slab and grass, and I thought of my father and what he had said that time about being a man and confronting the debris of your dreams. Without self-pity.

"Holly," I said.

Finally, she turned toward me—those lovely eyes, that curve of cheek. I had wondered before whether I was anywhere in her and now I hoped I wasn't.

"Yes?" she asked, mildly interested.

I wanted to say: "I'm sorry. I'm sorry for playing Santa Claus when I should have been a father. I'm sorry for wanting the whole world when I should have wanted only those who loved me. I'm sorry for the Rocket Ride—and all the Rocket Rides of your life that I didn't share."

Instead, I said: "I won't be coming to Monument for a while." I didn't allow her to answer but began to improvise quickly. "See, I've been thinking of leaving Boston, getting away from the rat race. I heard of a small-town newspaper up in Vermont—a weekly—that's looking for a man. Maybe I'll give it a whirl."

"That sounds interesting," she said, as if we were strangers on a plane.

"And if it works out, who knows? Maybe the Monument *Times* might have an opening someday."

Don't you see, my darling, what I'm trying to say?

"And I'll come home for good," I ventured.

She looked out over the cemetery, her face as bleak as any tombstone.

"Wouldn't you like that?" I asked.

At last, she looked at me again. "Yes," she said. For a moment, something raced across her face, something appeared in her eyes, perhaps an echo of the child I had known a long time ago. Then it faded. And the eyes were old. I knew I had done this to her. "Yes, that would be nice," she said, in that correct manner.

We drove away from the cemetery and to Spruce Street, and I parked in front of that house that once had been home. She kissed me dutifully on the cheek. I didn't blow the horn to provoke Alison or as a last attempt at amusing Holly. I drove away slowly, and I kept telling myself desperately that I wasn't saying goodbye.

Check Your Reading

1. What amusement park does Holly choose?

2. How does Holly describe Alison?

3. Where does Holly's father meet Sally? Why did they part?

4. What fears did Holly have in early childhood?

5. What excuse does Holly give for next Thursday?

Further Exploration

1. How does the narrator reveal his immaturity? Do you think Holly should forgive him for not going with her in the Rocket Ride? Explain your answer.

2. What clues suggest that Holly's father considers going on the Rocket Ride with her? How does he reveal his relief when the ride is over?

3. Holly's father describes his role as parent in terms of Superman, a comic strip character. How does Holly react to that description? How do children's perceptions of their parents change over the years?

4. What more might we have learned if Holly had been allowed, as a narrator, to express her inner feelings?

5. What kind of parent do you think Holly will become? What characteristics of her father are worth emulating? Which characteristics will Holly avoid?

Carson McCullers (1917–1967)

A native of Columbus, Georgia, who had come to seek fame and fortune in New York City, Carson Smith McCullers was no stranger to disappointment. Her heart set on attending Juilliard School of Music and becoming a concert pianist, she lost her tuition on the subway and forfeited her dream. The loss proved to be the literary world's gain as McCullers turned to writing, moved to North Carolina, and produced two sensitive, perceptive novels about young girls, *The Heart Is a Lonely Hunter* (1940) and *The Member of the Wedding* (1946), both of which have found their way to stage and screen adaptations. A third novel, *Reflections in a Golden Eye* (1941), and a collection of stories, *The Ballad of the Sad Cafe* (1951), reflect the macabre style known as Southern Gothic.

"Sucker" exemplifies McCuller's expert description of isolation and rejection as seen through the eyes of a young boy who has violated a sacred trust—the love of one who claims him for his brother.

Sucker
Carson McCullers

It was always like I had a room to myself. Sucker slept in my bed with me but that didn't interfere with anything. The room was mine and I used it as I wanted to. Once I remember sawing a trap door in the floor. Last year when I was a sophomore in high school I tacked on my wall some pictures of girls from magazines and one of them was just in her underwear. My mother never bothered me because she had the younger kids to look after. And Sucker thought anything I did was always swell.

Whenever I would bring any of my friends back to my room all I had to do was just glance once at Sucker and he would get up from whatever he was busy with and maybe half smile at me, and leave without saying a word. He never brought kids back there. He's twelve, four years younger than I am, and he always knew without me even telling him that I didn't want kids that age meddling with my things.

Half the time I used to forget that Sucker isn't my brother. He's my first cousin but practically ever since I remember he's been in our family. You see his folks were killed in a wreck when he was a baby. To me and my kid sisters he was like our brother.

Sucker used to always remember and believe every word I said. That's how he got his nick-name. Once a couple of years ago I told him that if he'd jump off our garage with an umbrella it would act as a parachute and he wouldn't fall hard. He did it and busted his knee. That's just one instance. And the funny thing was that no matter how many times he got fooled he would still believe me. Not that he was dumb in other ways — it was just the way he acted with me. He would look at everything I did and quietly take it in.

There is one thing I have learned, but it makes me feel guilty and is hard to figure out. If a person admires you a lot you despise him and don't care—and it is the person who doesn't notice you that you are apt to admire. This is not easy to realize. Maybelle Watts, this senior at school, acted like she was the Queen of Sheba and even humiliated me. Yet at this same time I would have done anything in the world to get her attentions. All I could think about day and night was Maybelle until I was nearly crazy. When Sucker was a little kid and on up until the time he was twelve I guess I treated him as bad as Maybelle did me.

Now that Sucker had changed so much it is a little hard to remember him as he used to be. I never imagined anything would suddenly happen that would make us both very different. I never knew that in order to get what has happened straight in my mind I would want to think back on him as he used to be and compare and try to get things settled. If I could have seen ahead maybe I would have acted different.

I never noticed him much or thought about him and when you consider how long we have had the same room together it is funny the few things I remember. He used to talk to himself a lot when he'd think he was alone—all about him fighting gangsters and being on ranches and that sort of kids' stuff. He'd get in the bathroom and stay as long as an hour and sometimes his voice would go up high and excited and you could hear him all over the house. Usually, though, he was very quiet. He didn't have many boys in the neighborhood to buddy with and his face had the look of a kid who is watching a game and waiting to be asked to play. He didn't mind wearing the sweaters and coats that I outgrew, even if the sleeves did flop down too big and make his wrists look as thin and white as a little girl's. That is how I remember him—getting a little bigger every year but still being the same. That was Sucker up until a few months ago when all this trouble began.

Maybelle was somehow mixed up in what happened so I guess I ought to start with her. Until I knew her I hadn't given much time to girls. Last fall she sat next to me in General Science class and that was when I first began to notice her. Her hair is the brightest yellow I ever saw and occasionally she will wear it set into curls with some sort of gluey stuff. Her fingernails are pointed and manicured and painted a shiny red. All during class I used to watch Maybelle, nearly all the time except when I thought she was going to look my way or when the teacher called on me. I couldn't keep my eyes off her hands, for one thing. They are very little and white except for that red stuff, and when she would turn the pages of her book she always licked her thumb and held out her little finger and turned very slowly. It is impossible to describe Maybelle. All the boys are crazy about her but she didn't even notice me. For one thing she's almost two years older than I am. Between periods I used to try and pass very close to her in the halls but she would hardly ever smile at me. All I could do was sit and look at her in class—and sometimes it was like the whole room could hear my heart beating and I wanted to holler or light out and run for Hell.

At night, in bed, I would imagine about Maybelle. Often this would keep me from sleeping until as late as one or two o'clock. Sometimes Sucker would wake up and ask me why I couldn't get settled and I'd tell him to hush his mouth. I suppose I was mean to him lots of times. I guess I wanted to ignore somebody like Maybelle did me. You could always tell by Sucker's face when his feelings were hurt. I don't remember all the ugly remarks I must have made because even when I was saying them my mind was on Maybelle.

That went on for nearly three months and then somehow she began to change. In the halls she would speak to me and every morning she copied my homework. At lunch time once I danced with her in the gym. One afternoon I got up nerve and went to her house with a carton of cigarettes. I knew she smoked in the girls' basement and sometimes outside of school—and I didn't want to take her candy because I think that's been run into the ground. She was very nice and it seemed to me everything was going to change.

It was that night when this trouble really started. I had come into my room late and Sucker was already asleep. I felt too happy and keyed up to get in a comfortable position and I was awake thinking about Maybelle a long time. Then I dreamed about her and it seemed I kissed her. It was a surprise to wake up and see the dark. I lay still and a little while passed before I could come to and understand where I was. The house was quiet and it was a very dark night.

Sucker's voice was a shock to me. "Pete? . . ."

I didn't answer anything or even move.

"You do like me as much as if I was your own brother, don't you Pete?"

I couldn't get over the surprise of everything and it was like this was the real dream instead of the other.

"You have liked me all the time like I was your own brother, haven't you ?"

"Sure," I said.

Then I got up for a few minutes. It was cold and I was glad to come back to bed. Sucker hung on to my back. He felt little and warm and I could feel his warm breathing on my shoulder.

"No matter what you did I always knew you liked me."

I was wide awake and my mind seemed mixed up in a strange way. There was this happiness about Maybelle and all that—but at the same time something about Sucker and his voice when he said these things made me take notice. Anyway I guess you understand people better when you are happy than when something is worrying you. It was like I had never really thought about Sucker until then. I felt I had always been mean to him. One night a few weeks before I had heard him crying in the dark. He said he had lost a boy's beebee gun and was scared to let anybody know. He wanted me to tell him what to do. I was sleepy and tried to make him hush and when he wouldn't I kicked at him. That was just one of the things I remembered. It seemed to me he had always been a lonesome kid. I felt bad.

There is something about a dark cold night that makes you feel close to someone you're sleeping with. When you talk together it is like you are the only people awake in the town.

"You're a swell kid, Sucker," I said.

It seemed to me suddenly that I did like him more than anybody else I knew—more than any other boy, more than my sisters, more in a certain way even than Maybelle. I felt good all over and it was like when they play sad music in the movies. I wanted to show Sucker how much I really thought of him and make up for the way I had always treated him.

We talked for a good while that night. His voice was fast and it was like he had been saving up these things to tell me for a long time. He mentioned that he was going to try to build a canoe and that the kids down the block wouldn't let him in on their football team and I don't know what all. I talked some too and it was a hard feeling to think of him taking in everything I said so seriously. I even spoke of Maybelle a little, only I made out like it was her who had been running after me all this time. He asked questions about high school and so forth. His voice was excited and he kept on talking fast like he could never get the words out in time. When I went to sleep he was still talking and I could still feel his breathing on my shoulder, warm and close.

During the next couple of weeks I saw a lot of Maybelle. She acted as though she really cared for me a little. Half the time I felt so good I hardly knew what to do with myself.

But I didn't forget about Sucker. There were a lot of old things in my bureau drawer I'd been saving—boxing gloves and Tom Swift books and second rate fishing tackle. All this I turned over to him. We had some more talks together and it was really like I was knowing him for the first time. When there was a long cut on his cheek I knew he had been monkeying around with this new first razor set of mine, but I didn't say anything. His face seemed different now. He used to look timid and sort of like he was afraid of a whack over the head. That expression was gone. His face, with those wide-open eyes and ears sticking out and his mouth never quite shut, had the look of a person who is surprised and expecting something swell.

Once I started to point him out to Maybelle and tell her he was my kid brother. It was an afternoon when a murder mystery was on at the movie. I had earned a dollar working for my Dad and I gave Sucker a quarter to go and get candy and so forth. With the rest I took Maybelle. We were sitting near the back and I saw Sucker come in. He began to stare at the screen the minute he stepped past the ticket man and he stumbled down the aisle without noticing where he was going. I started to punch Maybelle but couldn't quite make up my mind. Sucker looked a little silly—walking like a drunk with his eyes glued to the movie. He was wiping his reading glasses on his shirt tail and his knickers flopped down. He went on until he got to the first few rows where the kids usually sit. I never did punch Maybelle. But I got to thinking it was good to have both of them at the movie with the money I earned.

I guess things went on like this for about a month or six weeks. I felt so good I couldn't settle down to study or put my mind on anything. I wanted to be friendly with everybody. There were times when I just had to talk to some person. And usually that would be Sucker. He felt as good as I did. Once he said: "Pete, I am gladder that you are like my brother than anything else in the world."

Then something happened between Maybelle and me. I never have figured out just what it was. Girls like her are hard to understand. She began to act different toward me. At first I wouldn't let myself believe this and tried to think it was just my imagination. She didn't act glad to see me any more. Often she went out riding with this fellow on the football team who owns this yellow roadster. The car was the color of her hair and after school she would ride off with him, laughing and looking into his face. I couldn't think of anything to do about it and she was on my mind all day and night. When I did get a chance to go out with her she was snippy and didn't seem to notice me. This made me feel like something was the matter—I would worry about my shoes clopping too loud on the floor, or the fly of my pants or the bumps on my chin. Sometimes when Maybelle was around, a devil would get into me and I'd hold my face stiff and call grown men by their last names without the Mister and say rough things. In the night I would wonder what made me do all this until I was too tired for sleep.

At first I was so worried I just forgot about Sucker. Then later he began to get on my nerves. He was always hanging around until I would get back from high school, always looking like he had something to say to me or wanted me to tell him. He made me a magazine rack in his Manual Training class and one week he saved his lunch money and bought me three packs of cigarettes. He couldn't seem to take it in that I had things on my mind and didn't want to fool with him. Every afternoon it would be the same—him in my room with this waiting expression on his face. Then I wouldn't say anything or I'd maybe answer him rough-like and he would finally go on out.

I can't divide that time up and say this happened one day and that the next. For one thing I was so mixed up the weeks just slid along into each other and I felt like Hell and didn't care. Nothing definite was said or done. Maybelle still rode around with this fellow in his yellow roadster and sometimes she would smile at me and sometimes not. Every afternoon I went from one place to another where I thought she would be. Either she would act almost nice and I would begin thinking how things would finally clear up and she would care for me—or else she'd behave so that if she hadn't been a girl I'd have wanted to grab her by that white little neck and choke her. The more ashamed I felt for making a fool of myself the more I ran after her.

Sucker kept getting on my nerves more and more. He would look at me as though he sort of blamed me for something, but at the same time knew that it wouldn't last long. He was growing fast and for some reason began to stutter when he talked. Sometimes he had nightmares or would throw up his breakfast. Mom got him a bottle of cod liver oil.

Then the finish came between Maybelle and me. I met her going to the drug store and asked for a date. When she said no I remarked something sarcastic. She told me she was sick and tired of my being around and that she had never cared a rap about me. She said all that, I just stood there and didn't answer anything. I walked home very slowly.

For several afternoons I stayed in my room by myself. I didn't want to go anywhere or talk to anyone. When Sucker would come in and look at me sort of funny I'd yell at him to get out. I didn't want to think of Maybelle and I sat at my desk reading *Popular Mechanics* or whittling at a toothbrush rack I was making. It seemed to me I was putting that girl out of my mind pretty well.

But you can't help what happens to you at night. That is what made things how they are now.

You see a few nights after Maybelle said those words to me I dreamed about her again. It was like that first time and I was squeezing Sucker's arm so tight I woke him up. He reached for my hand.

"Pete, what's the matter with you?"

All of a sudden I felt so mad my throat choked—at myself and the dream and Maybelle and Sucker and every single person I knew. I remembered all the times Maybelle had humiliated me and everything bad that had ever happened. It seemed to me for a second that nobody would ever like me but a sap like Sucker.

"Why is it we aren't buddies like we were before? Why—?"

"Shut your damn trap!" I threw off the cover and got up and turned on the light. He sat in the middle of the bed, his eyes blinking and scared.

There was something in me and I couldn't help myself. I don't think anybody ever gets that mad but once. Words came without me knowing what they would be. It was only afterward that I could remember each thing I said and see it all in a clear way.

"Why aren't we buddies? Because you're the dumbest slob I ever saw! Nobody cares anything about you! And just because I felt sorry for you sometimes and tried to act decent don't think I give a damn about a dumb-bunny like you!"

If I talked loud or hit him it wouldn't have been so bad. But my voice was slow and like I was very calm. Sucker's mouth was part way open and he looked as though he'd knocked his funny bone. His face was white and sweat came out on his forehead. He wiped it away with the back of his hand and for a minute his arm stayed raised that way as though he was holding something away from him.

"Don't you know a single thing? Haven't you even been around at all? Why don't you get a girl friend instead of me? What kind of a sissy do you want to grow up to be anyway?"

I didn't know what was coming next. I couldn't help myself or think.

Sucker didn't move. He had on one of my pajama jackets and his neck stuck out skinny and small. His hair was damp on his forehead.

"Why do you always hang around me? Don't you know when you're not wanted?"

Afterward I could remember the change in Sucker's face. Slowly that blank look went away and he closed his mouth. His eyes got narrow and his fists shut. There had never been such a look on him before. It was like every second he was getting older. There was a hard look to his eyes you don't see usually in a kid. A drop of sweat rolled down his chin and he didn't notice. He just sat there with those eyes on me and he didn't speak and his face was hard and didn't move.

"No you don't know when you're not wanted. You're too dumb. Just like your name—a dumb Sucker."

It was like something had busted inside me. I turned off the light and sat down in the chair by the window. My legs were shaking and I was so tired I could have bawled. The room was cold and dark. I sat there for a long time and smoked a squashed cigarette I had saved. Outside the yard was black and quiet. After a while I heard Sucker lie down.

I wasn't mad any more, only tired. It seemed awful to me that I had talked like that to a kid only twelve. I couldn't take it all in. I told myself I would go over to him and try to make it up. But I just sat there in the cold until a long time had passed. I planned how I could straighten it out in the morning. Then, trying not to squeak the springs, I got back in bed.

Sucker was gone when I woke up the next day. And later when I wanted to apologize as I had planned he looked at me in this new hard way so that I couldn't say a word.

All of that was two or three months ago. Since then Sucker has grown faster than any boy I ever saw. He's almost as tall as I am and his bones have gotten heavier and bigger. He won't wear any of my old clothes any more and has bought his first pair of long pants—with with some leather suspenders to hold them up. Those are just the changes that are easy to see and put into words.

Our room isn't mine at all any more. He's gotten up this gang of kids and they have a club. When they aren't digging trenches in some vacant lot and fighting they are always in my room. On the door there is some foolishness written in Mercurochrome saying "Woe to the Outsider who Enters" and signed with crossed bones and their secret initials. They have rigged up a radio and every afternoon it blares out music. Once as I was coming in I heard a boy telling something in a low voice about what he saw in the back of his big brother's automobile. I could guess what I didn't hear. *That's what her and my brother do. It's the truth—parked in the car.* For a minute Sucker looked surprised and his face was almost like it used to be. Then he got hard and tough again. "Sure, dumbell. We know all that." They didn't notice me. Sucker began telling them how in two years he was planning to be a trapper in Alaska.

But most of the time Sucker stays by himself. It is worse when we are alone together in the room. He sprawls across the bed in those long corduroy pants with the suspenders and just stares at me with that hard, half sneering look. I fiddle around my desk and can't get settled because of those eyes of his. And the thing is I just have to study because I've gotten three bad cards this term already. If I flunk English I can't graduate next year. I don't want to be a bum and I just have to get my mind on it. I don't care a flip for Maybelle or any particular girl any more and it's only this thing between Sucker and me that is the trouble now. We never speak except when we have to before the family. I don't even want to call him Sucker any more and unless I forget I call him by his real name, Richard. At night I can't study with him in the room and I have to hang around the drug store, smoking and doing nothing, with the fellows who loaf there.

More than anything I want to be easy in my mind again. And I miss the way Sucker and I were for a while in a funny, sad way that before this I never would have believed. But everything is so different that there seems to be nothing I can do to get it right. I've sometimes thought if we could have it out in a big fight that would help. But I can't fight him because he's four years younger. And another thing— sometimes this look in his eyes makes me almost believe that if Sucker could he would kill me.

Check Your Reading

1. What is Sucker's real name?

2. Who comes between Sucker and Pete?

3. Where does Sucker sleep?

4. How is Sucker related to Pete?

5. What message does Sucker's gang put on the bedroom door?

Further Exploration

1. What age difference exists between the two boys? How does the difference affect Pete? If you could choose, would you rather be the older or younger sibling in the family? What are the benefits of each choice?

2. Is it the normal thing for the arrival of a girlfriend to disrupt a close relationship between two males in a family — or even two close friends? Support your answer.

3. How does Pete utter the words that cause the breach? Why does Pete fail to realize how damaging words can be? Relate an incident in your life when you have been wounded by words.

4. What line in the story suggests that Sucker feels a change in Pete? How do people give unspoken clues that they are losing their love for a friend?

5. How would you go about restoring the boys' friendship? Would a third party be able to patch things up? Will Sucker reach an age when he can understand Pete's feelings or is it too late for reconciliation?

Getting Along

Thinking It Over

These activities offer opportunities for you to consider how the stories in Part Five relate to one another and to the theme of *Getting Along*.

1. Which character from the four stories in this section is able to adjust most readily to a painful situation?

2. Which character do you think will make the best parent? What traits make the character a likely candidate for parenthood?

3. Compare the mother/daughter relationships in "From Mother. . . With Love" and "Mine on Thursdays." Which daughter seems to rely more on her mother?

4. Compare the weaknesses shown by the fathers in "From Mother. . . With Love" and "Mine on Thursdays." Which character seems most sincere in his efforts to be a father?

5. Which character has the greatest opportunity to make amends for faulty judgment or bad behavior? What actions or attitudes would prove that the change is real?

6. What have you learned from these stories that will help you in getting along with people? Support your opinion with specific examples from the stories.

Understanding
the Short Story

As you read a variety of stories, you will come to realize that each short work of fiction has its own style and its own emphasis, much like the characteristic set of fingerprints that every human being possesses. In most short stories there is a unique view of human life which must be examined for its own worth, just as individual people are judged on their separate merits. How is it posssible, then, to isolate a single set of characteristics which can be found in every story?

Several basic characteristics mark each narrative and place it in the single catagory or *genre* of short story. For example, every story contains *action*, external and/or internal. The *conflict* can originate between *characters*, within a single character, between a character and society, or between characters and nature or destiny.

The *setting* of the story, which is revealed through details that can be identified with a particular time and place, indicates where and when the story takes place. For example, a story that occurs in the earliest days of New York City would require a separate set of expectations from one set in the New York City of the next century. Both time and place can be pegged on obvious bits of information, such as the clothing people are wearing, application of modern discoveries, use of transportation and communication devices, style of speech, philosophies and political opinions of the participants, and general lifestyle of the characters. Setting also includes the *atmosphere* or mood that the writer creates.

The *exposition* is the part of the narration that provides information about the background of the characters and the action so that you can understand them. This does not always occur at the beginning of the story.

As the conflict develops (*rising action*), the struggle between opposing forces reaches a *climax*—a decisive moment or turning point in which the greatest amount of tension occurs. At this point the main character will have reached a decision about the situation.

The course of action taken by the characters forms the *plot*. Usually the situation in which the characters find themselves moves through *falling action* and *denouement* as the series of interrelated events reaches some identifiable conclusion. Sometimes the characters' arrival at the point of resolution occurs within their minds, where they experience a *revelation* or coming to knowledge about themselves or the world around them. The following diagram may help you to visualize the plot structure of most short stories.

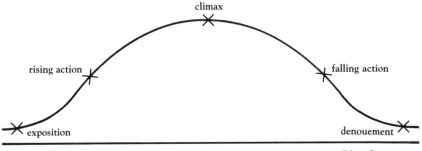

Plot Structure

The authors choice of a narrator or *point of view* is crucial to the impact of the action. Narrators may choose to stand outside the realm of the events and tell the story. When narrators know all the characters, their thoughts, and their motivations for action, they become *omniscient*, or all-knowing, like puppet masters working all the strings from behind the stage. Another possibility, *the third person narrator*, may speak in his or her own voice, separate from the author, and observe and describe the action from a limited sphere on the edge of the arena where the action occurs. The author may, on the other hand, want a more personal analysis of the events and select *a first person narrator* to tell the story as he or she watches or takes part. First person narrators refer to themselves as "I" and relate only the words and deeds that they can see and hear for themselves.

As the details of stories are woven together, the word choices of the authors indicate the *tone* or attitude they mean to convey. Authors have a wide array of possibilities: they can be amused or disgusted, teasing or shocked, terrified or outraged. Authors sometimes express *irony* by saying one thing and meaning something different. This discrepancy between what is apparent and what is real emphasizes more strongly what the authors think you should remember about the story.

One of the chief aspects of any story is the *theme*, or main idea, which inspires the story. As the experiences of the characters lead them to draw conclusions about themselves or about life, the broad idea takes shape in concrete form. A short story may include several interconnected themes, some of which may be in conflict with each other, which is often the case when a character faces a *dilemma*—a choice between equally unpleasant outcomes.

There are many other aspects of writing that can give you clues to meaning. The *title* should trigger some definite thoughts or pictures in your mind. *Symbols* or *images* that suggest universal meanings, such as food representing life and growth, may help you in interpreting details. Names for places and characters may have extra meaning beyond simple denotation and suggest a particular perception, such as the name "Scratchy" Wilson for the drunk in "The Bride Comes to Yellow Sky." There are additional places to look for meaning—repetition, rhythms of language, the sequence of events, dialect, graphic emphasis, contrast— in short, all the range of devices at the disposal of any artist.

Glossary

action   the happenings or series of events in a narrative

allusion   a brief, often indirect reference to something or someone in literature, mythology, or history which the author assumes the reader will recognize

analogy   a comparison of points of likeness between two otherwise dissimilar things. An analogy uses the more familiar to explain the less familiar

antagonist   the character that opposes the *protagonist*, or hero, in a narrative

atmosphere   the pervading emotional mood, often developed by the handling of the setting

caricature   a character development which satirizes a character by exaggerating his prominent features of appearance or behavior

character   a fictional personality created by an author

characterization   the techniques used by an author in creating and developing a character

climax   the decisive action or turning point in a narrative; the point of greatest intensity or interest

conflict   the struggle between opposing forces

connotation   the feeling or attitude associated with a word, related to but distinct from its *denotation*, or literal meaning

critic   a writer who studies, analyzes, and evaluates literary works

criticism   a specialized form of formal essay writing in which literature is analyzed and evaluated

denotation   the literal meaning of words

denouement   the last part of the *plot*, following the *climax*;
falling action; the outcome, solution, unraveling,
or clarification of the plot

description   the form of discourse which deals with the appearance of
a person, object, or place

dialogue   conversation between two or more characters

dialect   the imitation of regional speech in print, using altered,
phonetic spelling

diction   an author's choice of words, one aspect of his or her *style*

dilemma   a situation that requires one to choose between two equally
balanced alternatives

dramatic   the type of action that is presented directly, rather than told
about, often implying conflict and excitement

empathy   entering into the feelings or motives of characters

episode   an event in a narrative

episodic   a narrative largely composed of loosely related *episodes*

exposition   the part of a narrative, usually at the beginning, that
sketches in the background of the characters and the action so that the
reader can understand the situation

extended metaphor   a metaphor in which the main image or
comparison is extended and developed through several lines

falling action   the action in a narrative that follows the *climax* and
represents the working out of the decisive action of the *climax*; the
denouement

fiction   prose writings that tell about people and happenings which
have been created by an author

figurative language   language that departs from the strictly literal to
achieve special effects

figures of speech   an expression using words in an unusual or non-literal
sense to give beauty or vividness of style. The most common kinds of
figures of speech—*simile, metaphor, personification*—involve a
comparison of unlike things

flashback   an interruption in a narrative to show an episode that
happened before the story opens

folk lore   the customs, legends, songs, and tales of a people or nation

foreshadowing   suggestion, by the author, of events to come later in
a literary work

form   the arrangement of all aspects of a work of art to make a unified whole; the way the work is organized and designed

genre   literary form or type; e.g., poetry, novel, short story, drama

gothic   a type of fiction that aims at evoking terror through a gloomy, medieval setting, and sensational, supernatural action

idyl   any narrative dealing with an idealized picture of rural life

image   a word or phrase appealing to one or more of the senses

imagery   the use of vivid, concrete, sensory details

irony   a way of writing that depends on a discrepancy between what is apparent and what is real. There are three kinds of irony: (1)*verbal irony*, in which a writer says one thing and means another; (2)*dramatic irony*, in which a reader perceives a character's mistakes or misunderstandings; (3)*irony of situation*, in which there is a discrepancy between purpose and result

legend   a traditional story about a particular person, place, or deity, often popularly accepted as history

local color   in fiction, the use of speech, customs, and setting of a particular region for their own interest

metaphor   a figure of speech in which two unlike things are compared but in which no word of comparison (such as *like* or *as*) is used

myth   a traditional story connected with the religion of a people, frequently to explain some happening in nature or some specific belief

mythology   a complete group of closely connected myths

narrative   the kind of writing that relates to an event or series of events

narrative point of view   the relation assumed between the narrator and the characters, including the extent to which the narrator shows an awareness of what each character thinks and feels

narrator   the person who tells a story, usually a character

objective point of view   a narrative point of view in which the author does not presume to know the thoughts and feelings of the characters; the author simply reports what can be seen and heard

omniscient point of view   a narrative point of view in which the author may tell anything he wishes about the character's thoughts and feelings

parable   a short tale that illustrates a moral lesson

parody   imitates, mocks, or burlesques another usually serious work of literature. Like the caricature in art, a parody in literature mimics a subject or style

pathos   writer's tone which expresses pity and sorrow for the subject

periodic sentence   a sentence in which an important part of the meaning is withheld until the very end

personification   a figure of speech in which something nonhuman is given human qualities

plot   the sequence of events in a narrative

point of view   the relation between the narrator and the characters of a story

prose   the ordinary form of spoken or written language; language not arranged into verses

protagonist   the main character of a story

revelation   the moment of insight into a character or a situation as the climax of a short story

reversal   a point in a plot at which a force that has been dominant yields to another force

rising action   the first part of many narratives during which the tension between opposing characters or forces builds toward a climax

sarcasm   the use of exaggerated praise to insult

satire   a piece of writing which uses sarcasm or irony to hold up to ridicule or contempt the weaknesses of humanity in general. Satire often seeks to persuade through the force of laughter

scene   the specific setting for a given event in a narrative

sentimentalism   the attempt of an author to arouse more emotion in a work than the situation calls for

setting   the place, time, and mood of a story

short story   a type of prose fiction involving conflict, characters, situation, and scene, and setting forth the action in the form of a plot

simile   a *figure of speech* involving a comparison made explicit by the use of the word *like* or *as*

stock character   a definite type of character conventionally used in a particular literary form (e.g., the villain in a Western)

style   the distinctive use of language by a given author, including his or her choice of words, arrangement of words in sentences, and the relationship of the sentences to each other

symbol   a person, place, event, or object that represents something else, frequently an abstract quality or idea

technique   the conscious methods used by an author to shape his or her material

theme   the main idea or ideas of a literary work

tone   the author's attitude toward his or her material

unity   the interrelationship of the elements of a literary work as they form a complete whole

universal   a critical term employed to indicate the presence in a piece of writing of an appeal to all readers of all time

Credits

NTC LANGUAGE ARTS BOOKS

Business Communication
Business Communication Today! *Thomas & Fryar*
Handbook for Business Writing, *Baugh, Fryar, & Thomas*
Meetings: Rules & Procedures, *Pohl*

Dictionaries
British/American Language Dictionary, *Moss*
NTC's Classical Dictionary, *Room*
NTC's Dictionary of Changes in Meaning, *Room*
NTC's Dictionary of Debate, *Hanson*
NTC's Dictionary of Literary Terms, *Morner & Rausch*
NTC's Dictionary of Theatre and Drama Terms, *Mobley*
NTC's Dictionary of Word Origins, *Room*
NTC's Spell It Right Dictionary, *Downing*
Robin Hyman's Dictionary of Quotations

Essential Skills
Building Real Life English Skills, *Starkey & Penn*
English Survival Series, *Maggs*
Essential Life Skills, *Starkey & Penn*
Essentials of English Grammar, *Baugh*
Essentials of Reading and Writing English Series
Grammar for Use, *Hall*
Grammar Step-by-Step, *Pratt*
Guide to Better English Spelling, *Furness*
How to be a Rapid Reader, *Redway*
How to Improve Your Study Skills, *Coman & Heavers*
NTC Skill Builders
Reading by Doing, *Simmons & Palmer*
Developing Creative & Critical Thinking, *Boostrom*
303 Dumb Spelling Mistakes, *Downing*
TIME: We the People, *ed. Schinke-Llano*
Vocabulary by Doing, *Beckert*

Genre Literature
The Detective Story, *Schwartz*
The Short Story & You, *Simmons & Stern*
Sports in Literature, *Emra*
You and Science Fiction, *Hollister*

Journalism
Getting Started in Journalism, *Harkrider*
Journalism Today! *Ferguson & Patten*
Publishing the Literary Magazine, *Klaiman*
UPI Stylebook, *United Press International*

Language, Literature, and Composition
An Anthology for Young Writers, *Meredith*
The Art of Composition, *Meredith*
Creative Writing, *Mueller & Reynolds*

Handbook for Practical Letter Writing, *Baugh*
How to Write Term Papers and Reports, *Baugh*
Literature by Doing, *Tchudi & Yesner*
Lively Writing, *Schrank*
Look, Think & Write, *Leavitt & Sohn*
Poetry by Doing, *Osborn*
World Literature, *Rosenberg*
Write to the Point! *Morgan*
The Writer's Handbook, *Karls & Szymanski*
Writing by Doing, *Sohn & Enger*
Writing in Action, *Meredith*

Media Communication
Getting Started in Mass Media, *Beckert*
Photography in Focus, *Jacobs & Kokrda*
Television Production Today! *Kirkham*
Understanding Mass Media, *Schrank*
Understanding the Film, *Bone & Johnson*

Mythology
The Ancient World, *Sawyer & Townsend*
Mythology and You, *Rosenberg & Baker*
Welcome to Ancient Greece, *Millard*
Welcome to Ancient Rome, *Millard*
World Mythology, *Rosenberg*

Speech
Activities for Effective Communication, *LiSacchi*
The Basics of Speech, *Galvin, Cooper, & Gordon*
Contemporary Speech, *HopKins & Whitaker*
Dynamics of Speech, *Myers & Herndon*
Getting Started in Public Speaking, *Prentice & Payne*
Listening by Doing, *Galvin*
Literature Alive! *Gamble & Gamble*
Person to Person, *Galvin & Book*
Public Speaking Today! *Prentice & Payne*
Speaking by Doing, *Buys, Sill, & Beck*

Theatre
Acting & Directing, *Grandstaff*
The Book of Cuttings for Acting & Directing, *Cassady*
The Book of Scenes for Acting Practice, *Cassady*
The Dynamics of Acting, *Snyder & Drumsta*
An Introduction to Modern One-Act Plays, *Cassady*
An Introduction to Theatre and Drama, *Cassady & Cassady*
Play Production Today! *Beck et al.*
Stagecraft, *Beck*

For a current catalog and information about our complete line
of language arts books, write:
National Textbook Company
a division of NTC Publishing Group
4255 West Touhy Avenue
Lincolnwood (Chicago), Illinois 60646-1975 U.S.A.